Reconsidering Change Management

"This book offers a critical look at the assumptions underlying modern organization change efforts—a must for scholars and practitioners alike!"
—*Tonya L. Henderson, Principal-Gly Solutions, LLC, US*

Despite the popularity of organizational change management, the question arises whether its prescriptions and dominant beliefs and practices are based on solid and convergent evidence. Organizational change management entails interventions intended to influence the task-related behavior and associated results of an individual, team, or entire organization. There is a perception that a lot of change initiatives fail and limited understanding about what works and what does not and why.

Drawing on the field of psychology and based on primary research, *Reconsidering Change Management* identifies 18 popular and relevant commonly held assumptions with regard to change management that are then analyzed and compared to the four specific themes laid out in the book (people, leadership, organization, and change process), resulting in their own set of assumptions. Each assumption will have a brief introduction in which its relevance and popularity is explained.

By studying the scientific evidence, in particular meta-analytic evidence, the book provides students and academics in the fields of change management, organizational behavior, and business strategy the best available evidence for the acceptance or dropping of certain (change) management assumptions and their accompanying practices. By exploring the topics people, leadership, organization, and process, and the related assumptions, change management is restructured and reframed in a prudent, positive, and practical way.

Steven ten Have, PhD, is a full professor of strategy and change at the Vrije Universiteit Amsterdam, the Netherlands, visiting professor at the Nyenrode Business University, the Netherlands, chair of the Foundation the Center for Evidence-Based Management, and partner at TEN HAVE Change Management, the Netherlands.

Wouter ten Have, PhD, is a university lecturer of organization and change at the Vrije Universiteit Amsterdam, the Netherlands, visiting university lecturer of change management (MBA health care management) at the Amsterdam Business School, the Netherlands, and partner at TEN HAVE Change Management, the Netherlands.

Anne-Bregje Huijsmans is a consultant at TEN HAVE Change Management, the Netherlands.

Maarten Otto is a visiting university lecturer of organization and change (master of science in management) at the Hague University of Applied Sciences, the Netherlands, and a consultant at TEN HAVE Change Management, the Netherlands.

Routledge Studies in Organizational Change & Development

Series Editor: Bernard Burnes

For a full list of titles in this series, please visit www.routledge.com

9. **Change Competence**
   Implementing Effective Change
   Steven ten Have, Wouter ten Have, Anne-Bregje Huijsmans and Niels van der Eng

10. **Organizational Change and Global Standardization**
    Solutions to Standards and Norms Overwhelming Organizations
    David M. Boje

11. **Organizational Development and Change Theory**
    Managing Fractal Organizing Processes
    Tonya L. Henderson and David M. Boje

12. **The Leadership of Organizational Change**
    Mark Hughes

13. **Perspectives on Change**
    What Academics, Consultants and Managers Really Think About Change
    Edited by Bernard Burnes and Julian Randall

14. **Rethinking Organizational Change**
    The Role of Dialogue, Dialectic & Polyphony in the Organization
    Muayyad Jabri

15. **Organizational Change and Temporality**
    Bending the Arrow of Time
    Patrick Dawson and Christopher Sykes

16. **Reconsidering Change Management**
    Applying Evidence-Based Insights in Change Management Practice
    Steven ten Have, Wouter ten Have, Anne-Bregje Huijsmans, and Maarten Otto

Reconsidering Change Management

Applying Evidence-Based Insights in Change Management Practice

Steven ten Have, Wouter ten Have, Anne-Bregje Huijsmans, and Maarten Otto

NEW YORK AND LONDON

First published 2017
by Routledge
711 Third Avenue, New York, NY 10017

and by Routledge
2 Park Square, Milton Park, Abingdon, Oxon OX14 4RN

First issued in paperback 2018

Routledge is an imprint of the Taylor & Francis Group, an informa business

© 2017 Taylor & Francis

The right of Steven ten Have, Wouter ten Have, Anne-Bregje Huijsmans, and Maarten Otto to be identified as authors of this work has been asserted by them in accordance with sections 77 and 78 of the Copyright, Designs and Patents Act 1988.

All rights reserved. No part of this book may be reprinted or reproduced or utilised in any form or by any electronic, mechanical, or other means, now known or hereafter invented, including photocopying and recording, or in any information storage or retrieval system, without permission in writing from the publishers.

Trademark notice: Product or corporate names may be trademarks or registered trademarks, and are used only for identification and explanation without intent to infringe.

Library of Congress Cataloging-in-Publication Data
Names: Have, Steven ten, author. | Have, Wouter ten, author.
Title: Reconsidering change management : applying evidence-based insights in change management practice / by Steven ten Have, Wouter ten Have, Anne-Bregje Huijsmans, and Maarten Otto.
Description: First Edition. | New York : Routledge, 2016. | Series: Routledge studies in organizational change & development ; 16 | Includes bibliographical references and index.
Identifiers: LCCN 2016007378 | ISBN 9781138183148 (hardback : alk. paper) | ISBN 9781315646015 (ebook)
Subjects: LCSH: Organizational change. | Management.
Classification: LCC HD58.8 .H3887 2016 | DDC 658.4/06—dc23
LC record available at http://lccn.loc.gov/2016007378

ISBN 13: 978-1-138-34003-9 (pbk)
ISBN 13: 978-1-138-18314-8 (hbk)

Typeset in Sabon
by Apex CoVantage, LLC

Contents

List of Tables and Figures   vii
Foreword   ix
List of Contributors   xiii

1 Introduction   1
2 Why Reconsider Change Management?   15
3 Story of Change: 18 Leading Assumptions in Change Practice   29
4 Methodology   62
5 Examining the Story of Change: Part I   70
6 Examining the Story of Change: Part II   102
7 Examining the Story of Change: Part III   136
8 The Story of Change Reconsidered   176

Appendix A: Overview of Authors and Researchers   181
Appendix B: Allocation of Researchers Per Assumption   183
Appendix C: List of Firms Referred to in Chapter 3   185
Appendix D: Bibliography   187
Index   211

Tables and Figures

Tables

1.1	Full List of the Assumptions	4
3.1	Books and Book Chapters Reviewed	30
4.1	Six Levels to Determine the Methodological Appropriateness of the Research Design of the Studies Included	66
B.1	Overview of Researchers Per Assumption	183

Figures

4.1	Overview of the Research Steps	65
5.1	A Simplified Version of the Model of Organizational Trust Based on Mayer et al. (1995)	85
7.1	Assumed Framework of the Relationship between Culture and Performance	147

Foreword

Organizational change is risky. At least, that is what many change experts including well-known global consultants and management gurus would have us believe. It is often claimed that 70 percent of all change initiatives fail. For most experts, the reasons for this high failure rate are obvious. Change initiatives fail because there is no sense of urgency. Change only succeeds when there is a clear vision, a guiding coalition, or a strong commitment to the change goals. Change projects break down because change leaders lack emotional intelligence (EI) or fail to deal with resistance to change among employees. Such a litany of expert claims is not unique to organizational change: Whether it's strategy, marketing, or human resources, such experts make many (sometimes conflicting) claims about what does and doesn't work without explaining the basis for their assumptions.

In all areas of management practice, there are large discrepancies between the assumptions that experts do and what current academic research suggests. Studies indicate that even highly educated, experienced managers are largely unaware of key research findings that are relevant to their everyday decisions and that they often place too much trust in so-called best practices or what just feels 'right' (Carless, Rasiah, & Irmer, 2009; Rynes, Colbert, & Brown, 2002; Sanders, van Riemsdijk, & Groen, 2008).

The gap between research and practice in management is profound. The way managers are educated is partly to blame. There are major differences between what is taught in MBA classrooms and what the research evidence shows (Brown, Charlier, Rynes, & Hosmanek, 2013). A review of more than 800 course syllabi from 333 management programs showed that only a minority (26 percent) made use of scientific evidence in any form (Charlier, Brown, & Rynes, 2011)—suggesting that business schools inhabit the world of folk wisdom rather than the domain of science (Pfeffer, 2012). Thoughtful managers who think critically are therefore ill equipped to know whether the claims and beliefs that dominate management practice are true or important and whether they should guide their actions.

One hopeful response to this dilemma is a call for evidence, that is, information, facts, or data supporting a claim, belief, or assumption. This call is largely inspired by the evidence-based management movement and its emphasis on the explicit use of the current, best evidence in making managerial and business decisions. It is part of a broader movement advocating evidence-based practice (EBP) that is being increasingly used in medicine, policing, education, criminology, social work, and public policy. An important premise of EBP is that all types and sources of evidence—whether they relate to professional experience, organizational data, or scientific research findings—must be critically appraised for reliability and trustworthiness. This critical appraisal of evidence is at the heart of EBP.

As ambassadors of the EBP movement in management, we advocate the integration of EBP in management education. Future managers should be taught to ask their teachers and management gurus critical questions that challenge assumptions and critically appraise the reliability of evidence. Learning such skills makes people reflective, active, and critical. In management education and practice, too much attention is paid to unfounded beliefs, 'new' insights, and success stories from famous business leaders. Instead, managers always need to ask whether the underlying evidence bears scrutiny.

In recent years we have taught hundreds of managers and management students how to appraise the quality of evidence. When teaching these skills, we mainly focus on the use of evidence from the scientific literature—findings from empirical studies published in peer-reviewed academic journals—as these appear to be the sources that managers use the least (Dunnette & Brown, 1968; Gabriel, Kottasz, & Bennett, 2006; Howells, Nedeva, & Georghiou, 1998; Rynes et al., 2002). Using their own questions as a starting point, we teach managers how to search for relevant studies in online databases and to critically appraise the relevance and trustworthiness of research findings. Importantly, the same skills that are used when thinking about the validity, reliability, and relevance of evidence are useful for evaluating other kinds of evidence such as organizational data and personal opinions. As academics we have taught these skills to students at universities and business schools and, as members of the Center for Evidence-Based Management (CEBMa), we have taught the same skills in workshops in companies.

One company we have trained is actively facilitating the management of change from an evidence-based perspective. TEN HAVE Change Management is a Dutch consulting firm whose professional consultants specialize in the management of organizational change. As a consultancy firm giving expert advice to others, TEN HAVE Change Management considers it their moral obligation to ensure that their advice stands up to evidence-based scrutiny. By training their consultants in the principles of EBP, they have taken an important first step.

The partners of TEN HAVE Change Management also decided to further enhance the EBP skills of their consultants while making a substantial contribution to the application of EBP in change management. They have done this by first identifying 18 widespread assumptions about the management of change. To do this they assessed popular business books and the Web sites of highly reputed consulting firms. Next, they and their consultants adopted an evidence-based approach by conducting a rapid assessment of the research evidence for each of these assumptions. This book is the outcome of their work. TEN HAVE Change Management has performed the service of separating the wheat from the chaff around these claims, clearly identifying what is known, what is not known, and the level of trustworthiness of the evidence for each of these critical change management assumptions.

TEN HAVE Change Management consultants are first and foremost practitioners. Although most have advanced academic degrees, their daily practice is about helping clients solve tough problems in their businesses rather than conducting research and writing academic papers. To identify the evidence for each assumption and its trustworthiness, they sifted through many academic articles. We have seen them make sense of each study (What kind of research design is this? How was this outcome measured? How should we interpret this effect size?) and watched the sometimes heated discussions about what conclusions can reasonably be drawn from the findings. Their efforts have paid off in two important ways.

The first concerns the management profession itself. Several authors argue that management is not really a profession, even though it should be (Barker, 2010; Khurana, Nohria, & Penrice, 2005; Sutton, 2007). A profession is defined by several features, the most important of which is having a formal shared body of knowledge. In management—and change management in particular—such a formal body of knowledge has been lacking. Through the research reported in this book, TEN HAVE Change Management has made a substantial contribution by providing professional managers with a carefully scrutinized and actionable body of knowledge.

The second contribution concerns the employees who are those most affected by change. Organizational change can have a truly profound impact on the lives and well-being of employees and their families. As practitioners affecting the lives of so many, change managers have a moral obligation to use the best available evidence. In that regard, this book, which was created by a small consulting firm, is a truly important contribution. May many such contributions follow.

Eric Barends, PhD, managing director of CEBMa.
Rob Briner, PhD, professor of organizational psychology at the International Centre for Higher Education Management (ICHEM), Division Strategy and Organisation, and scientific director of CEBMa.
Denise M. Rousseau, PhD, professor of organizational behavior and public policy at Carnegie Mellon University's H. John Heinz III College and the Tepper School of Business and president of the Academic Council of CEBMa.

References

Barker, R. (2010). No, management is not a profession. *Harvard Business Review*, 88(7/8), 52–60.

Brown, K. G., Charlier, S. D., Rynes, S. L., & Hosmanek, A. (2013). What do we teach in organizational behavior? An analysis of MBA syllabi. *Journal of Management Education*, 37(4), 447–472.

Carless, S. A., Rasiah, J., & Irmer, B. E. (2009). Discrepancy between human resource research and practice: Comparison of industrial/ organisational psychologists and human resource practitioners' beliefs. *Australian Psychologist*, 44(2), 105–111.

Charlier, S. D., Brown, K. G., & Rynes, S. L. (2011). Teaching evidence-based management in MBA programs: What evidence is there? *Academy of Management Learning & Education*, 10(2), 222–236.

Dunnette, M., & Brown, Z. (1968). Behavioral science research and the conduct of business. *Academy of Management Journal*, 11(2), 177–188.

Gabriel, H., Kottasz, R., & Bennett, R. (2006). Advertising planning, ad-agency use of advertising models, and the academic practitioner divide. *Marketing Intelligence & Planning*, 24(5), 505–527.

Howells, J., Nedeva, M., & Georghiou, L. (1998). *Industry academic links in UK*. Retrieved February 8, 2016, from https://www.google.nl/url?sa=t&rct=j&q=&esrc=s&source=web&cd=2&ved=0ahUKEwjG4Kv79ufKAhXGwxQKHYqbC3AQFggnMAE&url=http%3A%2F%2Fwww.ibrarian.net%2Fnavon%2Fpaper%2FIndustry_Academic_Links_in_the_UK.pdf%3Fpaperid%3D13710593&usg=AFQjCNFWk8qk5QNnVSE-MRJYRbznTr3Gnw&cad=rja

Khurana, R., Nohria, N., & Penrice, D. (2005). Management as a profession. In J. W. Lorsch, L. Berlowitz, & A. Zelleke (Eds.), *Restoring trust in American business* (pp. 43–62). Cambridge, MA: MIT Press.

Pfeffer, J. (2012). Foreword. In D. M. Rousseau (Ed.), *The Oxford handbook of evidence-based management* (pp. VII–X). New York, NY: Oxford University Press.

Rynes, S. L., Colbert, A. E., & Brown, K. G. (2002). HR professionals' beliefs about effective human resource practices: Correspondence between research and practice. *Human Resource Management*, 41(2), 149–174.

Sanders, K., Van Riemsdijk, M., & Groen, B. (2008). The gap between research and practice: A replication study on the HR professionals' beliefs about effective human resource practices. *The International Journal of Human Resource Management*, 19(10), 1976–1988.

Sutton, B. (2007, September 17). *Why management is not a profession*. Retrieved February 8, 2016, from http://bobsutton.typepad.com/my_weblog/2007/09/more-evidence-t.html

Contributors

Vittorio Busato

Marieke Dresmé

Niels van der Eng

Ernst Graamans

Kim Grinwis

Leonard Millenaar

Lianne Ossenkoppele

Lisa van Rossum

Sjoerd Segijn

Stefan Smit

Ton Speet

Cornell Vernooij

Joris Westhof

With support of the CEBMa (www.cebma.org).

1 Introduction

Separating the Wheat From the Chaff

> Billions of dollars have been spent in the last two decades on management and organizational development activities purportedly designed to change organizations. These include programs to introduce management by objectives (MBO), organization development programs, the managerial grid, leadership training, strategic planning models, and more recently, quality circles. Virtually none of these efforts has any systematic monitoring or evaluation associated with it. This leads to an unfortunate state of affairs where the waxing and waning of organizational improvement remedies are associated with limited understanding of what works and what does not and why.
>
> (Tichy, 1983, p. 363)

In the 1970s, inmates serving life sentences at a prison in New Jersey started a program known as 'Scared Straight' to deter at-risk or delinquent children from a future life of crime. The inmates used aggressive presentations depicting the worst of life in adult prisons, including exaggerated stories of rape and murder, to discourage at-risk juveniles visiting the prison facility from committing future criminal offenses. Programs such as this are rooted in deterrence theory. Even though research has indicated that such programs are not effective, jurisdictions across the country continue to use Scared Straight and related programs. Moreover, a recent meta-analysis has revealed that these programs actually increased crime and delinquency. Nevertheless, Scared Straight was recently presented as a successful intervention in a television documentary broadcast in the Netherlands (Petrosino, Turpin-Petrosino, Hollis-Peel, Lavenberg, & Stern, 2004).

In the early 1980s a new drug (Tambocor) was found to be highly successful in suppressing arrhythmias. Not until a randomized control trial was performed did it become clear that although these drugs do indeed suppress arrhythmias, they also increase mortality. The CAST trial revealed excess mortality of 56/1000. By the time the results were published, at least 100,000 patients had been taking this drug (Moore, 1995).

2 Introduction

In 1998, teaching methods in the final three years of secondary education in the Netherlands (Grades 9 to 12) were overhauled by the introduction of two major new educational formats—'Nieuwe Leren' (New Learning) and 'Studiehuis' (Independent Self-Study)—for which no academic basis whatsoever was available. The reform was motivated by the idea that 'senior' pupils in secondary education should be given more freedom to choose their own learning methods on the assumption that this would smooth their transition to higher education. In October 2005, the Dutch Education Ministry published a damning assessment of the reform, saying that many first-year students in higher education lacked the required entry-level qualifications for their chosen course. Due to an emphasis on skills and competence building, students simply had not learned enough at secondary school (Busato, 2014).

The North American Free Trade Agreement (NAFTA) passed Congress amid contentious debate in 1993. Detractors argued that it would produce an exodus of jobs, whereas proponents argued that it would create jobs. The economist Samuelson stated:

> What we're being told is that free trade with Mexico would devastate the U.S. economy. With its low wages, Mexico would unleash a flood of cheap imports into our markets. There would be a mass exodus of U.S. factory jobs, as hordes of American companies fled across the border. "Save Your Job, Save Our Country: Why NAFTA Must Be Stopped—Now" is the book by Ross Perot and Pat Choate that captures the worst fears. Many unions make similar arguments. . . . The alarmism about jobs is actually an assault on the president's authority to make foreign policy. The economic logic against NAFTA is weak as is the political logic. Congressional opposition is a wrecking operation.
> (Samuelson, 1993)

Claims of influential people like Perot and Choate were suspect; they ignored evidence and economic models (Samuelson, 1993). For example, the available evidence indicated that whereas the employment effects have been small, NAFTA has caused an explosion of trade (Thorbecke & Eigen-Zucchi, 2002). Many studies sought to predict the effects of NAFTA on low-skilled labor. As Burfisher, Robinson, and Thierfelder (2001) discussed, the consensus of these studies was that the negative effects on low-skilled workers would be negligible.

The evidence-based paradigm for practitioners—accounting for a particular course of action by referring to academic data in combination with professional judgment and experience, organizational data, and the concerns and values of stakeholders (Center for Evidence-Based Management, n.d.)—has been gaining ground in recent decades. An attempt has been made to improve the quality of outcomes in a variety of areas, including policy making, education, and clinical health care, to name but a few. Medical practice, for example, relies on scientific research. Clearly, doctors want answers to two questions: What is the available scientific evidence, and how strong is it?

Might the evidence-based paradigm also be applicable in management and more specifically in change management? What would happen if consultants, executives, and managers also base their recommendations and decisions on behavioral research findings that are evidence based? Would this measurably improve organizational performance and reduce reliance on all kinds of popular but poorly founded ideas about effective management and effective change management in particular (what we call the *providence-based approach*)? Would this paradigm encourage executives and managers to distinguish between evidence-based and providence-based thinking? Would it perhaps help executives and managers to learn to appreciate that some management interventions are made merely on the recommendation of some authority figure or management guru (what we call the *eminence-based approach*)?

These questions and the conviction that it may be dangerous or unprofessional to apply unproven ideas or concepts—or old ideas or concepts that have been refuted—motivated us to write the book that you now hold in your hands: *Reconsidering Change Management—Applying Evidence-Based Insights in Change Management Practice*.

In our consulting practice, we frequently come across managers who make unnecessary mistakes, for example, because they cling to management theories that can quite easily be disproved. Frequently, such management theories address symptoms rather than root causes, are downright flawed, or obstruct the search for real solutions.

Over the years, the pseudo-academic nature of many popular management theories has been criticized by authors such as Jeffrey Pfeffer, Robert Sutton, Sumantra Ghoshal, and Phil Rosenzweig. In our prior articles (Barends & Ten Have, 2008; Barends, Janssen, Ten Have, & Ten Have, 2013, 2014) we have also questioned the validity of many popular change management theories. For this book, we brought together a team of 17 academics and practitioners, all trained in evidence-based methodology, to examine the academic basis for the practical application of 18 popular management assumptions—for example, the idea that participation is the key to successful change or that a fair change process is what matters for successful change (see Table 1.1 for a full list of the assumptions discussed in detail in this book). A systematic review (see Chapter 4) served as the methodological basis for the book: Identify all relevant pieces of academic research related to these assumptions, assess their validity, and rank them by strength of evidence. It should be emphasized that behavioral researchers do not set out to 'prove' their theories in the way that, for example, mathematicians do; instead, they provide support for their assertions and attach a degree of probability to the random nature, or otherwise, of their findings.

4 Introduction

Table 1.1 Full List of the Assumptions

1	Seventy percent of all change initiatives fail.
2	A clear vision is essential for successful change.
3	People will not change if there is no sense of urgency.
4	Trust in the leader is needed for successful change.
5	When managing change, a transformational leadership style is more effective than a transactional one.
6	Organizational change requires leaders with strong emotional intelligence.
7	Supervisory support is critical for the success of change.
8	To realize change in organizations, a powerful guiding coalition is needed.
9	Employees' capabilities to change determine the organization's capacity to change.
10	Participation is key to successful change.
11	Resistance to change is detrimental to the success of change.
12	A fair change process is important in achieving successful change.
13	Changing organizational culture is time-consuming and difficult.
14	Organizational culture is related to performance.
15	Goal setting combined with feedback is a powerful tool for change leaders.
16	Commitment to change is an essential component of a successful change initiative.
17	Financial incentives are effective ways to encourage change and improve performance.
18	Self-managing teams perform better in realizing change than traditionally managed teams.

This book provides managers with digestible summaries of relevant scientific evidence related to change (rather like the medical Cochrane reviews, which make current information about effectiveness in health care accessible to doctors by providing systematic overviews of available literature; Higgins & Green, 2006). It thus bridges the gap between research and practice, with a view to bringing about tangible improvements in management, and change management in particular, as well as in organizations. In this way it makes a meaningful contribution to the maturing profession of change management and to responsible change management in practice.

Why This Book?

In Formula 1 racing, for some teams a key criterion for innovation is that it should make the car go faster (Pettit, 2006). But there have been instances where the fastest driver didn't win the race, for example, because his or her engine blew up. So we need a more inclusive definition of what constitutes successful innovation. This illustrates precisely what evidence-based change management is not, but should be. With a more inclusive definition, you will see that you're not in the business of owning and operating fast cars but rather in the business of winning races. We want to contribute with evidence-based change management to enable practitioners to win their races. Scientific knowledge can be compared to speed in Formula 1. However, what ultimately wins the race for you is far more complex. Science is not an end in itself but merely a means toward an end. This is not 'art for art's sake' but a new contribution to 'management technology,' as Peter Drucker (2010) puts it. It's a positive development, and its application will contribute to economic growth, our common well-being, and quality of life while preventing unnecessary economic, social and social-emotional damage. In other words, we want to be in the business of providing the right solutions that help improve working practices and, hence, our lives. That's our guiding principle.

Our central research aim is to understand the key issues in change management. But it's important to expose the views of gurus and commercial service providers who burden organizations with invalid and irresponsible ideas. We do not level charges against such people but rather showcase validated knowledge and know-how. For our research, we identified the main issues that managers struggle with. Some of the answers they seek can be found in popular management books. Our team has analyzed more than 50 of such books to identify the key concepts and views related to change management. Our research shows that in some cases, messages do indeed stand up to critical assessment. But often the stated claims go way beyond what the available evidence supports. And sometimes, either there's no supporting evidence whatsoever, or assertions are in conflict with available evidence. In other cases, new hypotheses are presented as the evidence-based answers can easily be found.

About 10 years ago, when one of our former colleagues was a senior manager in a large health care organization, his CEO strongly advised him to read Jim Collins's book *Good to Great* (Collins, 2001). In this best seller, Collins reveals the principles behind growth, financial performance, and shareholder value. On closer inspection, however, his claims and assertions turn out to be true in the same way that a horoscope is true: They are all quite generic, so most readers will be inclined to interpret them in a way that makes them sound true. The CEO was absolutely convinced that this book revealed a higher truth, not because he was naive or gullible but because he read it in a way that confirmed his existing beliefs. Because he believed the claims in the book to be true, he 'saw' that they were consistent with his own professional experience. What we see is often what we want to see: We are inclined to interpret evidence in ways that confirm our existing beliefs and to ignore contrary evidence. For years, our former colleague also based his decisions on knowledge gained from popular business books. His favorite was Peters and Waterman's *In Search of Excellence* (1982), another best seller. For a long time, he used their '7S' Model to analyze organizations simply because it was the model that best reflected his professional beliefs. What he did learn was that asking for evidence to back up claims—especially when made in a professional context—is the first and possibly most important step toward EBP. And asking critical questions does not require a Harvard degree. Everyone can do it.

Within a few years after the book of Peters and Waterman (1982) was published, all the 'great' and excellent companies cited in them fell into decline. One, Fannie Mae, was even bailed out by the government. In fact, 14 of the 43 companies were in serious trouble only a few years after the book came out. Tom Peters admitted the 'fraud' he had committed in the December 2001 Issue of *Fast Company*: "This is pretty small beer, but for what it's worth, okay, I confess: We faked the data" (Peters, 2001, confession number three).

Practitioners tend to ignore this. Many serious organizations facing serious issues rely on superficial and intuitively attractive approaches. This clearly applies to change processes as well. The solutions provided tend to be merely entertainment or infotainment at best—and in the 'song-and-dance' category at that. Words like *inspiration, collaboration,* and *vision* apparently give consultants a license for making virtually boundless assertions. Those who make them seem to think that ineffective fads can do no damage. Sometimes that may indeed be the case. At least something happens as the result of the chosen intervention; the organization is 'shaken up.' So be it—organizations are playing with their own time and money, or so one would assume. But it's another matter if valid expertise in change management is callously discarded at the expense of clients (e.g., patients)—those who are dependent and vulnerable during reorganization. 'Professionals' can and should be subjected to performance criteria because others depend on their expertise and moral standards. Courts and disciplinary boards are quite rightly alert and ready to intervene when there is professional malpractice, especially when vulnerable people are affected.

Some regret the emergence of EBP. 'Never let the truth waste a good story' has a nice ring to it, whereas the evidence-based approach does not. It's rather like the two basic tendencies that are said to dominate historiography: Some historians produce broad-sweeping and inspiring stories that are fun to read, whereas others take a skeptical view and fillet myths and magic with sobering facts and critical arguments. Although their popular appeal differs, both fulfil a need. There is a need for attractive stories as well as for solid knowledge and facts. The trick is to strike a balance between story and knowledge. As John Malkovich once explained in an interview the difference between a magician and an actor: "The first shows you magic and lets you believe it is reality. The second shows you reality and lets you believe it's magic."

Is Change Management 'Maturing'?

Like clinical psychology several decades ago, change management is now in the process of emerging from the phase of theory development. There are many original insights into how best to change organizations, and there are also many change management gurus. This diversity does not need to be an obstacle; often it's the precursor of the next phase. An evidence-based approach can herald the end of the old phase, which is mainly characterized by personal convictions held by experts.

If change management is to develop like clinical psychology, it will next enter a phase of 'cautious' research, for example, observational and retrospective studies that identify all kinds of correlations without offering a plausible explanatory theory. That's fine, but a further methodological step will be needed for the field to become 'mature': Insights, models, and interventions related to change should, in principle, always be tested empirically.

To do that, we will need a solid methodology as well as databases for recording the outcome of empirical research. But that's not all. The managers and executives of the future will need to be trained, much more than in the past, in how they can critically assess such research and its methodological value. Research by Pfeffer and Sutton (2006), among others, has identified a growing demand in the field of management and organization for an academic basis to theories and models.

Our own research shows that most managers favor evidence-based management (Barends, Villanueva, Briner, & Ten Have, 2015). They are convinced that this can improve the quality of their work. Whether that's wishful thinking, or whether perhaps they are merely paying lip service to the notion of evidence-based management, we don't know. Managers also sometimes say that evidence-based management takes up too much time. That's remarkable if we consider how much time is devoted to legal and financial matters to prevent hasty and careless decision making. Why not adopt a similar attitude toward management theories that are of questionable benefit to the organization? At any rate, our approach is in line with a movement that has been long underway in 'practical disciplines' such as medicine, clinical psychology, pedagogy, policy making, and education.

The Challenge of Management

The world of change management has become utterly commercialized, rather like the medical world, with all those diets and food supplements and the (largely) unsubstantiated claims made about them. It's an illusion to think that big consulting firms advertise their wares simply with the intent of improving organizations. There are major financial interests at stake. They do not hesitate to sell new methods, models, or insights, regardless of whether their effectiveness has been established. Many consulting firms also latch onto trends. Ten years ago business process redesign was all the rage; five years ago it was lean management, and Six Sigma. Subsequently, these were merged (to milk them even more). Nowadays, it's said that organizations need to be *agile*. If you search for that term on Google, you'll find dozens of firms that will offer to help your organization become agile. Boards and managers are being bombarded with propositions that are peddled very convincingly. Our method should give them the tools that will enable them to challenge such propositions.

It's pretty fashionable nowadays to be contemptuous about managers and executives, to look down on them as the source of all evil, to engage in management bashing, or to make a caricature of managers. There are indeed many poor managers, people who are incompetent, morally reproachable, or overly narcissistic. Sometimes they are redundant. With or without conventional managers, the function of manager still has to be fulfilled. Organizations, teams, and individuals require direction, coordination, steering, encouragement to collaborate, and feedback. The function of management must be fulfilled, whether it be via the hierarchy or via interaction in the community, with formal or informal leadership, by means of systems or by means of shared values. That's not easy to do, and it requires solid knowledge. But conventional managers often are attracted by or turn to 'revolutionary' concepts and 'best practices' that emerge. Managers are aware of their responsibility, have their ambitions, and feel they have to act. Moreover, they are expected to keep a steady hand on the rudder and to know what they're doing. These managers have to take their responsibility in uncertain, demanding, dynamic, and often difficult circumstances. Solid knowledge and the time to reflect are often lacking. That explains their vulnerability and openness to new concepts or models that promise easy solutions or quick fixes in complex situations.

The Role of Business Schools

Business schools are major driving forces behind these tendencies. Management education is one of the world's largest industries, involving billions of dollars. Jeffrey Pfeffer (2015) has characterized this industry as an entertainment industry and for a reason. It's not in the interest of a business school that makes millions in profit to adjust the curriculum to an evidence-based approach. That goes against their revenue model. Ghoshal (2005), writing in the professional magazine *Academy of Management Learning and Education*, noted as early as 2005 that renowned business schools teach pseudo-academic management models and theories. And they still do.

Medical schools and medical practitioners, in contrast, aim to do things differently. The question is why business schools and the management profession in general—and change management in particular—do not adopt sound guidelines similar to those that are now provided, for example, by the Cochrane reviews (Higgins & Green, 2006). Why is there so much resistance? After all, management *is* a profession. There are few professions where so many ill-conceived and barely substantiated interventions are put to practice without careful consideration. All too often, the importance of solid managerial and organizational knowledge and science is underplayed. Managers need to be like good parents: They have to think and act responsibly; they have to provide a safe and stimulating environment and allocate resources in a proper way. They must act knowledgeably and dedicated and be professional, that is to say, deal professionally and ethically with that which has been entrusted to them, with those who depend on them, and for whom they are responsible. If they don't, they may well cause social, emotional, and economic damage and loss by causing personal suffering and stress, leading to fear, dysfunction, and disaffection. For example, a major reorganization at France Telecom caused a great deal of anguish—and even suicides—among the staff (Hoheb, 2014). This is at least partly due to changes in the company leading to a dysfunctional working environment.

The Role of Consultants

Should consultants base their recommendations on the best available evidence instead of merely relying on the 'tool kit' routinely applied in earlier engagements? Yes. Consultants and managers are often perceived as merchants of hope, and people look to them for guidance—all the more reason to analyze the specific context of challenges faced by the company concerned, to develop insights on the basis of the most convincing data available, and to translate these insights into appropriate interventions and recommendations to managers. When evidence is hard to come by, insights based on providence and eminence may be useful. But those insights will need to be qualified and explicitly positioned for the client. If no tried, tested, and proven method is available, other avenues that might lead to a solution will need to be explored: trial-and-error, experiments. But experimentation and prototyping are governed by other criteria than tried-and-tested methods and 'proven concepts.' Knowing and using the available evidence is not nice-to-haves; they are must-haves: a moral and professional obligation. Professionals owe it to themselves and to the clients, customers, or patients in their care. A court verdict in the Netherlands on the application of alternative medical practice may serve to illustrate this. In this particular case, the court ruled that practitioners of alternative medicine are not at liberty to give incorrect or incomplete information to their patients but in fact are under an obligation to ". . . alert [their patients], if necessary, to the (limited) possibilities, effectiveness and risks of the diagnosis, prescribed medication, or therapy . . ." (Rechtbank Amsterdam, 2009). Moreover, the court ruling stated that if the effectiveness of a particular therapy had not properly been demonstrated, practitioners had the obligation to explain this clearly and up front to their patients or clients. The key is to separate the wheat from the chaff.

That's indeed what we aim to achieve in change management, but how do you do it? Many organizations don't even try and lack the necessary awareness to do this. They tend to choose the easy way: the intuitively attractive course of action. In many organizations, information is judged rather like 14-year-olds do when they simply go with the very first attractive hit they find in Google and don't probe any further.

Organizations tend to engage outside help without any prior reflection or diagnosis, let alone gathering and assessing available evidence. With all those 'best practices,' kickoffs, references, benchmarks, and so on, reflection and evidence are woefully lacking. Organizations need to be like a monastery but end up as an amusement park.

Our approach has been described as an *activist* one. That's fine with us. Activist is not a form of abuse but a way to describe those who take up a cause. It means being committed, dedicated, wanting to do something about and for things that can be done better, and having a clear 'voice.' But it also implies doing more than merely being critical. The evidence-based approach offers a well-considered, positive, and dedicated way of thinking and acting whereby the academic knowledge and profound expertise of experienced professionals are made available to management practitioners.

Exposing the Quacks in Change Management

In this book, we aim to present a more effective—and more honest—type of management practice. In our view, quacks and pseudo-professionals are ineradicable. Given human nature and the urge felt by managers to act, there will always be a market for stories that are too good to be true and for those who tell such stories. But with growing awareness among 'practitioners'— and evidence continuing to flow—the nature of that 'show' will become increasingly evident. We aren't there yet; there's still too much damage being done. Evidence-based management and change management can be used to denounce questionable ideas and replace them with insights based on hard facts and solid research. The paradigm is one of a basic academic attitude designed to raise the profession of management to a higher level.

This book is intended first and foremost to be a sober call for well-considered, careful, and prudent change management. It offers a new perspective by showing how a systematic and methodical assessment of relevant knowledge and experience can offer answers to questions that really matter. This is not to suggest that managers, with their characteristic urge to act, should go about their business like natural scientists. But it does mean that they should make their professional decisions on the basis of the best available evidence, the relevant experiences of peers, their own carefully considered experiences and options, and the specific characteristics and contexts of the organizations in which they work.

Evidence-Based Change Management Has Academic Roots and a Pragmatic Orientation

The function of evidence-based management is to provide practice and practitioners with a better basis for their decisions and action. Following the CEBMa, the guiding principle is:

> . . . that management decisions should be based on a combination of critical thinking and the best available evidence. And by 'evidence,' we

mean information, facts or data supporting (or contradicting) a claim, assumption or hypothesis. Evidence may come from scientific research, but internal business information and even professional experience can count as 'evidence.' In principle, then, all managers base their decisions on some kind of 'evidence.' Many managers, however, pay little or no attention to the quality of the evidence they rely on to make decisions. As a result management decisions are often based on unfounded beliefs, so-called 'best practice,' fads, ideas popularized by management gurus, and success stories of famous CEOs.

(Center for Evidence-Based Management, n.d.)

Evidence-based practice seeks to improve the way decisions are made. It is an approach to decision making and day-to-day work practice that helps practitioners to critically evaluate the extent to which they can trust the evidence they have at hand. It also helps practitioners to identify, find, and evaluate additional evidence relevant to their decisions. "Evidence-based practice seeks to address this state of affairs by helping managers to critically evaluate the validity, generalizability, and applicability of the evidence they have in hand and how to find the 'best available' evidence" (Center for Evidence-Based Management, n.d.).

Based on research Barends, Rousseau, and Briner (2014) state that:

> . . . most practitioners pay little or no attention to evidence from the scientific literature or from the organization, placing instead too much trust in low-quality evidence, such as personal judgment and experience, 'best practices' and the beliefs of corporate leaders. As a result, billions of dollars are spent on management practices that are ineffective or even harmful to organizations, their members and their clients. (p. 6)

As CEBMA states (Barends, Rousseau, & Briner, 2014):

> When we say 'evidence,' we mean information, facts or data supporting (or contradicting) a claim, assumption or hypothesis. Evidence may come from scientific research suggesting generally applicable facts about the world, people, or organizational practices. Evidence may also come from local organizational or business indicators, such as company metrics or observations of practice conditions. Even professional experience can be an important source of evidence, for example an entrepreneur's past experience of setting up a variety of businesses should indicate the approach that is likely to be the most successful. Think of it in legal terms. In a court of law, evidence is presented in a variety of forms, from eyewitness testimonies and witness statements to forensic evidence and security-camera images. All this evidence helps the judge or jury to decide whether a person is innocent or guilty. The same is true

for management decisions. Regardless of its source, all evidence may be included if it is judged to be trustworthy and relevant. (p. 5)

To illustrate, Michael Frese (2015) put it as follows:

> People always consider their own knowledge to be more important than any other knowledge. In discussion with managers, we need to point out that there are numerous biases in their intuitions, remembered experiences, and approaches. The n = 1 experience is always more powerful than pretty much anything else. And often these experiences are based on defunct theories. Thus, we need to tell practitioners: "don't fall prey to the latest fad—or your (distorted) memories—rather, check also the academic evidence yourself."

This of course, is why we say that practitioners should be able to change their views when the evidence contradicts their experience. Or like John Maynard Keynes—although views differ on who said it (first)—wrote: "When the facts change, I change my mind. What do you do, sir?" (Quote Investigator, n.d.). Rob Briner (2015) adds:

> We need to critically appraise evidence from whatever sources it comes—our experience, industry 'standards,' claims by consultancies, management gurus, academic research, anecdotes, success stories, organizational data, etc. One reason for getting practitioners to do this is that we believe it makes them *active* and also critical users of evidence. We are trying to make sure that people always question evidence and data, and ask if it's relevant and trustworthy from *wherever* it comes. We don't want practitioners just to assume something is true' or correct or valid, without critically appraising it.

Rationalizations such as 'It's best practice,' 'It's all in the textbooks,' 'A big consultancy firm does it,' or 'Steve Jobs did it' belong to the preadult phase of evidence-based change management.

The Structure of This Book

In recent decades many popular change management textbooks have been written, and consultancy firms have flourished with their ideas and 'best practices' on change management. A great deal of scientific research has also been carried out in this period involving issues relevant to change management practice. The main purpose of this book is to confront both disciplines and further develop change management as a professional discipline.

Chapter 2 describes the existing paradigms of providence, eminence, and evidence. It explains the necessity of applying the evidence-based approach within the field of management and in particular change management. In

Chapter 3, the 'Story of Change' is introduced and exemplified based on 18 relevant and widespread assumptions regarding change management that we identified by assessing the most popular books on change management and analyzing a large number of Web sites of consultancy firms. The methodology used to examine the academic basis of these assumptions is described in Chapter 4. In Chapters 5, 6, and 7, the assumptions are appraised and evaluated, mainly by testing them against the scientific evidence (scientific literature) available. Taking this evidence-based perspective, we as experienced change management practitioners also reflect on the conclusions drawn from our own professional expertise. As a result, we reconsider change management leading to the final Chapter (8), wherein the 'Story of Change' is reconsidered. We create an evidence-based perspective on change management and organizational change. In doing so we provide practitioners with a frame of reference that can be used to evaluate popular assumptions and use them as a basis for their own practice and interventions.

References

Barends, E., & Ten Have, S. (2008). Op weg naar evidence-based verandermanagement. *Holland Management Review*, 120, 15–21.

Barends, E., Janssen, B., Ten Have, W. D., & Ten Have, S. (2013). Effects of change interventions: What kind of evidence do we really have? *Journal of Applied Behavioral Science*, 50(1), 5–27.

Barends, E., Janssen, B., Ten Have, W. D., & Ten Have, S. (2014). Difficult but doable: Increasing the internal validity of organizational change management studies. *The Journal of Applied Behavioral Science*, 50(1), 50–54.

Barends, E., Rousseau, D. M., & Briner, R. B. (2014). *Evidence-based management: The basic principles*. Amsterdam, NL: Center for Evidence-Based Management.

Barends, E., Villanueva, J., Briner, R. B., & Ten Have, S. (2015). Managers' attitudes and perceived barriers to evidence-based management: An international survey. In E. Barends (Ed.), *In search of evidence. Empirical findings and professional perspectives on evidence-based management* (pp. 143–178). Amsterdam, NL: VU University Press.

Briner, R. (2015, November 27). *Why the CEBMa model is misleading—further comments* [Blog post]. Retrieved January 4, 2016, from https://groups.google.com/forum/#!msg/evidence-based-management/Gjj2B_Qeav4/uG8pDs_rCAAJ

Burfisher, M. E., Robinson, S., & Thierfelder, K. (2001). The impact of NAFTA on the United States. *Journal of Economic Perspectives*, 15(1), 125–144.

Busato, V. (2014). *Psychologie al dente*. Amsterdam, NL: Uitgeverij Fosfor.

Center for Evidence-Based Management (CEBMa). (n.d.). *What is evidence-based management?* Retrieved January 14, 2016, from http://www.cebma.org/frequently-asked-questions/evidence-based-management/

Collins, J. C. (2001). *Good to great: Why some companies make the leap . . . and others don't*. New York, NY: HarperCollins Publishers.

Drucker, P. F. (2010). *Technology, management, and society*. Boston, MA: Harvard Business Press.

Frese, M. (2015, November 27). *Re: Why the CEBMa model may, for some people, be misleading—some suggestions for improvement* [Blog post]. Retrieved December 15, 2015, from https://groups.google.com/forum/#!msg/evidence-based-management/Gjj2B_Qeav4/eKV65-7sCAAJ

Ghoshal, S. (2005). Bad management theories are destroying good management practices. *Academy of Management Learning & Education, 4*(1), 75–91.

Higgins, J. P. T., & Green, S. (2006). *Cochrane handbook for systematic reviews of interventions 4.2.6* [updated September 2006]. Retrieved September 1, 2015, from http://community.cochrane.org/sites/default/files/uploads/Handbook4.2.6Sep 2006.pdf

Hoheb, C. (2014, January 29). *Lessons learned from France Telecom: Stress in the workplace*. Retrieved January 13, 2016, from http://www.corporatewellnessmagazine.com/focused/france-telecom-layoffs/

Moore, T. J. (1995). *Deadly medicine: Why tens of thousands of heart patients died in America's worst drug disaster*. New York, NY: Simon & Schuster.

Peters, T. J. (December, 2001). *Tom Peters' true confessions*. Retrieved January 12, 2016, from http://www.fastcompany.com/44077/tom-peterss-true-confessions

Peters, T. J., & Waterman, R. H. (1982). *In search of excellence: Lessons from America's best-run companies*. New York, NY: Harper & Row.

Petrosino, A., Turpin-Petrosino, C., Hollis-Peel, M. E., Lavenberg, J. G., & Stern, A. (2004). *Scared straight and other juvenile awareness programs for preventing juvenile delinquency*. Retrieved July 19, 2015, from http://www.campbellcollaboration.org/lib/download/13/Scared+Straight_R.pdf

Pettit, R. (2006, December 3). *The agile manager: It might make the car go faster, but does it make the car more competitive?* Retrieved January 12, 2016, from http://www.rosspettit.com/2006/12/it-might-make-car-go-faster-but-does.html?m=1

Pfeffer, J. (2015). *Leadership BS: Fixing workplaces and careers one truth at a time*. New York, NY: Harper Business.

Pfeffer, J., & Sutton, R. I. (2006). *Hard facts, dangerous half-truths, and total nonsense: Profiting from evidence-based management*. Boston, MA: Harvard Business School Press.

Quote Investigator. (n.d.). *When the facts change, I change my mind. What do you do, sir?* Retrieved December 14, 2015, from http://quoteinvestigator.com/2011/07/22/keynes-change-mind/

Rechtbank Amsterdam. (2009, June 12). *ECLI:NL:RBAMS:2009:BI7370*. Retrieved January 12, 2016, from http://deeplink.rechtspraak.nl/uitspraak?id=ECLI:NL:RB AMS:2009:BI7370

Samuelson, R. J. (1993, September 15). *Scare talk about NAFTA*. Retrieved January 12, 2016, from https://www.washingtonpost.com/archive/opinions/1993/09/15/scare-talk-about-nafta/82a1c705-732c-499c-80bc-e63fd74e5942/

Thorbecke, W., & Eigen-Zucchi, C. (2002). Did NAFTA cause a "giant sucking ground?" *Journal of Labor Research, 23*(4), 647–658.

Tichy, N. M. (1983). *Managing strategic change: Technical, political, and cultural dynamics*. New York, NY: John Wiley & Sons.

2 Why Reconsider Change Management?

Eminence, Providence, and Evidence

Like the seafarers of old, managers are constantly searching the horizon for dependable clues that can help them navigate what they often experience as treacherous environments. The challenges related to change management are often seen as *wicked problems*: problems that "cannot be easily and objectively defined . . . and that are open to interpretation from a virtually endless variety of angles. The same is true for possible solutions" (De Wit & Meyer, 1999, p. 60). These challenges are not hypothetical; for the managers involved they are real, and they have to act on them. As Bower (2000) states:

> It's one thing to recognize that a corporation is a complex nonlinear system interacting with a very rich and changing environment. It is another to provide a map of that system that permits managers to act in an intentionally rational fashion. (p. 91)

The need for such a map increases with the pressure, challenges, and competition managers and their people face. This makes them prone to stories and models that promise to tackle the complex problem of changing organizations and people. These ambitious, struggling, and sometimes insecure managers are the first 'targets' of authors producing books with promising titles such as *Managing at the Speed of Change* (Conner, 1992), *Teaching the Elephant to Dance* (Belasco, 1990), *The Change Leaders Roadmap* (Anderson & Anderson, 2010), and *Taking People With You* (Novak, 2012). Despite all the theories, models, and stories about change management, crafting organizational and behavioral change is not a trivial task.

Managers are thus susceptible to popular management books and concepts published by gurus, reputed consultants, and other management thinkers. Influential thinkers Jim Collins and Daniel Goleman, for example, provide us with concepts such as *level-five leadership* and *emotional intelligence (EI)*. In describing a successful change manager, Bower (2000) uses words such as *engaged*, *mobilized*, *steered*, *oversaw*, and *wielded*. These verbs are the characteristics and artistic skills of a great leader of change. Such leaders, according to Bower, energize and focus the efforts of the organization on all levels in a coherent way.

Gurus such as John Kotter (2008) present us with a 'sense of urgency' and 'leading coalitions' as 'givens' in developing successful change. Consultants also enthusiastically provide navigational guidelines and pointers. They bring evidence to bear, or so one would assume, in their efforts to help managers reduce uncertainty when implementing change. When evidence is hard to come by, insights based on providence and eminence may be useful, but these must be applied carefully and conscientiously.

Managing change in organizations is a difficult, risky, and demanding task involving tough, intricate, multidimensional challenges. It's a small wonder that consultants are frequently called on to contribute their presumably objective and experienced analytical perspectives and thus help managers see the wood for the trees when mapping a path toward organizational change. The same goes for famous management thinkers and gurus, the prophets and preachers of our time. These consultants and gurus (and managers, too, for that matter) are often perceived as merchants of hope: People look to them for guidance. Many like to think they are indeed just that. Armed with a broad, fresh perspective, promising alternatives, and simple, effective solutions, they provide managers with an attractive, simple approach to complex matters or a welcome, can-do outlook on the business challenges at hand.

Managers tend to respond enthusiastically to the straightforward solutions of consultants and the intuitive, attractive messages of management gurus, both of which are typically well packaged and eloquently delivered. Relieved to see a way forward between a rock and a hard place, they eagerly take action to implement the recommendations (thus enhancing the market reputation of the consultants and the popularity of gurus). After a while, however, much enthusiastically embraced advice proves to be little more than shallow uncertainty reduction peddled by unscrupulous consultants whose elegantly presented solutions frequently address symptoms rather than root causes and sometimes only make matters worse for their clients. And the followers of gurus such as Kotter and Goleman experience—and sometimes deny—that believing is not a guarantee for performing, changing, or improving. More worrying still is that managers and consultants may derive their 'solutions' from some 'successful and proven' management concept that they happen to have heard about without asking themselves whether the recommendations in question fit the specific organizational context they are dealing with and without testing these 'solutions' in advance by confronting them against the relevant evidence that is available. Beliefs and convictions—providence—and the mesmerizing and rhetoric qualities of gurus—eminence—often prove to be stronger and more attractive than evidence. The willingness to act combined with the availability and attractiveness of ideas advocated and promoted by 'professionals' and 'thinkers' is in most cases stronger than critical reflection, contextual sensitivity, and good thinking. This is a serious problem.

This is why consultants and managers alike have a moral obligation to investigate the specific context of the challenges they face, to develop relevant insights based on the hardest facts available, and to translate these insights into suitable interventions and recommendations. Gurus need to be aware of the way their ideas and concepts are likely to influence their followers, the believers. They must also be clear with regard to the characteristics and qualities of their insights. These may be creative and inspiring but also tentative or not so well grounded. Or they may be intuitive, attractive, and promising or well-defined, tested, validated, and clear with regard to the level of evidence, the contextual limitations, and risks that apply to their ideas. This is the evidence-based approach, whereby managers and consultants develop their decisions and actions from the most reliable pieces of evidence they can find, looking at findings from scientific research, their own carefully considered experience, and whatever they have available to them, as well as the specific characteristics and context of the organization they serve, helped by reliable thinkers who not only brilliantly communicate the strong, attractive characteristics of their messages but also the level of evidence, limitations, risks, downsides, and possible collateral damage when applying them. However, this evidence-based approach is often obstructed by what Schramade (2006, 2014) calls *providence-based thinking*, that is, decision making and actions inspired by popular beliefs or ideologies rather than available evidence. Providence-based thinking tends to manifest itself in the myths and misconceptions that exist in many professions and fields of expertise (Lilienfield, Lynn, Ruscio, & Beyerstein, 2010) and practitioners who refer to providence typically justify their approaches by citing a lack of reliable evidence.* Finally, in addition to evidence and providence as a basis for management intervention, there is the earlier mentioned *eminence-based approach*, that is, thinking and doing based on the opinion some authoritative figure or specialist rather than careful consideration of the available evidence. Knowing, and using, the available evidence is not something that is nice to have; it is essential. It is a moral and professional obligation for the professional and reflects care and responsibility toward clients, customers, and patients.

Why Do Fashionable Ideas Often Carry So Much Weight?

Several factors may explain the popularity of a broad category of management books with one-sided, unproven, or even demonstrably erroneous opinions and the professional actions inspired by them. First of all, reputable publishers can promote the distribution of pseudo-academic management theories and models (Clark & Greatbach, 2004; Micklethwait & Wooldridge, 1998). The many books on General Electric and Jack Welch are cases in point. Second, there is the word-of-mouth or social virus phenomenon: Flawed and sometimes downright folkloristic convictions are often distributed across professional and other communities, assuming a life of their own—and, when this happens, their familiarity is easily mistaken for credibility. One example of this is the oft-stated assertion that 70 percent of all change efforts fail, a popular but nevertheless rash statement (Ten Have & Visser, 2004). A third explanation concerns the selectiveness of our personal perceptions and memories. Human perception of reality tends to be flawed; we perceive reality through our own 'lenses,' and these are skewed by our prejudices and expectations, producing a naive realism (Ross & Ward, 1996) that makes us unwittingly vulnerable to misconceptions. An example of the selectiveness of human perception and memory is our tendency to focus on hits, that is, remarkable coincidences, instead of misses. Many people, for example, will readily recall this or that greedy executive while ignoring the existence of many decent managers, as the latter do not fit their preconceptions. Yet another example is the perception shared by most people that change is difficult or even painful, a view proposed by (the writings of) professionals such as therapists and management consultants whose working days are routinely filled with arduous and painful change efforts. Such professionals—and those who read their books—effectively rule out another reality, which is that many people and organizations are capable of realizing both smaller and larger changes in a natural and harmonious way without suffering major traumas or emotional upheaval. Obviously, successful cases of do-it-yourself change have little to offer to those seeking more sensational outcomes. The fourth and last possible explanation for the popularity of thinly supported management interventions (other than the influence exerted by publishers, folklore, and the selectiveness of human perception and memory) has to do with the easy solutions or quick fixes alluded to earlier. People have a tendency to favor such solutions for their real or perceived problems as they require the least effort. Many dieting regimes, for example, are popular in spite of the fact that the overwhelming majority of adepts quickly regain their former weight once they stop following the regime (Brownell & Rodin, 1994). Similarly, many organizations are addicted to popular management approaches, applying one after the other—TQM, BPR, lean—without ever achieving substantial or lasting improvement.

The latter explanation highlights the deeply felt need that makes professionals embrace ideas, concepts, opinions, and convictions that have little to do with either evidence or the context of the specific organization concerned. It is a tendency witnessed among suppliers of solutions and buyers alike. Solution suppliers tend to promise more than they can deliver, and their clients typically are all too happy to buy the promise. This dynamic is not exclusive to management and consulting, of course; it can also be witnessed in other professional contexts. In her newspaper columns, the Dutch writer Asha ten Broeke often discusses the practices of academics and journalists (e.g., Ten Broeke, 2015). In her search to explain why these professionals and their customers or audiences behave the way they do, she prefers looking for clues in the human condition and social dynamics to easily blame malpractice on the inevitable 'rotten apples in the barrel' and the gullibility of the general public.

Academics and journalists are indeed looking for reliable glimpses of reality or the truth, she says, but they also have an innate desire to 'score.' Managers and consultants, too, want to score while searching for those reliable glimpses of truth that will allow them to get a grip on the reality of their organizational and business processes. Ten Broeke (2015) points to an important problem in this respect: Truth is not easily captured because it is contradictory, complicated, and messy. "That is why solid academic and journalistic research is so time-consuming," Ten Broeke (2015) says, noting that there is no ready market for 'slow messiness' and citing journalist Felix Salmon's observation that contemporary culture will only allow for stories that make sense from A to Z. Salmon has dubbed this the *TED culture*, after the annual Technology, Entertainment and Design (TED) meetings in California, where thinkers and practitioners are given 18 minutes in front of the audience to expound their ideas or experience. In other words, we live in a world where everything is supposed to fit, make sense, and function properly, based on established or emerging 'thought leaders' and their 'ideas worth spreading.' Sagan's (1996) notion that something which is too good to be true usually is, is rejected in this TED culture. Until their protagonists are found out, 'realistic-sounding fairy tales' appear to be the norm—whether they be spectacular research findings in psychology, astonishing revelations by journalists, stories of heroic acts, or the next trailblazing management concept.

So What's the Problem With Eminence?

Many pretentious insights generated by managers and consultants have failed the test of closer inspection. When asked to cite inspiring management research, management students typically refer to the Hawthorne studies (Mayo, 1933), Peters and Waterman's *In Search of Excellence* (1982), Jim Collins's (2001, 2009) work, and Geert Hofstede's (1980) cultural dimensions. Although not entirely without evidence, these studies primarily owe their attractiveness to the eminent names associated with them: Their credibility is eminence based. Furthermore, they have in common that (a) they are all, directly or indirectly, about culture and (b) that the data (and data analysis) and research support for the purported findings are, at the very least, open to question. In all of these cases, the evidence is limited or insubstantial.

Let us briefly look at each of them:

- *Hawthorne Studies*

The original sources showed no systematic change in production levels whatsoever following any of the interventions studied (Franke & Kaul, 1978; McQuarrie, 2005).

- *In Search of Excellence*

The claim was certainly impressive: 'Excellence' in performance allegedly could be traced back to, and explained by, eight specific organizational characteristics. It seemed to be a blueprint for success—at least it was received as such, and the authors did little if anything to deny that it was. Here again, the lofty claim was in shrill contrast to the feeble underlying research and the limited and largely anecdotal evidence. Peters and Waterman's (1982) book contains 140 anecdotes, mostly about the heroics of specific managers. Whereas the book and its message were hugely successful, the alleged excellence of the 43 companies featured in Peters and Waterman's review left something to be desired. Only one in three outperformed the S&P 500 during the first half of the 1980s. Most of the companies discussed suffered a decline in profitability and one decade on were performing below the market average. In fact, 14 of the 43 companies were in serious trouble only a few years after the book came out. Tom Peters (2001) admitted the 'fraud' as cited in Chapter 1.

- *The Work of Jim Collins*

Jim Collins's influential studies, which are among the most popular in management over the past 15 years, have been scrutinized by Rosenzweig (2007). Collins in essence wanted to find out why certain 'ordinary' companies managed to make the transition to excellent performance levels, while others did not. Rosenzweig shows that much of Collins's data came from problematic sources—the general media and interviews with managers from the companies concerned looking back on past achievements—that is, retrospective reports, a type of source vulnerable to distortion and prejudice (Miller, Cardinal, & Glick, 1997). In his books, Collins 2001, 2009) primarily relates the views of specific 'insiders' and observers of the companies reviewed, offering no solid foundations for his assertions, thoroughly crafted answers to the central question, solid research, nuance, or adequate descriptions of the 'limitations' of the research employed.

- *Hofstede's Cultural Dimensions*

Hofstede's approach, too, has been the subject of considerable criticism. According to Schein (1990):

> The problem with this approach is that it assumes knowledge of the relevant dimensions to be studied. Even if these are statistically derived from large samples of items, it is not clear whether the initial item set is broad enough or relevant enough to capture what may for any given organization be its critical cultural themes. Furthermore, it is not clear

whether something as abstract as culture can be measured with survey instruments at all. (p. 110)

Schein (1996) later added the following about Hofstede's research:

We have gone too quickly to formal elegant abstractions that seemingly could be operationally defined and measured, i.e., centralization-decentralization, differentiation-integration, power, etc., and failed to link these to observed reality. I say 'seemingly' because in the effort to define such concepts, we often relied on further abstractions, i.e., questionnaire responses, and began to treat the abstractions as the reality. Not only does this create fuzzy theory and research that is made significant only by massaging the data statistically, but the results are often useless to the practitioner. (p. 232)

Work-related dimensions are deduced from 'lots of data' on the highly dubious assumption that "cultures really are identifiable and exist independently of behavior, so that behavior is molded in the 'template' of the culture" (Voestermans & Verheggen, 2007, p. 21). Further criticism of Hofstede's work relates to flaws in the design process for his five cultural dimensions, the fact that they cannot be replicated, and the notion that his research probably does not touch on culture but most probably relates more to socio-economic factors instead (Baskerville, 2003).

Although typically astonished when first confronted with it, students and practitioners tend to respond with remarkable cheerfulness to such criticism of ostensibly leading management research. In the end, many seem to think that these studies still represent a good 'yarn.' It reminds us of that famous Italian expression: *se non è vero, è ben trovato*—even if it is not true, it is well conceived. As Karmakar and Datta (2012) put it: "[And yet,] the Hawthorne experiments have opened up a new dimension in the field of management . . ." Admittedly, there is some truth in that: An insight or idea can be tremendously valuable in academia and daily practice, irrespective of its theoretical foundations. *Not theory* (Sutton & Staw, 1995)—that is, initial hypotheses, a set of intertwined insights, or a diagram—can often lead to research that produces solid (either confirming or disproving) evidence and possibly the development of well-founded theory. The issues related to the work of Collins and others would be less serious if their 'new dimensions' or 'not theories' had been presented as providence based. But they were not. On the contrary, in all the cases cited here, references to mountains of data, the scientific method, and research constitute important elements of the story, creating the impression that the insights presented are based on solid, methodologically sound reasoning and, as such, high-quality evidence. In short, studies like these are unprofessional in their approach and presentation, to say the least, and potentially damaging in those cases where managers and organizations decide to heed the recommendations provided.

Why Is Providence Sometimes Questionable?

For an examination of providence-based advice and interventions, we will now take a closer look at two specific examples of management practice: the 'new way of working' and employee satisfaction surveys—both based on the premise that the recommended approach enables organizations to improve performance by making staff happier, more committed, or more inspired. The leading assumptions and fashionable ideas by which these two examples are defined are tested from an evidence-based perspective. The 18 selected change management assumptions related to questions relevant from a practitioner's perspective and popular management books in this book are evaluated in a comparable way.

The 'New Way of Working'

Many organizations have by now embraced the new way of working, typically heeding consultants' advice or enlisting their support in the implementation of the approach, whereby individual, confined work spaces are replaced by open-plan offices and flexible workstations. It is a modern layout, and authoritative consulting firms say it produces results. As the number of organizations adopting the approach swells, it increasingly becomes the obvious act to follow for organizations with mounting financial challenges or ambitions—and little or no time for reflection. Very few indeed ever seem to ask whether the presumed effectiveness of the new way of working stands up in the face of rigorous academic research. Similarly, rarely if ever do organizations seem to take the time to investigate specific dimensions of the intervention, for example, under which types of conditions the approach has proven effective and whether there are undesirable side effects. The same probably applies to the consultants who propagate the new way of working, as to do so would be contentious and would 'open a can of worms.'

However, available scientific research does indeed point to undesirable side effects. A meta-analysis of 49 existing studies showed as long as a decade ago that the introduction of open-plan offices resulted in a sharp increase in the number of interruptions to people's work routines (De Croon, Sluiter, Kuijer, & Frings-Dresen, 2005). Also, a considerable body of research has shown that such interruptions undermine performance, particularly in knowledge work. For example, every single interruption, even when lasting only seconds, has been found to double the risk of mistakes. It also typically takes more than 20 minutes on average before work on an interrupted task is resumed (De Croon et al., 2005). In other words, if the new way of working amounts to no more than creating open-plan offices, there is a more than even chance that cost savings owing to a reduction in the required floor space are undone by a drop in employee productivity. To what extent are the consultants who propagate the new way of working familiar with these research findings? Will they openly share the risks and possible side effects with their clients? Managers may still decide to implement the new way of working, even when told about the risks and side effects, as they may well conclude that the expected benefits outweigh those disadvantages. Also, a proper understanding of possible drawbacks or downsides should inspire preventive measures or carefully crafted risk management. The potential damage of providence in this example is mainly caused by consultants who unscrupulously *sell* the new way of working without appraising available knowledge and contraindications.

Measuring Employee Satisfaction

In our second case example of providence-based management thinking and doing, we look at the practice of measuring employee satisfaction, which over the past two decades or so, has grown into a multimillion-dollar industry for management consultants who conduct annual job or employee satisfaction surveys for corporations. When asked why they have their employee satisfaction measured each year, executives and human resource managers tend to respond with indignation, arguing that employee satisfaction is an important indicator and therefore must be measured at regular intervals. But when asked to probe more deeply and explain what precisely this 'important indicator' stands for, the initial indignation gives way to hesitation, and after some prodding, the answer typically includes a reference to 'performance.' That is also the stated claim on the Web sites of many consulting firms who carry out employee satisfaction surveys: the idea that happy employees are productive employees.

Many executives and human resource managers seem to accept that statement at face value. Also, they seem to think that many other organizations measure employee satisfaction, and so it must be worth the effort. But why, precisely, should happy employees put in more effort than unhappy ones? Also, how exactly does employee satisfaction relate to productivity? Is there a linear relationship? In other words, if satisfaction, expressed on a scale from 1 to 10, drops by one point, does that imply that productivity drops by 10 percent? Or is there a threshold value involved; for example, productivity will only start declining once employee satisfaction has fallen below 6 on a 10-point scale? And conversely, if managers or frontline supervisors make their staff happier, will the latter work even harder? More fundamentally, is satisfaction really the most important indicator for employee performance? Or are there other, more powerful indicators? Consultants tend to shy away from such probing questions—and so do their clients. Neither does anyone ever ask about the scientific evidence for the assertions published on consultants' Web sites. Executives and human resource managers would do well, however, to ask these questions and take the trouble of personally appraising the available academic literature. Even in a review of the topic 'job satisfaction' on Wikipedia, it is noted:

> . . . job satisfaction has a rather tenuous correlation to productivity on the job. This is a vital piece of information to researchers and businesses, as the idea that satisfaction and job performance are directly related to one another is often cited in the media and in some non-academic management literature.
>
> (Job satisfaction, 2016)

In support of this view, reference is made to a meta-analysis (Judge, Thoresen, Bono, & Patton, 2001) that reports a very weak correlation between employee satisfaction and performance. In fact, in this particular analysis (based on 254 studies comprising a total sample of more than 54,000 employees), a correlation of no more than 0.3 was found. In other words, a mere 9 percent of organizational performance can be traced to employee satisfaction—the remaining 91 percent being attributable to other factors. Moreover, the authors correctly point out that there may well be an inverse relationship, that is, that high performance may result in high levels of satisfaction. For more than 30 years now, scientific research has found a weak relationship at best between employee satisfaction and performance. In fact, no such relationship exists at all when outcomes are corrected for variables such as personality (Bowling, 2007). The same goes for other factors that are often measured in organizations, such as *commitment* or *involvement*. For these, too, correlations of 0.2 or less have been found (Riketta, 2002). At the same time, high correlations with performance—notably among knowledge workers—have been found for certain other factors that are rarely, if ever, measured in organizations, one example being *social cohesion*, for which a correlation of 0.7 has been found (Chiocchio & Essiembre, 2009). In spite of all these findings, organizations continue to spend large sums of money each year on employee satisfaction and commitment surveys. Once more, one wonders to what extent the external providers of such surveys are aware of the available scientific evidence. Do they tell their clients, professionally and honestly, about the limited added value of this annual ritual? Or do they merely collect the proceeds of providence that is so eagerly embraced by their needy clients?

The Journey: One Purpose—18 Destinations

Despite reportedly high failure rates (e.g., Beer & Nohria, 2000; Kotter, 2008; Smith, 2002), the popularity of organizational change management continues unabated. In 1980, the database ABI/INFORM contained 426 articles on the subject in scholarly journals. This figure had risen to more than 1,700 by 1990 and to more than 6,800 by 2000. As of 2012, this database contained more than 20,000 articles on organizational change management. Despite this publication boom, questions remain as to whether and how well change management practices work and whether the underlying assumptions and ideas are true or evidence based. Research in 2014 therefore addressed the question whether change management's prescriptions are based on solid, convergent evidence—in particular scientific evidence—a very important but not exclusive dimension of evidence-based change management (Barends, Janssen, Ten Have, & Ten Have, 2014). To answer this question, a systematic review was conducted of organizational change management research published in scholarly journals over the past 30 years. The assessment of 563 carefully selected studies shows a predominance of one-shot studies with low internal validity. Replication studies are rare. The findings of Barends et al. (2014) suggest that scholars and practitioners should be skeptical about research published in the field of organizational change management. The paradoxical effect of these findings could be reliance on providence and eminence. Practitioners confronted with real-life change management challenges could reason: If academia and research do not provide answers, we have to look for other navigational guidelines. These other guidelines are often provided from the perspectives of providence and eminence and found in popular management books. An important principle of evidence-based practice is the notion of 'best' available evidence: the most valid and reliable evidence given the type of question or problem at hand.

Providence and eminence can be important and useful alternatives when there is little or no evidence available to those seeking to address the challenges they face. Providence, eminence, and evidence can also reinforce and supplement each other. By way of illustration, let us contrast eminence, providence, and evidence with ethos, pathos, and logos. *Ethos* involves an attempt to convince one's audience by referring to an authoritative source. *Pathos* involves an appeal to the audience's emotions or its affective dimension by presenting an image, a conviction, a perspective, or a metaphor. *Logos*, then, is about rational reasoning, employing facts, knowledge, and findings from research in combination with the reliability of the sources referred to. Proposals for employing specific therapies or management interventions may, conceivably, fail to appeal to and convince the target audience when the argumentation is entirely based on logos and content—particularly when the proposed therapy or intervention has a bearing on human interaction and the social environment. The proposed intervention may be more readily accepted when proposed by someone in authority who is credibly linked to its content. The effect may be stronger still if content and authority are coupled in an appealing manner so that the content and the solution are connected (in an honest fashion) with the target audience's feelings and deeper needs, for example, a desire to be guided forward and being able to believe in something. In short, eminence and providence can strengthen the presentation of evidence—but without evidence, they risk being toxic.

Our contention, therefore, is not that evidence is admissible, whereas eminence and providence are not, but rather that corrupt or unscrupulous manifestations exist, not least in the world of management and organizations, causing those in need of guidance to embrace 'authorities' and 'broadly shared views' that rest on flimsy or contentious grounds at best. There is also the possibility of eminence and providence being called on to support assertions that have already been put to rest by powerful evidence. That would always be an unprofessional act, whether committed wittingly (in the case of unscrupulous practitioners) or unwittingly (by amateurs).

The norm should be to make a professional commitment to a conscientious, evidence-based approach—in the interests of the client, other stakeholders, the profession at large, and one's own professional and personal integrity. This is no small ambition, for it could sound the death toll for entire industries, for example the employee satisfaction measurement community. Major interests, sums of money, and 'players' are at stake. Whistleblowers face potentially disturbing consequences, as Rosenzweig (2007) can confirm: According to reports, he has been receiving far fewer invitations to management gatherings since his debunking of popular misconceptions about companies. Notwithstanding that, the mission and purpose of this book is to reconsider change management by making a professional, scientific, and moral commitment to a conscientious and evidence-based approach. After a further introduction to the evidence-based approach, we will continue our journey to the 18 leading assumptions in the next chapter and reconsider change management in a thoughtful, transparent, and conscientious way.

Note

* Evidence tends to be in short supply for emerging methods or technologies, for example, or when circumstances change rapidly. Barends, Rousseau and Briner (2014) point out, however, that it would be wrong even then to assume that there is nothing one can do or that one has no option but to rely on providence. Under such circumstances, the way forward is to learn by doing in the most structured way possible, constantly experimenting and systematically assessing the outcomes of experiments and critically studying what works and what doesn't. This way, organizations create their own evidence. Pfeffer and Sutton (2006b) even regard this sort of prototyping as the essence of evidence-based management.

References

Anderson, L. A., & Anderson, D. (2010). *The change leader's roadmap*. San Francisco, CA: Jossey-Bass.

Barends, E., Janssen, B., Ten Have, W. D., & Ten Have, S. (2014). Difficult but doable: Increasing the internal validity of organizational change management studies. *The Journal of Applied Behavioral Science, 50*(1), 50–54.

Barends, E., Rousseau, D. M., & Briner, R. B. (2014). *Evidence-based management: The basic principles*. Amsterdam, NL: Center for Evidence-Based Management.

Baskerville, R. F. (2003). Hofstede never studied culture. *Accounting, Organizations and Society*, 28(1), 1–14.
Beer, M., & Nohria, N. (2000). Cracking the code of change. *Harvard Business Review*, 78(3), 133–141.
Belasco, J. A. (1990). *Teaching the elephant to dance. Empowering change in your organization.* New York, NY: Crown Publishers.
Bower, J. L. (2000). The purpose of change: A commentary on Jensen and Senge. In M. Beer, & N. Nohria (Eds.), *Breaking the code of change* (pp. 83–95). Boston, MA: Harvard Business School Press.
Bowling, N. A. (2007). Is the job satisfaction-job performance relationship spurious? A meta-analytic examination. *Journal of Vocational Behavior*, 71(2), 167–185.
Broeke, Ten A. (2015). *De verleiding van de TED-cultuur.* Retrieved January 2, 2016, from https://blendle.com/i/de-volkskrant/de-verleiding-van-de-ted-cultuur/bnl-vkn-20150102-3826828
Brownell, K. D., & Rodin, J. (1994). The dieting maelstrom: Is it possible and advisable to lose weight? *American Psychologist*, 49(9), 781–791.
Chiocchio, F., & Essiembre, H. (2009). Cohesion and performance: A meta-analytic review of disparities between project teams, production teams, and service teams. *Small Group Research*, 40(4), 382–420.
Clark, T., & Greatbach, D. (2004). Management fashion as image-spectacle: The production of best-selling management books. *Management Communication Quarterly*, 17(3), 396–424.
Collins, J. C. (2001). *Good to great: Why some companies make the leap . . . and others don't.* New York, NY: HarperCollins Publishers.
Collins, J. C. (2009). *How the mighty fall: And why some companies never give in.* New York, NY: HarperCollins Publishers.
Conner, D. R. (1992). *Managing at the speed of change: How resilient managers succeed and prosper where others fail.* New York, NY: Random House.
De Croon, E. M., Sluiter, J. K., Kuijer, P. P., & Frings-Dresen, M. H. (2005). The effect of office concepts on worker health and performance: A systematic review of the literature. *Ergonomics*, 48(2), 119–134.
De Wit, B., & Meyer, R. (1999). *Strategy synthesis: Resolving strategy paradoxes to create competitive advantage.* London, UK: International Thompson Business Press.
Franke, R. H., & Kaul, J. D. (1978). The Hawthorne experiments: First statistical interpretation. *American Sociological Review*, 43(5), 623–643.
Hofstede, G. (1980). *Culture's consequences: International differences in work-related values.* London, UK: Sage Publications.
Job satisfaction. (2016, January 27). In *Wikipedia*. Retrieved January 27, 2016, from http://en.wikipedia.org/wiki/Job_satisfaction
Judge, T. A., Thoresen, C. J., Bono, J. E., & Patton, G. K. (2001). The job satisfaction-job performance relationship: A qualitative and quantitative review. *Psychological Bulletin*, 127(3), 376–407.
Karmakar, A., & Datta, B. (2012). *Principles and practices of management and business communication.* New Delhi, IN: Dorling Kindersley.
Kotter, J. P. (2008). *A sense of urgency.* Boston, MA: Harvard Business Review Press.
Lilienfield, S. O., Lynn, S. J., Ruscio, J., & Beyerstein, B. L. (2010). *50 great myths of popular psychology. Shattering widespread misconceptions about human behavior.* Chichester, UK: Wiley-Blackwell.
Mayo, E. (1933). *The human problems of an industrial civilization.* New York, NY: Macmillan.

McQuarrie, F. A. E. (2005). How the past is present(ed): A comparison of information on the Hawthorne studies in Canadian management and organizational behavior textbooks. *Canadian Journal of Administrative Sciences, 22*(3), 230–242.

Micklethwait, J., & Wooldridge, A. (1998). *The witch doctors: Making sense of the management gurus.* New York, NY: Three Rivers Press.

Miller, C., Cardinal, L. B., & Glick, W. H. (1997). Retrospective reports in organizational research. A reexamination of recent evidence. *Academy of Management Journal, 40*(2), 189–204.

Novak, D. (2012). *Taking people with you: The only way to make big things happen.* New York, NY: Portfolio/ Penguin.

Peters, T. J. (2001, December). *Tom Peters' true confessions.* Retrieved January 12, 2016, from http://www.fastcompany.com/44077/tom-peterss-true-confessions

Peters, T. J., & Waterman, R. H. (1982). *In search of excellence: Lessons from America's best-run companies.* New York, NY: Harper & Row.

Pfeffer, J., & Sutton, R. I. (2006b). Treat your organization as a prototype: The essence of evidence-based management. *Design Management Review, 17*(3), 10–14.

Riketta, M. (2002). Attitudinal organizational commitment and job performance: A meta-analysis. *Journal of Organizational Behavior, 23*(3), 257–266.

Rosenzweig, P. (2007). *The halo effect . . . and the eight other business delusions that deceive managers.* New York, NY: Free Press.

Ross, L., & Ward, A. (1996). Naive realism in everyday life: Implications for social conflict and misunderstanding. In T. Brown, E. S. Reed, & E. Turiel (Eds.), *Values and knowledge* (pp. 103–135). Hillsdale, NJ: Erlbaum.

Sagan, C. (1996). *The demon-haunted world: Science as a candle in the dark.* New York, NY: Random House.

Schein, E. H. (1990). Organizational culture. *American Psychologist, 45*(2), 109–119.

Schein, E. H. (1996). Culture: The missing concept in organization studies. *Administrative Science Quarterly, 41*(2), 229–240.

Schramade, P. W. J. (2006). Tussen providence- en evidence-based HRD. *Opleiding & Ontwikkeling, 19*(3), 10.

Schramade, P. W. J. (2014). Laveren tussen Evidence- en providence-based management. *Holland Management Review, 157*(Sep-Oct), 3.

Smith, M. E. (2002). Success rates for different types of organizational change. *Performance Improvement, 41*(1), 26–33.

Sutton, R. I., & Staw, B. M. (1995). What theory is not. *Administrative Science Quarterly, 40*(3), 371–384.

Ten Broeke, A. (2015). *De verleiding van de TED-cultuur.* Retrieved January 2, 2016, from https://blendle.com/i/de-volkskrant/de-verleiding-van-de-ted-cultuur/bnl-vkn-20150102-3826828

Ten Have, S., & Visser, C. (2004). Naar een productief veranderperspectief: Van mislukking naar succes. *Holland Management Review, 98*, 32–47.

Voestermans, P., & Verheggen, T. (2007). *Cultuur en lichaam: Een cultuurpsychologisch perspectief op patronen in gedrag.* Malden, MA: Blackwell Publishing.

3 Story of Change
18 Leading Assumptions in Change Practice

Story of Change

> *Given the fact that 70 percent of all change initiatives fail, we clearly need an effective professional framework to manage change. Because it's important to know where we are heading, there must be a clear vision. Another prerequisite is to establish a sense of urgency to fuel change and motivate people. Leaders are immensely important in implementing change, and trust is essential. When managing change, a transformational leadership style is more effective than a transactional one. Organizational change also requires leaders with strong emotional intelligence (EI). Supervisory support is critical for the success of change. A leader cannot succeed on his or her own—a powerful guiding coalition is needed. Furthermore, employees' capabilities to change determine the organization's capacity to change. Also, participation is key to successful change. Resistance to change is detrimental to the success of change. A fair change process is important in achieving successful change. It's all about behavior. Organizational culture can be an effective tool for stimulating performance, but it's difficult—and time-consuming—to change the organizational culture. However, goal setting combined with feedback is a powerful tool for change leaders. Employee commitment to change is an essential component of a successful change initiative, and commitment is positively correlated with performance. Financial incentives are an effective way to encourage and improve performance. Self-managing teams perform better in realizing change than traditionally managed teams.*

This integral model of the 'Story of Change' is based on the selection of 18 leading assumptions in the field of change management, as described in the following paragraph. It seems to be an ideal, simple, and clear story, grounded in the messages conveyed by popular management books and consultancy firms in the last decades.

Our Approach

Important indicators of the attractiveness or popularity of these management books and ideas are the issues, uncertainties, and questions that managers raise when asked what is critical, difficult, or decisive in their ability to do their jobs. In this book the focus is on a particular activity, namely change management. We have collected the most influential ideas and the most critical and widespread questions from managers relating to behavioral change and organizations. In prior research, Ten Have, Ten Have, and Janssen (2009) gathered the questions or problems related to change management that are most relevant and critical from a practitioner's perspective, in which 262 managers from 43 large organizations were interviewed and surveyed, including Philips, DSM, Baker & McKenzie, a Dutch ministry, and several municipalities. In our current research, questions were selected that were most clearly defined from a practitioner's and an academic perspective.

Moreover, we followed Lewis, Schmisseur, Stephens, and Weir (2006) and replicated their search strategy as we generated the sample of books on organizational change. To identify the books that have had the most influence on managerial practice, we sampled from best-selling books. From the top 100 best-selling books on organizational change (from a total base of 17,559 as indicated by Amazon), we included books that (1) focus on *how* to change organizations rather than *what* to change, (2) take a position rather than provide an overview (as handbooks do), and (3) provide advice and guidance to practitioners. From these best-selling books in 2015 we selected 23 books. To extend the time period and scope, we also reviewed the 2006 selection of Lewis et al. and added 31 books relevant to change management to the definitive selection. This process resulted in the list in Table 3.1:

Table 3.1 Books and Book Chapters Reviewed

Allen, R. C. (2002). *Guiding change journeys: A synergistic approach to organization transformation.* San Francisco, CA: Jossey-Bass and Pfeiffer Publishers.

Anderson, L. A., & Anderson, D. (2010). *The change leader's roadmap.* San Francisco, CA: Jossey-Bass Publishers.

Augustine, N. R. (1998). Reshaping an industry: Lockheed Martin's survival story. In *Harvard Business Review on Change* (pp. 159–187). Boston, MA: Harvard Business School.

Beer, M., & Nohria, N. (2000). *Breaking the code of change* (pp. 83–95). Boston, MA: Harvard Business School Press.

Belasco, J. A. (1990). *Teaching the elephant to dance. Empowering change in your organization.* New York: Crown Publishers.

Blanchard, K., & Miller, M. (2014). *The secret: What great leaders know and do.* San Francisco, CA: Berrett-Koehler Publishers.

(Continued)

Table 3.1 (Continued)

Bridges, W., & Mitchel, S. (2002). Leading transition: A new model for change. In F. Hesselbein & R. Johnson (Eds.), *On leading change* (pp. 33–47). San Francisco, CA: Jossey-Bass Publishers.

Bridges, W. (1991). *Managing transitions: Making the most of change.* Reading, MA: Perseus Books.

Brown, T. (2009). *Change by design: How design thinking transforms organizations and inspires innovation.* Broadway, NY: HarperCollins Publishers.

Cameron, K., & Quinn, R. (2011). *Diagnosing and changing organizational culture.* Reading, MA: Addison Wesley Longman.

Collins, J. C. (2001). *From good to great.* New York: HarperCollins Publishers.

Collins, J. C. (2009). *How the mighty fall: And why some companies never give in.* New York: Random House.

Collins, J. C., & Porras, J. I. (1996). Building your company's vision. *Harvard Business Review, 74*(5), 65.

Conner, D. (2006). *Managing at the speed of change.* New York: Random House.

Connors, R., & Smith, T. (2011). *Change the culture, change the game: The breakthrough strategy for energizing your organization and creating accountability for results.* New York: Random House.

Davidson, J. (2002). *The complete idiot's guide to change management.* Indianapolis: Alpha Books.

Duck, J. D. (1998). Managing change: The art of balancing. In *Harvard business review on change* (pp. 55–83). Boston, MA: Harvard Business School.

Dupuy, F. (2002). *The chemistry of change.* New York: John Wiley & Sons.

Eckes, G. (2001). *Making Six Sigma last: Managing the balance between cultural and technical change.* New York: John Wiley and Sons.

Ghoshal, S, & Bartlett, C. A. (2000). Rebuilding behavioural context: A blueprint for corporate renewal. In M. Beer & N. Nohria (Eds.), *Breaking the code of change* (pp. 195–222). Boston, MA: Harvard Business School.

Goss, T., Pascale, R., & Athos, A. (1998). The reinvention roller coaster: Risking the present for a powerful future. In *Harvard business review on change* (pp. 83–112). Boston, MA: Harvard Business School.

Goleman, D. (2015). *On emotional intelligence.* Boston, MA: Harvard Business Review Press.

Heath, C., & Heath, D. (2010). *Switch: How to change things when change is hard.* New York: Broadway Books.

Heifetz, R. A., Grashow, A., & Linsky, M. (2009). *The practice of adaptive leadership: Tools and tactics for changing your organization and the world.* Boston, MA: Harvard Business Press.

Heller, J. (1998). *Essential managers: Managing change.* New York: D. K. Publishing.

Hesselbein, F. (2000). The key to cultural transformation. In F. Hesselbein & R. Johnston (Eds.), *A leader to leader guide* (pp. 1–6). San Francisco, CA: Jossey-Bass Publishers.

Hirschhorn, L. (2000). Changing structure is not enough: The moral meaning of organizational design. In M. Beer & N. Nohria (Eds.), *Breaking the code of change* (pp. 161–176). Boston, MA: Harvard Business School.

(*Continued*)

Table 3.1 (Continued)

Holman, P., & Devane, T. (Eds.). (1999). *The change handbook*. San Francisco, CA: Berrett-Koehler Publishers.

Humble, J., Molesky, J., & O'Reilly, B. (2015). *Lean enterprise: How high performance organizations innovate at scale*. Sebastopol, CA: O'Reilly Media.

Ibarra, H. (2015). *Act like a leader, think like a leader*. Boston, MA: Harvard Business Review Press.

Kanter, R. M. (2002). The enduring skills of change leaders. In F. Hesselbein & R. Johnston (Eds.), *On leading change* (pp. 47–61). San Francisco, CA: Jossey-Bass Publishers.

Kegan, R., & Lahey, L. (2001). *How the way we talk can change the way we work*. New York: John Wiley & Sons.

Kegan, R., & Lahey, L. (2009). *Immunity to change: How to overcome it and unlock the potential in yourself and your organization*. Boston, MA: Harvard Business Press.

Kimsey-House, K., & Kimsey-House, H. (2015). *Co-active leadership: Five ways to lead*. San Francisco, CA: Berrett-Koehler Publishers.

Kotter, J. P. (1996). *Leading change*. Boston, MA: Harvard Business Press.

Kotter, J. P. (1998). Leading change: Why transformation effort fail. In *Harvard business review on change* (pp. 1–21). Boston, MA: Harvard Business School.

Kotter, J. P., & Cohen, D. S. (2004). *The heart of change: Real-life stories of how people change their organizations*. Recording for the Blind & Dyslexic.

Kouzes, J., & Posner, B. (2012). *The leadership challenge: How to make extraordinary things happen in organizations*. San Francisco, CA: Jossey-Bass Publishers.

Kriegel, R. J., & Brandt, D. (1996). *Sacred cows make the best burgers*. New York, NY: Warner Books, Inc.

Laloux, F. (2014). *Reinventing organizations: A guide to creating organizations inspired by the next stage of human consciousness*. Brussel: Nelson Parker.

Langley, G. J., Moen, R., Nolan, K. M., Nolan, T. W., Norman, C. L., & Provost, L. P. (2009). *The improvement guide: A practical approach to enhancing organizational performance*. San Francisco, CA: Jossey-Bass Publishers.

Larkin, T., & Larkin, S. (1994). *Communicating change: Winning employee support for new business goals*. New York: McGraw-Hill.

Lewis, L. K., Schmisseur, A. M., Stephens, K. K., & Weir, K. E. (2006). Advice on communicating during organizational change the content of popular press books. *Journal of Business Communication, 43*(2), 113–137.

Liedtka, J., & Ogilvie, T. (2011). *Designing for growth: A design thinking tool kit for managers*. New York: Columbia University Press.

Lipman-Blumen, J. (2002). The age of connective leadership. In F. Hesselbein & R. Johnston (Eds.), *On leading change* (pp. 89–102). San Francisco, CA: Jossey-Bass Publishers.

Martin, R. (1998). Changing the mind of the corporation. In *Harvard business review on change* (pp. 113–138). Boston, MA: Harvard Business School.

Maurer, R. (2010). *Beyond the wall of resistance: Why 70% of all changes still fail—and what you can do about it*. Austin, TX: Bard Press.

Miller, K. (2002). *The change agent's guide to radical improvement*. Milwaukee: American Society for Quality.

(*Continued*)

Table 3.1 (Continued)

Mourier, P., & Smith, M. R. (2001). *Conquering organizational change. How to succeed where most companies fail.* Atlanta, GA: CEP Press.

Novak, D. (2012). *Taking people with you: The only way to make big things happen.* New York: Portfolio and Penguin.

Oakley, E., & Krug, D. (1991). *Enlightened leadership: Getting to the heart of change.* New York: Fireside.

Robertson, B. J. (2015). *Holacracy: The new management system for a rapidly changing world.* New York: Henry Holt and Company.

Watkins, M. D. (2013). *The first 90 days: Proven strategies for getting up to speed faster and smarter, updated and expanded.* Boston, MA: Harvard Business Review Press.

Zaffron, S., & Logan, D. (2009). *The three laws of performance: Rewriting the future of your organization and your life.* San Francisco, CA: Jossey-Bass Publishers.

Four independent reviewers, all practitioners and researchers (PhDs or PhD candidates), reviewed the 54 books. They focused on identifying underlying or explicit assumptions about organizational change. Each reviewer prepared a data sheet for each book with notes, quotations, assumptions, and lists of critical elements such as advice and positions taken. Each reviewer was asked to define and list the 30 to 40 most relevant assumptions and recommendations. Relevance was established by scoring them (in addition to their popularity) by answering the question of how robust and convincing the assumption or advice was (or how robustly and convincingly it was presented) and how visible or present it might be if put into practice. Working from the data sheets, a discussion and process of validation was started, leading to a selection of 25 assumptions. For practical reasons, 18 of these were selected and further described as follows.

To illustrate the 18 assumptions, we have added claims and statements from influential consultancy firms advising on organizational change. We analyzed a large number of their Web sites, as well as the claims and statements they present. These illustrate the influence of the selected assumptions, highlighting the diffusion of certain ideas. As it is not our intention to pillory specific firms, we will use descriptions such as 'an international strategy firm' and 'a human resource consultancy.' In the appendix a list with references to the corresponding sources is presented.

18 Key Assumptions

1 70 Percent of All Change Interventions Fail

A reputed consultancy firm founded by a change management guru states that "change practitioners have some culpability for the atrocious 70% failure rate of change initiatives." An international strategy firm notes: "A recent survey of business executives indicates that the percentage of change programs that are a success today is . . . still 30%." One of the leading management journals (Beer & Nohria, 2000): "The brutal fact is that about 70% of all change initiatives fail." The assumption that 70 percent of all change interventions fail seems to be ubiquitous. On the back cover of the bestseller *Conquering Organizational Change. How to Succeed Where Most Companies Fail*, Mourier and Smith (2001) claim that "over 70% of all change efforts fail." They also provide an overview of success rates for various types of organizational change based on 35 studies.

The studies focus on, for example, technology change, culture change, mergers and acquisitions, and strategy deployment. Consultancy firms are responsible for most of the studies. The success rates vary with the kind of change; many report a success rate of around 30 percent, but strategy deployment, for example, has a success rate of 58 percent. Maurer (2010) notes on the cover of his *Beyond the Wall of Resistance*: "Why 70% of All Changes *Still* Fail—and What You Can Do About It." Maurer refers to the development of change management in practice: "Over the past fifteen years most of the large consulting firms have created change management practices. Boutique firms were created just to address the challenges of change" (p. 11). He states that in 1995, about 70 percent of all major change initiatives failed and also refers to a more recent study (Keller & Aiken, 2009), which showed that the failure rate was still around 70 percent. Maurer calls this 'sobering statistics.' He rightly articulates the negative impact of failure: cynicism, missed opportunities, and false starts "with time and limited resources going into trying to manage resistance and indifference" (Maurer, 2010, p. 12). Kriegel and Brandt (1996) also introduce the question why change fails with statistics. In their book, Leo Lewis, president of the Tandy Computer Users Group, notes: "Re-engineering is not a bed of roses. . . . Some statistics say seven out of ten reengineering initiatives fail" (p. 3).

2 A Clear Vision Is Essential for Successful Change

Ibarra (2015) refers to the importance of having a clear and inspiring vision. She states that "across studies and research traditions, vision has been found to be a defining feature of leadership" (Ibarra, 2015, p. 41). Bridges (1991) emphasizes the importance of clarifying the purpose: What is the idea behind what you're doing? People need a picture of how the outcome will look; participation asks for imagination. Bridges attributes terrible obstacles in change processes to having no discernible purpose behind the proposed changes. Belasco (1990) says his experience tells him that an energizing, inspiring vision is the key to mobilizing support: "This vision is the picture that drives all action" (p. 11). Belasco defines the vision as focus and inspiration that empower people to change. A prestigious international consulting firm states the following:

> In our experience, two issues are particularly pressing for CEOs and top teams. One is setting an appropriate and inspiring aspiration, or vision,

for change—and making it come alive for everyone. The other is mobilizing and sustaining the transformation 'engine': the flow of energy and ideas needed to drive the organization forward.

Another well-known international consulting firm says the following about vision: "A clear vision that answers the questions 'What does success look like for the organization?' and 'How does the change affect each stakeholder?' is the first step in achieving a successful transformation."

A third large international consulting firm states that vision is important:

> Any disruptive change needs to be communicated in a way that aligns all constituents and staff to the new direction. Creating a compelling story for transformation helps to get a faster buy-in from stakeholders. Such a story is predicated on a strong vision that the leader must build to set new goals. Additionally, stripping the vision down to simple messages is an effective way to engage a variety of stakeholders—from donors to peer organizations—amidst competing causes. When communicating the compelling story, both internally and externally, nonprofit CEOs need to have a flexible style to counter the inevitable pockets of resistance to change.

And a fourth well-known international consulting firm has a statement on vision:

> Analysis is about assessing the risk and cultural readiness of the organization for change while concurrently laying the foundation for a compelling vision and executable change strategy, as tailored to the unique context of the organization. Following key areas may be addressed in the analysis phase. Business Case and Vision for Change: Why do we need to change, what are the desired benefits, and how does it impact us?

Maurer (2010) also underlines the importance of a vision that must be clear and compelling to get people deeply involved. In *Guiding Change Journeys*, Allen (2002) describes the achievement of a change vision as new emergence or discovery that is an essential part of the change journey. She notes that a key task when guiding change is to help clarify goals: "Change intention shapes the course and quality of a change journey. Intention is like the needle of a compass. It points you in the right direction, no matter what the circumstances" (Allen, 2002, p. 67). Zaffron and Logan (2009) talk about the creation of a new game by declaring that something is important. By using future-based language, you invite others to commit to the game. Watkins (2013) pleas for an inspiring vision, built on a foundation of intrinsic motivators, making people part of the story, and containing evocative language to inspire and motivate people. Hesselbein and Johnston (2002) consider a compelling aspiration as a condition sine qua non in change; without it you will not overcome the many sources of resistance. Lippitt (1999) considers a vision, among others, as a necessary part of the 'change equation' to overcome resistance.

3 People Will Not Change If There Is No Sense of Urgency

Kotter (1996) is very outspoken: "By far the biggest mistake people make when trying to change organizations is to plunge ahead without establishing a high enough sense of urgency in fellow managers and employees" (p. 4). Consultants consider sense of urgency to be an essential part of their change approach. A famous international consultancy firm writes: "Our approach helps management understand and control the integration process, retain a sense of urgency, identify and respond to execution problems, and extract real value from the deal." Another consultancy firm states: "A sense of urgency can come from an external source or it can come from within; either way, far more will be accomplished once you have it." A partner in a US consultancy firm repeats the following project manager's antidote to corporate inertia: "Inject a spirit of urgency into your team. This 'urgency' is not a panicky, anxious urgency, but a spirited, engaged urgency that propels people to move ideas along and get busy."

Ibarra (2015) provides the following reflection: "It's all too easy to fall hostage to (giving priority to) the urgent over the important" (p. 1). Conner (1992) states that the urgency of 'burning-platform' situations motivates major change. Urgency can be generated by the high price of unresolved problems or the high cost of missed opportunities. Novak (2012) refers to the tendency to 'sugarcoat' things, whereas Kriegel and Brandt (1996) consider urgency as one of the four keys to lighting a firestorm in your organization (the other three are inspiration, ownership, and rewards and recognition). Heifetz, Grashow, and Linsky (2009) also discuss urgency, in particular the negative or crisis variant, and they give a warning: "There is a myth that drives many change initiatives into the ground: that the organization needs to change because it's broken" (p. 17). Heath and Heath (2010) also give a warning. A cliché commands people to 'raise the bar' (p. 129) to motivate them to change. But they emphasize the fact that you sometimes need to lower the bar, to 'shrink the change' to motivate people who are reluctant to change. However, Bridges (1991) emphasizes the importance of conveying the necessity of change; people don't act if they can't see, acknowledge, and understand the problem.

4 Trust in the Leader Is Needed for Successful Change

Kouzes and Posner (2012) state that exemplary leaders create a climate of trust. Without trust you simply cannot accomplish extraordinary things. They state: "Trust is a strong, significant predictor of employee satisfaction, the quality of communication, honest sharing of information, acceptance of change, acceptance of the leader's influence, and team and organizational performance" (Kouzes & Posner, 2012, pp. 219–220). Maurer (2010) states that "trust can make or break a change. But sadly, many who lead change seem to ignore this critically important ingredient. They seem to believe that a good idea will win the day. It won't" (p. 14). A human resource consultancy firm underlines the importance of leadership and trust:

> So, management often asks, "how can we build trust in the workforce, and how can we avoid losing it?" Well, it starts at the very top, since trustfulness—and trustworthiness—can exist only if top management sets the example, and then builds that example into every department and unit.

And:

> Consider the great military leaders of history (e.g., Augustus Caesar, Oliver Cromwell, and George Washington), as well as the genuinely beloved political leaders (yes, there actually have been some: Joan of Arc, Peter the Great, Gandhi . . .). And then there are the highly respected industrial leaders (Henry Ford, Lee Iacocca, and Jack Welch). All of these great leaders built trust among their superiors, peers and subordinates, and it was this that spurred success and greatness for themselves, their units, alliances and companies.

Kriegel and Brandt (1996) emphasize the fact that resistance to change increases as trust in an organization's leader decreases. Trustworthiness and believability are seen as the foundations of leadership. Watkins (2013) emphasizes the importance of credibility and trust in demanding situations: "As people come to trust your judgment, your ability to learn accelerates, and you equip yourself to make sound (judgment) calls on tougher issues" (p. 8).

5 When Managing Change, a Transformational Leadership Style Is More Effective Than a Transactional One

Based on his research, Collins (2001) defines five levels of executive capabilities. On Level 3 we find the so-called competent managers who organize people and resources toward the effective and efficient pursuit of predetermined objectives. Their perspective is mainly a transactional one. On the higher levels of the 'effective leader' (4) and ideal typical 'executive' (5), we find leaders who are (more) transformational. They, in particular on Level 5, are the leaders whose companies 'make the leap, where others don't.' The Level 5 leader "builds enduring greatness through a paradoxical blend of personal humility and professional will" (Collins, 2001, p. 20). On Level 4 is the 'effective leader' who "catalyzes commitment to and vigorous pursuit of a clear and compelling vision, stimulating higher performance standards" (Collins, 2001, p. 20). These transformational leaders have the personality and ability to inspire. Heifetz et al. (2009) state: "To lead your organization through adaptive change, you need the ability to inspire. Adaptive challenges involve values not simply facts or logic. And resolving them engages people's beliefs and loyalties, which lie in their hearts, not their heads" (p. 263).

Ibarra (2015) states that charismatic leaders are excellent at sensing the environment and (therefore) able to generate sounder, more appealing ideas.

Maxwell (2013) writes: "The single biggest way to impact an organization is to focus on transformational leadership. There is almost no limit to the potential of an organization that recruits good people, raises them up as leaders and continually develop them" (p. 185). A leading international strategy firm also underscores the importance of transformational leadership: "Despite widespread evidence that 'transformational leaders' are essential building blocks of every high-performing school, school districts often fail to prioritize leadership development." One consultancy firm places transformational leadership even at the heart of their philosophy. They state:

> Our vision is of a world in which all life matters: sustainability is at the core of what we do. Our intention is to be a force for good, creating transformational leadership and whole system transformation. Organizations have previously existed primarily to create profit but now their remit is being widened by employees who want to find fulfilment and purpose in their work and a society which demands that companies act with integrity. Meeting these demands requires transformational leaders at the top who are able to help their teams develop and rise to new challenges rather than leaders who solely help their teams at the technical level.

Research by a leading strategy firm links transformational change to performance and the health of the organization. The research reports:

> Eighty-three percent of all respondents say their companies' transformations focused wholly or in part on changing the organizations' long-term health by building capabilities, changing mindsets or culture, or developing a capacity for continuous improvement. Transforming leadership capacity seems to be particularly significant in transformations that succeeded in improving long-term health: 63 percent of executives who say their companies' transformations had a significant impact on leadership capacity indicate that the transformation improved both short-term performance and long-term health. By contrast, a third of those who say their companies' transformations had no significant effect on leadership capacity nonetheless succeeded in transforming short-term performance—a rate of success almost as high as the rate for any transformation.

6 *Organizational Change Requires Leaders With Strong Emotional Intelligence*

Goleman (2015) has found that the most effective leaders are alike in one crucial way: "They all have a high degree of what has come to be known as *emotional intelligence*" (p. 1). He says that his research, along with other recent studies, clearly show that this kind of intelligence is the sine qua non of leadership. EI is related to self-awareness, self-regulation, motivation, empathy, and social skill. Kriegel and Brandt already expressed this idea way back in 1996: "Offer respect, understanding, and acknowledgement and you'll foster incredible loyalty, enough to propel you through incremental or transformative organizational change" (p. 185). Talking about EI, an international prestigious consulting firm states:

> In any industry that offers a service (or sells a product with an 'embedded' service element), there are moments when the long-term relationship between a business and its customers can change significantly—for better or for worse. By supporting and developing the frontline emotional intelligence of its employees, it can ensure that more of those moments have a positive outcome.

The importance of EI and how to enhance it is highlighted by the research of another international consulting firm:

> While recent research has shown the importance Emotional Intelligence (EI) plays in effective leadership, a large question remained: How quickly and effectively can leaders who lack key EI competencies develop them?

New studies by [a consultancy firm] show that managers and executives can effectively enhance critical EI competencies through a combination of workshops and ongoing personal development. Yet another international consulting firm also emphasizes the importance of emotionally intelligent leaders:

> They must be self-aware, self-regulating, and empathetic. Leaders need to understand their own moods and motivations, and appreciate how their own emotions may color their perspective. Leaders must keep those emotions in check, as well, suspending judgment and thinking before acting, so that the discussion moves toward agreement, instead of toward increasingly angry debate.

They need the capacity to put themselves in another person's shoes and understand and respond fairly to positions that differ from their own. Building consensus and formulating a coherent and viable strategy requires an intimate understanding of everything that is going on beneath the surface of an organization. Emotionally intelligent leaders keep their antennae finely tuned to such undercurrents. A final quote from an international consulting firm subscribes the latter, stating that EI is a key factor in successful organizations: "To reach your full potential, you need to build your emotional intelligence. There is now a significant body of research showing that emotional intelligence is linked to successful performance in the workplace."

7 Supervisory Support Is Critical for the Success of Change

The vital role and position of (frontline) supervisors in change was illustrated by Larkin and Larkin (1994) when talking about communication: "Frontline employees distrust information from senior managers, don't believe employee publications, hate watching executives on video, and have little or no interest in corporate-wide topics" (p. ix).

> Supervisors are the opinion leaders for frontline behaviour. Supervisors are not just one of the receivers—they are the receivers. The consultants, the CEO, the VP for marketing or finance are never going to change the way frontline employees act.
> (Larkin & Larkin, 1994, p. 10)

Supervisors are in the position to influence the feelings, perceptions, and judgment of their employees. Kriegel and Brandt (1996) note that people often misunderstand how much change is involved in change. To correct this, "leaders should not point out just what will be altered but also what will stay the same. That bi-focus puts a more balanced spin on plans for change and reduces anxiety" (p. 225). Eckes (2001) in his book *Creating the Six Sigma Culture* identifies 'maladaptive behaviors' such as 'No Follow Through' (not completing action items) and the 'Interruptor.' He emphasizes the importance of facilitative skills needed to change these behaviors. Kouzes and Posner (2012) emphasize the importance of supervisory support focused on creating a climate in which people are fully engaged and feel in control of their own lives. "In a climate of competence and confidence, people don't hesitate to hold themselves personally accountable for results, and they feel profound ownership for their achievements" (Kouzes & Posner, 2012, p. 243). Kouzes and Posner emphasize the fact that leaders must "invest in strengthening the capacity and the resolve of everyone in the organization" (p. 256), especially in situation of change. Exemplary leaders strive to create conditions in which people perform effortlessly and expertly despite challenging situations.

A global consultancy network writes:

> When change happens, people go through a very natural and completely common emotional transition. Once they have personally navigated that transition, they naturally become committed to any positive change they see as relevant and meaningful. . . . Until they have navigated that transition, they may be confused, aloof, afraid, angry, or resistant. These are all natural reactions that any person in a similar circumstance may go through.

The key for leaders is to understand this natural emotional transition and set up their organizational change efforts to minimize it in people while promoting positive ways to help them move through it. However, most leaders do not adequately understand or embrace the human dynamics of change. They are uncomfortable with people's negative emotional reactions and would prefer to ignore them or give them to the human resource department to handle. Neither works. Instead, leaders must design organizational change to address the human dynamics overtly and early. This will minimize people's resistance and maximize their understanding, alignment, ability, and willingness to change. A prestigious international consulting firm states:

> Survey results point to three critical areas where women in the middle of their careers report more negative experiences and perceptions than those who have just entered the workforce: a clash with the stereotype of the ideal worker, a lack of supervisory support and too few role models in senior-level positions.

The same consulting firm stresses the importance of supervisory support:

> They must believe that their compensation and benefits are fair, and they must trust their supervisors and managers. In eNPS companies, employees must also feel that managers listen and support them, that their huddles are effective and that they are rewarded for doing the right things for customers.

Another international firm views supervisor support as critical to success:

> A leader with high supervisor support is one that makes employees feel heard, valued, and cared about. Although it sounds simple, providing this kind of support is one of the hardest transitions to make when promoted from employee to supervisor. The move from 'process expert' to 'motivational leader' is possibly one of the largest steps one can take in his/her working life. . . . So why is supervisor support so important for effective leadership? Because it's one of the key behaviors that effective leaders develop as soon as they move from individual contributor to manager.

8 To Realize Change in Organizations, a Powerful Guiding Coalition Is Needed

The importance of top managers as leaders of change is emphasized in many books. As Kotter (2012) remarks, "Major transformations are often associated with one highly visible individual" (p. 53). Another way of leading change is by way of a guiding coalition. A reputed Dutch consultancy firm considers the 'Gideon's mob' approach to be an essential driver of cultural change. But Kotter criticizes the belief that change can come from a single larger-than-life person. He explains:

> Because major change is so difficult to accomplish, a powerful force is required to sustain the process. No one individual, even a monarch-like CEO, is ever able to develop the right vision, communicate it to large numbers of people, eliminate all the key obstacles, generate short-term wins, lead an manage dozens of change projects, and anchor new approaches deep in the organization's culture. Weal committees are even worse. A strong guiding coalition is always needed—one with the right composition, level of trust, and shared objective. Building such a team is always an essential part of the early stages of any effort to restructure, reengineer, or retool a set of strategies. (p. 51)

Several consultancies and learning and development firms embrace the idea of the guiding coalition. A change agent at such a firm writes:

> It's never a good idea to go it alone, even if you are the top dog of the organization. If you are the sole owner of the vision, the direction and the message, (which you most certainly are if you haven't involved other voices in the process), then you can expect to see a marked dilution of that vision as it's communicated downward by other levels of leadership and management who may not fully understand your vision or desired outcomes—and who may not share your level of commitment!

And, the 'agility ladder' of a software consultancy firm shows:

> Your agile transformation needs a leading coalition that makes the transformation happen. The leading coalition consists of skilled, credible and influential leaders. These leaders are convinced that an 'Agile transformation' is essential and they do whatever is needed to make the change happen. Next to sponsorship from senior managers, the leading coalition needs a transformation team that does the work to guide the transformation in its various stages.

Hesselbein (2002) states that the process of change often starts with a passionate few initiators. He introduces a more 'organic,' strong, meritocratic variant of the guiding coalition:

> Leaders (and teachers) spend too much time trying to remediate weaknesses and too little building on strengths. Remember Georg Solti, conductor of the Chicago Symphony, who found 20 musicians who had passion to do something new: Rather than trying to push the entire organization forward, he focused on the top performers. It's an atypical strategy, but it's the most effective one. (p. 27)

9 Employees' Capabilities to Change Determine the Organization's Capacity to Change

A highly reputable international consulting firm claims that "change management begins and ends with your people. Whereas in the past we talked about managing people through change, today we manage change through our people—putting the capacity to change in their hands." Talking about capacity Conner (1992) also focuses on people, he writes:

> People can only change when they have the capacity to do so. *Ability* means having the necessary skills and knowing how to use them. *Willingness* is the motivation to apply those skills to a particular situation. If you lack either ability or willingness, it's unlikely that you will successfully adapt to a change. (p. 129)

Kriegel and Brandt (1996) advise:

> Emphasizing strengths builds esteem and encourages people to do better in everything, including those things that give them trouble. When you're introducing change, remind people of their competence. Show them how the skills they already have will help them to excel in the new task. (p. 209)

Talking about change capacity, Heifetz et al. (2009) underline the importance of individual employees and their attitude and orientation: "In an organization with a high capacity to adapt, people share responsibility for the larger organization's future in addition to their identification with specific roles and functions" (p. 103). They also point at the importance of extending your 'bandwidth'; "your repertoire for moving adaptive change in your organization. . . . Depending on the situation and people involved, you have to be able to mix and match techniques as needed. That requires a broad bandwidth" (Heifetz et al., 2009, p. 205). Kegan and Lahey (2009) link the challenge of change to a need to develop as a person and 'care' about change rather than having to deal or cope with it. According to them the last two skills are valuable but insufficient for meeting today's change challenges. A proposition by Mourier and Smith (2001) focuses on change capacity: "Change efforts have the highest likelihood of success when they are driven by visible support from the sponsor, employees know what they have to do to support the change, and adequate resources are dedicated to the change" (p. 19). For the Dutch financial sector an organization's capacity for change is:

> The extent to which groups of people within that organization are willing and able to effectively implement ambitions and objectives and ensure they succeed. It also includes the ability to adjust the process

of change if the approach does not seem to be working or if there is a drastic change in circumstances.

(AFM, & DNB, n.d.)

A consultancy network also focuses on the people side:

> Capacity issues are exacerbated by unrealistic timelines and insufficient resources. When people do not have the time or tools to achieve expected results, they take shortcuts that lead to failure or unnecessary rework. By adjusting timelines to fit your capacity, you can ensure better performance and higher morale in your employees. In short, do not make the mistake of neglecting capacity as you set due dates.

The president of a US-based consulting firm asks:

> What can organizations do to be ready for the phenomenal amount of change that they are lining up for their future? My view is that they need to build greater change capacity, to be change ready and change agile. Having the ability to manage many changes concurrently is a challenge—I remember a change register holding over 300 initiatives at one organization—but if you build a dispersed capacity, to support, assist and enable change at all levels, then you will have a ready build network for greater change capacity. To build this capacity you need to recognize that organizations are best served by a mix of individual involvement. Many employees with varying levels of change responsibility need to be included.

Based on a survey a leading strategy firm claims that ". . . three-quarters of the respondents whose companies broke down their change process into clearly defined smaller initiatives and whose transformations were 'extremely successful' say that staff members were entirely or very able to participate in shaping those change initiatives."

10 Participation Is Key for Successful Change

Talking about the ideal typical 'good-to-great leaders,' Collins (2001) emphasizes the importance of voice and the participation of employees. He puts it this way:

> Yes, leadership is about vision. But leadership is equally about creating a climate where the truth is heard and the brutal facts confronted. There's a huge difference between the opportunity to 'have your say' and the opportunity to be *heard*. The good-to-great leaders understood this distinction, creating a culture wherein people had a

tremendous opportunity to be heard and, ultimately, for the truth to be heard. (p. 74)

Talking about culture change, Connors and Smith (2011) define five principles that should guide encouraging full employee engagement. The fifth is: Design for maximum involvement and creativity. They state: "Culture change is a highly collaborative effort and requires the engagement of everyone at every level as co-creators of the culture. You must design the enrolment to achieve this maximum involvement and creativity from everyone in the organization" (Connors & Smith, 2011, p. 209). Zaffron and Logan (2009) point out the positive effects of participation: "When you share, other people take on performance challenges with you and form a network. In this community everyone is learning and working together to achieve what once looked impossible" (p. 202). Watkins (2013) talks about the use of consultation to maximize commitment: "Be clear on which elements of your vision are non-negotiable, but beyond these, be flexible enough to consider the ideas of others and allow them to have input and to influence the shared vision. In that way, they share ownership" (p. 187). Brown (2009) advocates an inspiration space in which insights are gathered from every possible source to develop good designs. He also gives an example of a school that developed a philosophy of investigative learning that engages people as seekers of knowledge. This participatory design mirrored the end product: a participatory teaching and learning environment.

11 Resistance to Change Should Be Defused Early on in the Change Process

Bridges (1991) emphasizes the importance of understanding resistance and its causes:

> It's the process of letting go that people resist, not the change itself. Their resistance can take the form of foot-dragging or sabotage, and you have to understand the pattern of loss to be ready to deal with the resistance and keep it from getting out of the hand. (p. 15)

Kriegel and Brandt (1996) refer to the classic paper "How to Deal With Resistance to Change" (1954) by Harvard Business School professor Paul Lawrence. Lawrence describes "how failing to understand workers' resistance can sabotage the whole effort" (p. 187). Heifetz et al. (2009) plead for the protection of the voices of dissent. They put it this way:

> The voices of dissent are the naysayers, the skeptics, who not only question this initiative but question whatever is on the agenda of today. They are princes of darkness, often resting on the negative. But they are valuable

for implementing adaptive change because they are canaries in the coal mine, early-warning systems, and because in addition to being unproductive and annoying much of the time, they have the uncanny capacity for asking the really tough key question that you have been unwilling to face up yourself or that others have been unwilling to raise. In many organizations dissenters get marginalized, silenced, or even fired, which deprives the organization of their valuable, if unpopular service. (p. 145)

Belasco (1990) poses some essential questions about dealing with resistance:

When and how can I talk to my critics directly? When I do, what will my approach be? . . . How can I share power with the critic? What does the critic want that I can provide in return for his/her support for my vision? (p. 45)

Davidson (2002) gives an initial answer that focuses on defusing resistance: "Even if you do not intellectually and emotionally agree with you staff's viewpoint, give them validation to their feelings. That will prove to be a most helpful gesture in inducing them to move on to what is next" (p. 45). Resistance is often seen as an obstacle. Zaffron and Logan (2009) explain that "if something occurs to you and others as an obstacle, you'll push back by playing on the obstacle terms. Instead, make the obstacles conditions of the game" (p. 201). Maurer (2010) writes:

. . . [P]rogress without resistance is impossible. People will always have doubts and questions. Even when you are the champion of change, you will still have doubts. Will this really work? Have I given the idea sufficient thought? Resistance is a natural part of any change. (p. 35)

An international consultant writes: "Change is not the problem. Resistance to change is the problem." He adds:

Expecting resistance to change and planning for it from the start of your change management programme will allow you to effectively manage objections. Understanding the most common reasons people object to change gives you the opportunity to plan your change strategy to address these factors.

An international consultancy firm furthermore writes:

Change occurs in all organizations, so successful leaders and managers need to master the skill of leading and managing change, including being able to recognize and manage resistance to change. Resistance to change is the response that many employees have when managers introduce change. While change can be an exciting opportunity for some, it can be a time of loss, disruption or threat for others. This is why change and resistance often go hand in hand. Resistance is the most common issue that managers encounter when implementing change and the problem that causes them the most frustration.

12 A Fair Change Process Is Important in Achieving Successful Change

A reputed author and consultant claims on his Web site:

> How you lead the change—not what you are changing—is the key to raising the success rate of change projects to 8 out of 10 . . . rather than 3 out of 10 that 30 years of research indicates is the average success rate.

He explains both the concept of fair process and its effects in a very clear way:

> What is Fair Process? Simply put, fair process is honest communication about 1) What is already decided and 2) What your employees can influence (or decide for themselves) and 3) By what criteria their input to your decisions will be judged. . . . The most common effects of a fair process is building employees' trust in you as a manager and an increase in employee engagement and inner motivation to develop solutions and implement decisions. The tangible results are quicker and better implementation.

A consulting firm describes:

> What this means for developers is that they can certainly placate people by allowing them to have their voices heard through the entitlement process. More importantly, they are putting their projects at risk if people don't perceive that they are being treated fairly. After all, even the best projects with potentially great outcomes can be derailed by a few critical missteps.

A consulting firm specializing in family business explains: "We have adopted the procedural approach, known as Fair Process, because the complexities of the family business systems make this the only workable solution."

Several leading authors also advocate a fair change process. As Kriegel and Brandt (1996) write: "The way you introduce change makes a world of difference in how people feel about it" (p. 218). They explain that if major changes are implemented, employees will be less resistant when they understand the decision in its context and feel that they are being treated

48 Story of Change

honestly. However, in practice a fair process is often lacking, and employees feel as if a bombshell has been dropped. According to Kriegel and Brandt:

> Many companies simply announce a downsizing scheme such as it was a new health plan or accounting procedure. No input. No Q&A. No dialogue. It's not just the bad news, but the form of delivery that bends employees out of shape. No wonder people feel victimized and disrespected. The rumor mills start racing and the resistance starts rising. (p. 219)

They emphasize the importance of providing a structure for employees to express their natural disappointment and a sense of loss. This is not the same as involving people in the creation of change but helping them move toward acceptance. It's about acknowledging their feelings. Ibarra (2015) refers to the importance of engaging people in the change by developing supportive processes by stating that "naïve leaders act as if the idea itself is the ultimate selling point. Experienced leaders, on the other hand, understand that the process is just as important, if not more so" (p. 45). Brockner (2006) builds the 'business case for fair process'; fair process makes great 'business sense.' He writes: "From minimizing costs to strengthening performance, process fairness pays enormous dividends in a wide variety of organizational and people-related challenges" (p. 123). According to Brockner process fairness has three drivers: (1) how much input employees believe they have in the decision-making process, (2) how employees believe decisions are made and implemented (e.g., consistent, accurate, transparent, and not biased), and (3) how managers behave. He claims that change will go more smoothly if process fairness is in place. Leaders have to express authentic interest to create a trusting environment in which people feel that they can safely voice their anxieties, objections, and worries about the change at hand. Brockner not only builds the business case for fair process. He advocates that there is a moral imperative for companies to practice process fairness as the right thing to do. Collins (2001) also emphasizes the importance of processes that guarantee that people will be heard in the right way. His 'good-to-great leaders' lead with questions (not answers), engage in dialogue and debate (not coercion), and build 'red flag' mechanisms. ". . . [R]ed flag mechanisms give you a practical and useful tool for turning information into information that can't be ignored and for creating a climate where the truth is heard" (p. 80).

13 Organizational Culture Is Difficult and Time-Consuming to Change

Both authors and consultants emphasize the difficult and time-consuming character of cultural change. An international strategy firm states:

> But culture change doesn't come easily. Lou Gerstner, who transformed IBM's fortunes in the '90s, says, "Fixing culture is the most critical—and

the most difficult—part of a corporate transformation." Carly Fiorina, the ex-HP boss reflects, "The soft stuff is actually the hard stuff." They are right, too. The truth is that more than 70 percent of large-scale change efforts fail, and of these failures more than 70 percent are due to culture-related issues: employee resistance to change and unsupportive management behavior. Executives try a variety of initiatives to create high-performance environments. More often than not, however, the results are disappointing. Cultural interventions are often not clearly linked to business performance and value creation. Such initiatives also frequently fail to explicitly address the often hidden mindsets and attitudes of employees. Finally, dysfunctional cultures are simply tough to fix. How do you get thousands of employees to suddenly change their most basic assumptions about their company when these filter through everything the company does?

Davidson (2002) considers cultural change as a major issue: "Inducing cultural change can take many years, hundreds of thousands of dollars, outside consultants, and team members working at the full bore to implement" (p. 19). Watkins (2013) is very clear:

> To change your organization, you will likely have to change its culture. This is a difficult undertaking. Your organization may have well-ingrained bad habits that you want to break. But we know how difficult it is for one person to change habitual patterns in any significant way, never mind a mutually reinforcing collection of people. (p. 135)

Humble, Molesky, and O'Reilly (2015) state: "Culture is the most critical factor in an organization's ability to adapt to its changing environment. However, being intangible, it is hard to analyze and even harder to change" (p. 209). They put forward the idea that it is hard to achieve sustained, systemic change without a crisis and present Schein's (2009) answer on the question as to whether a crisis is a necessary condition of successful transformations. Schein (2009) answers:

> Because humans (mostly) avoid unpredictability and uncertainty, hence create cultures, the basic argument for adult learning is that we indeed need some new stimulus to upset the equilibrium. The best way to think about such a stimulus is as *disconfirmation*: something is perceived or felt that is not expected and that upsets some of our beliefs or assumptions. . . . [D]isconfirmation creates *survival anxiety*—that something bad will happen if we don't change—or *guilt*—we realize that we are not achieving our own ideals or goals. (p. 106)

An international change management expert emphasizes: "Changing an organization's culture is one of the most difficult leadership challenges.

That's because an organization's culture comprises an interlocking set of goals, roles, processes, values, communications practices, attitudes, and assumptions." On behalf of a leading international strategy firm, an expert explains:

> Success in the past always becomes enshrined in the present by the overvaluation of the policies and attitudes which accompanied that success. As long as the environment and competitive behavior do not change, these beliefs and policies contribute to the stability of the firm. However, with time these attitudes become embedded in a system of beliefs, traditions, taboos, habits, customs, and inhibitions which constitute the distinctive culture of that firm. Such cultures are as distinctive as the cultural differences between nationalities or the personality differences between individuals. They do not adapt to change very easily.

A popular tool kit includes the following statement:

> Cultural change efforts seem to fail as often as they succeed. Knowing the reasons for both success and failure before a project starts can prevent problems and make a faster transition. Cultural change is neither easy nor fast. It requires concentrated and focused effort over the long haul. It also requires a widespread belief that change is necessary, and the willingness to critically examine current beliefs, values, and practices.

14 Organizational Culture Is Related to Performance

"Culture is it!" says Belasco (1990, p. 201). He claims that every organization has a culture that shapes behavior, culture calls the tune, and the challenge is to create the culture you want—one that empowers using the vision. Cameron and Quinn (2011) claim that they provide "a critically important strategy in an organization's repertoire for changing culture and improving performance" (p. 24) and are also quite outspoken:

> Since culture is such a crucial factor in the long-term effectiveness of organizations, it's imperative that the individuals charged with studying or managing organizational culture be able to measure key dimensions of culture, develop a strategy for changing it, and begin an implementation process. (p. 8)

And, explaining the 'extraordinarily' successful performance of companies such as Walmart, Apple and Pixar, "The major distinguishing feature in these companies—their most important competitive advantage, the most powerful factor they all highlight as a key ingredient in their success—is their organizational culture" (Cameron & Quinn, 2011, p. 5). Cameron and Quinn (2011) also link culture to a specific kind of organizational performance, namely achieving organizational change. Referring to several studies, they identify a neglect of corporate culture as the main reason for failure; "failure to change the organization's culture doomed the other kinds of organizational changes that were initiated" (Cameron & Quinn, 2011, p. 2). They state that without "a change in organizational culture, there is little hope of enduring improvement in organizational performance" (p. 12). Connors and Smith (2011) also describe culture as decisive in their best seller *Change the Culture, Change the Game*. Changing culture is "the breakthrough strategy for energizing your organization and creating accountability for results" (Connors & Smith, 2011, cover). Their claim is clear and outspoken: "The most compelling reason to work on your culture? Culture produces results" (p. 29). Kotter (2012) calls culture 'powerful' and 'influential'; therefore, "the new practices created in a reengineering or a restructuring or an acquisition must somehow be anchored in it; if not, they can be very fragile and subject to regression" (p. 159). Conner (1992) agrees: "Whenever a discrepancy exists between the current culture and the objectives of your change, the culture always wins" (p. 179). Keller and Aiken talk about 'performance culture' and explain in their article:

> Most business leaders know intuitively what academic research has consistently confirmed—that cultural factors are powerful drivers of business performance. Larry Bossidy, reflecting on his turnaround of Allied Signal, says that "the soft stuff is at least as important as the hard stuff." Jack Welch, after he masterminded GE's corporate transformation in the '80s and '90s, said, "No company can sustain high productivity without culture change." They are right. McKinsey research has found that companies with strong performance cultures have 11 percent higher annual total return to shareholders (TRS) and 5.2 percent higher return on investment capital (ROIC) than those with weak performance cultures.
>
> (Keller & Aiken, 2014, p. 1)

Kouzes and Posner (2012) present a corporate leader who focuses on a 'safety culture' and writes: "We believe that culture is key to preventing incidents and injuries. When we proactively look out for ourselves, our co-workers, our friends and families, then we can get closer to the reality of zero incidents and injuries" (p. 215). Talking about lean management, Humble et al. (2015) consider the ability to 'grow an innovation culture' as the key to successful performance. They state: ". . . [O]rganizational culture determines not just the productivity and performance of the people working in it, but also their ability to gain new skills, their attitude to failure and new challenges, and their goals" (p. 222). Cameron and Quinn (2011) state: "Modifying organizational culture, in other words, is a key to the successful implementation of major improvement strategies (TQM, downsizing, re-engineering) as well as adaptation to the increasing turbulent environment faced by modern organizations" (p. 13).

15 Goal Setting Combined With Feedback Is a Powerful Tool for Change Leaders

Consultants and leading authors alike emphasize the importance of measuring results and providing feedback. Novak (2012), author and famous CEO, tells us:

> Recognizing the behaviors you want and those you don't is essential to keeping your people on track toward achieving your Big Goal. It's important to do this formally, with things like performance reviews and raises, but even informal recognition can have a big impact. (p. 193)

An international consultant adds:

> Organizations should really focus on two kinds of factors to change their employees' behavior, whether that be with a reward structure of their choosing or the way that they're providing feedback to employees. . . . Another piece that is really important for changing employee behavior is immediate, on-the-job feedback that individuals can identify while they're performing the behavior.

Mourier and Smith (2001) underline the importance of measurement, feedback, and consequences: "Provide positive recognition when expectations are met and negative consequences when expectations aren't met" (p. 32). Kouzes and Posner (2012) state: "People need to know if they're making progress toward the goal or simply marking time. Their motivation to perform a task increases only when they have a challenging goal *and* receive feedback on their progress" (p. 282).

Heller (1998) addresses measuring results and providing feedback as ways to influence or change employee behavior by presenting the concept of goal setting. He advises: "Set personal objectives for people so they focus their minds on performance; reaching the goals will reinforce their enhanced drive" (p. 51). On feedback, he states: "Commend people, publicly or privately, to strengthen commitment. Be sure to set high standards, and never ignore mistakes" (p. 51). Watkins (2013) also advocates the definition and monitoring of goals and performance metrics: "On the push side, establishing—and sticking to—clear and explicit performance metrics is the best way to encourage accountability" (p. 183). Laloux (2014) is less instrumental and considers feedback as an essential element in work and organizations. He links feedback deprivation to the psychological phenomenon of sensory deprivation: "Our egos may be wary of feedback, but we are relational beings that thrive on honest feedback. I've seen organizations where no feedback is ever exchanged 'go mad' because of it" (p. 125). Sometimes people believe a change is good, in itself, for the organization or even for themselves, but they will resist when they feel that they are not up to the task." Kriegel and Brandt (1996) plead for 'honest feedback that builds confidence': "Neutralizing fear-driven resistance to change requires managers to help their people believe in themselves. Confidence is a fear killer" (p. 207).

Kegan and Lahey (2001) warn us about the use of indirect, nonspecific feedback, and they provide the alternative of *ongoing regard*. Ongoing regard is direct and specific, and it is about appreciation and admiration of employees' behavior, choices, and intentions at work. Jackman and Strober (2003) talk about the 'fear of feedback' and define the importance and characteristics of good feedback:

> Fears and assumptions about feedback often manifest themselves in psychologically maladaptive behaviors such as procrastination, denial, brooding, jealousy, and self-sabotage. But there's hope. Those who learn adapt to feedback can learn to acknowledge negative emotions, constructively reframe fear and criticism, develop realistic goals, create support systems, and reward themselves for achievements along the way. (p. 127)

Looking at managing changes, Bridges (1991) links feedback to reinforcement through consistency and reward:

> It's common and always disastrous to tell people to act and react in new ways—and then to reward them for the old actions and reactions. You won't manage to hold a new beginning for long if you preach teamwork and the reward individual contribution, if you preach customer service and then reward following the rules, if you preach risk taking and then reward no mistakes. (pp. 61–62)

Ibarra (2015) refers to the lack of change or progress notwithstanding the fact that feedback is available and given. Often people lack a sense of urgency to do something about the feedback. Ibarra (2015) writes: "[T]he problem is that the carrot-and-stick theory of self-motivation rarely works, because change is so difficult. The statistics are depressing. Some 80 percent of people who make New Year's resolutions fall of the wagon by mid-February. Two-thirds of dieters gain back any lost weight within a year" (p. 166).

16 Commitment to Change Is an Essential Component of a Successful Change Initiative

In sports, the importance of commitment is undisputed. According to White (2011) the legendary athlete Haile Gebrselassie tells us: "You need three things to win: discipline, hard work and, before everything maybe, commitment. No one will make it without those three. Sport teaches you that." And the world-champion racing driver Mario Andretti would have once said: "Desire is the key to motivation, but it's determination and commitment to an unrelenting pursuit of your goal—a commitment to excellence—that will enable you to attain the success you seek" (Mario Andretti Quotes, n.d.). Employee *commitment* to change objectives often is considered a prerequisite for successful change. Conner (2006) is very clear:

> Successful change is rooted in commitment. Unless key participants in a transition are committed to both attaining the goals of the change and paying the price those goals entail, the project will ultimately fail. In fact, most change failures trace back to this lack of commitment, with obvious symptoms such as sponsors terminating projects and more subtle signs such as target apathy as leading indicators. (p. 147)

And:

> Given that committed people will devote the time, money, endurance, persistence, loyalty, and ingenuity necessary, it's easy to see why commitment is critical for successful change. It's the glue that provides the vital bond between people and change goals. It's the source of energy that propels resilient people and organizations through the process as the fastest, most effective pace possible—the optimum speed of change. (Conner, 2006, p. 148)

An international consultancy firm agrees: "Organizations are under constant pressure to change. Employee commitment to necessary changes is of paramount importance for such changes to be effective." According to executives, the key to an effort's success or failure is commitment to change—or the lack thereof. When asked about company efforts that met their goals and those that did not, executives most often cited organization-wide ownership of and commitment to change as a capability responsible for either outcome.

Today some people prefer to talk about engagement instead of commitment. Several experts see the difference between the two as a matter of semantics. One could say that, if there is any difference, engagement is a variant of or on commitment going a step further; commitment is about being emotionally bound, and engagement is about being passionate. Maurer (2010) prefers to talk about engagement. He considers underestimating the potential power of employee engagement as an important mistake in change processes. He refers to the 'extensive research' of the Gallup organization:

> [I]n average organizations the ratio of engaged to actively disengaged employees is near 8:1. . . . Actively disengaged employees erode an

organization's bottom line, while breaking the spirits of colleagues in the process. Within the U.S. workforce, Gallup estimates this cost to be more than $300 billion in lost productivity alone. (p. 13)

Langley et al. (2009) emphasize the fact that people need to cooperate to make effective change, but that commitment to change is not a given: "People will usually have some reaction to change. This reaction can range from total commitment to open hostility" (p. 46). Kegan and Lahey (2001) talk about the "chance to bring vitalizing energy of commitment into the workplace" (p. 30). Bridges (1991) emphasizes how important it is to take that chance:

> Maybe you don't care. Maybe in the old days when you learned how to manage people, you learned to give orders and to crack the whip if they weren't carried out. Compliance was enough in those days because there wasn't much competition and it took only half of the people's energy and intelligence to do a decent job. Today's different. Compliance isn't enough. You need everyone's commitment because only with commitment you get people to give 100%. (p. 22)

Commitment is not only viewed as essential in realizing change but also associated with performance gains. In their paper Fredberg, Beer, Eisenstat, Foote, and Norrgren (2008) point out the critical relationship between commitment and performance. They state that it

> ... is intuitively attractive to think that if a CEO is able to engage people in the development of the organization he/she leads, there is a greater likelihood that a strategic change initiative will reach its full potential. Indeed, research has shown that a high level of engagement from employees is positively correlated with financial performance. (p. 3)

Earlier engagement was introduced as a variant on commitment. Talking about engagement and performance, an international consultancy firm tells us:

> Employee engagement has become a top business priority for senior executives. In this rapid-cycle economy, business leaders know that having a high-performing workforce is essential for growth and survival. They recognize that a highly engaged workforce can increase innovation, productivity, and bottom-line performance, while reducing costs related to hiring and retention in highly competitive talent markets.

17 Financial Incentives Are an Effective Way to Encourage Change and Improve Performance

With respect to financial incentives and rewards as a way to reinforce commitment to change, Heller (1998) advises very clearly: "Be willing to pay generously for achievement. People may change their behavior radically for significant pay rewards" (p. 51). He explains: "People want to feel that their reward will match their efforts; if it does, this will reinforce their commitment to the new ways" (p. 51). Kriegel and Brandt (1996) are also very straightforward: "The most obvious way to motivate employees to get excited about your plans is through rewards" (p. 260). But they also are more specific:

> There are two kinds of rewards: extrinsic incentives, such as the corner office, money, gifts, and titles, and intrinsic rewards, which appeal to more abstract personal needs. People do things not just to get an object or the cash to buy it. They're also motivated by such intangibles as recognition, fairness, flexibility, creativity, meaningfulness, ad freedom. These internal factors have more impact on readiness for change than traditional extrinsic rewards do. (p. 261)

Conner (2006) writes: "A lack of willingness stems from a shortage of motivation and should be addressed through consequence management (the combination of rewards and punishments)" (p. 129). An international consultant writes:

> Employees are going to inevitably repeat behaviors for which they are rewarded. For example, if an employee is rewarded for their productivity, he or she is going to focus on productive behaviors and, as a result, this will help to drive productivity.

Watkins (2013) talks about 'aligning incentives' and a 'baseline question': "how best to incentivize team members to achieve desired goals. What mix of monetary and nonmonetary rewards will you employ?" (p. 183). A consultancy network adds: "Financial incentives can be important, but don't always work and are most effective if combined with non-financial incentives."

18 Self-Managing Teams Perform Better in Realizing Change Than Traditionally Managed Teams

Evan Williams, cofounder of Blogger, Twitter, and Medium tells that people romanticize start-up cultures and their lack of structure, while they create tons of anxiety and inefficiency. Referring to the work of Robertson (2015), about the 'Holacracy,' he pleas for clarity without neglecting flexibility: who is in charge of what and who makes each kind of decision. Novak (2012) says: "Once you have your strategy for your Large Goal, you have to put structure in place to make it happen. That means having the resources, organization, and processes you need to execute your strategy" (p. 135). Williams both underlines the role and importance of structure and indirectly warns for structures which are too 'fluid,' 'organic,' or 'over-flexible.' Robertson puts emphasis on the role of one of the essential building blocks of an effective structure, the job description:

> ... [J]ob descriptions contain relevant, accurate, clear and useful information about what it makes sense to do and expect. This means that the way we actually work together (the extant structure) more closely reflects what's documented (the formal structure), which more closely reflects what's best for the organization (the requisite structure). (p. 38)

Watkins (2013), talking about the 'organizational architect,' also underlines the importance of structure; the architect is responsible for:

> ... creating and aligning the key elements of the organizational system: the strategic direction, structure, core processes, and skill bases that provide the foundation for superior performance. No matter how charismatic you are as a leader, you can't hope to do much if your organization is fundamentally out of alignment. (p. 140)

Miller (2002, p. 271) refers to Deming, who writes: "96 percent of all problems can be attributed to the system and 4 percent to the people." Having noticed this, one could state that today the most popular concept to structure, align, execute, and solve system problems is that of the team or, more precisely, the self-managing team. Talking about change campaigns, Davidson (2002) pleas for a 'team-based culture.'

A popular blog reads:

> Employees are the most important asset of an organization and teams are the building blocks of its success. A person's quality to be a good team player and leader determines how well he or she can contribute to achieving the company's objectives. To compete effectively in today's markets, organizations have turned their focus on building self-motivated and efficient teams so as to maximize the use of their resources and employee talents. Businesses across industry verticals are giving increasing importance to put in place flexible teams that are more responsive to changing environments. The importance of a team comes into play when business processes need a coordinated and collective effort from the employees, which in turn creates a positive impact on the entire organization.
>
> (Richa, 2014, para 1)

Laloux (2014) provides us with "A Guide to Creating Organizations Inspired by the Next Stage of Human Consciousness" and considers self-management (structures) and self-managing teams as defining elements.

A team-based organization (TBO) is often described in very positive, attractive terms; an example of this can be found in the business dictionary:

> a traditional, innovative work environment relying on teams to achieve its objectives. TBO's major characteristics include (1) mutual trust, (2) employee empowerment in planning, organization, and goal-setting, (3) shared responsibility for self-management, (4) shared accountability for performance, and (5) shared leadership.
> (Team based organization, n.d.)

A reputed international strategy firm also underlines the potential of teams:

> There are very few tricks for improving organizational performance left in the management deck of cards. In recent years, many eager corporate hands have played the organization redesign card; others, strategic planning; still others, value-based management. If they played them well, their companies are now fitter, stronger, more flexible, and more focused. But so too are their competitors. Sloppy strategies have been tightened; yawning skill gaps closed; troubled economies made healthy; and bloated organizations made lean. What remains—the trump card— is the effort to coax exceptional levels of performance from all the pieces now in place. And that means learning how to build and lead world-class—or what McKinsey's Jon Katzenbach and Doug Smith refer to as 'high-performing'—teams.

To Sum Up

Our team has identified a collection of assumptions grounded in the popular management books and the practice of—mainly—highly influential consultants and consultancy firms. Eighteen of them were selected to be analyzed and to be judged with the help of an evidence-based management approach. In doing this we focus on the academic perspective of this approach and combine it with the professional and academic knowledge and experience in our team. Before presenting our analyses, we elaborate on our methodology in the next chapter.

References

AFM & DNB (n.d.). *Capacity for change in the financial sector*. Retrieved February 3, 2016, from https://www.afm.nl/~/profmedia/files/brochures/2014/verandervermogen-banken-verzekeraars-2.ashx

Allen, R. C. (2002). *Guiding change journeys: A synergistic approach to organization transformation*. San Francisco, CA: Jossey-Bass and Pfeiffer.

Beer, M., & Nohria, N. (2000). Cracking the code of change. *Harvard Business Review*, 78(3), 133–141.

Belasco, J. A. (1990). *Teaching the elephant to dance. Empowering change in your organization.* New York, NY: Crown Publishers.

Bridges, W. (1991). *Managing transitions: Making the most of change.* Reading, MA: Perseus Books.

Brockner, J. (2006). Why it's so hard to be fair. *Harvard Business Review, 84*(3), 122–129.

Brown, T. (2009). *Change by design: How design thinking transforms organizations and inspires innovation.* Broadway, NY: HarperCollins Publishers.

Cameron, K., & Quinn, R. E. (2011). *Diagnosing and changing organizational culture: Based on the competing values framework.* Reading, MA: Addison Wesley Longman.

Collins, J. C. (2001). *Good to great: Why some companies make the leap . . . and others don't.* New York, NY: HarperCollins Publishers.

Conner, D. R. (1992). *Managing at the speed of change: How resilient managers succeed and prosper where others fail.* New York, NY: Random House.

Conner, D. R. (2006). *Managing at the speed of change: How resilient managers succeed and prosper where others fail.* New York, NY: Random House.

Connors, R., & Smith, T. (2011). *Change the culture, change the game: The breakthrough strategy for energizing your organization and creating accountability for results.* New York, NY: Random House.

Davidson, J. (2002). *The complete idiot's guide to change management.* Indianapolis, IN: Alpha Books.

Eckes, G. (2001). *Making Six Sigma last: Managing the balance between cultural and technical change.* New York, NY: John Wiley & Sons.

Fredberg, T., Beer, M., Eisenstat, R., Foote, N., & Norrgren, F. (2008). *Embracing commitment and performance: CEOs and practices to manage paradox.* Retrieved October 17, 2015, on http://www.hbs.edu/faculty/Publication%20Files/08-052_18284f5a-c48b-45e9-acfd-8b3d3242514e.pdf

Goleman, D. (2015). *On emotional intelligence.* Boston, MA: Harvard Business Review Press.

Heath, C., & Heath, D. (2010). *Switch: How to change things when change is hard.* New York, NY: Broadway Books.

Heifetz, R. A., Grashow, A., & Linsky, M. (2009). *The practice of adaptive leadership: Tools and tactics for changing your organization and the world.* Boston, MA: Harvard Business Press.

Heller, J. (1998). *Essential managers: Managing change.* New York, NY: D. K. Publishing.

Hesselbein, F., & Johnston, R. (2002). *On leading change: A leader to leader guide.* San Francisco, CA: Jossey-Bass.

Humble, J., Molesky, J., & O'Reilly, B. (2015). *Lean enterprise: How high performance organizations innovate at scale.* Sebastopol, CA: O'Reilly Media.

Ibarra, H. (2015). *Act like a leader, think like a leader.* Boston, MA: Harvard Business Review Press.

Jackman, J. M., & Strober, M. N. (2003). Fear of feedback. *Harvard Business Review, 81*(4), 101–108.

Katzenbach, J. R., & Smith, D. K. (1992). Why teams matter. *McKinsey Quarterly, 3*, 3–27.

Kegan, R., & Lahey, L. (2001). *How the way we talk can change the way we work.* New York, NY: John Wiley & Sons.

Kegan, R., & Lahey, L. (2009). *Immunity to change: How to overcome it and unlock the potential in yourself and your organization*. Boston, MA: Harvard Business Press.

Keller, S., & Aiken, C. (2009). *The inconvenient truth about change: Why it isn't working and what to do about it*. Retrieved July 10, 2015, from http://www.aascu.org/corporatepartnership/McKinseyReport2.pdf.

Keller, S., & Aiken, C. (2014). *On performance culture*. Retrieved November 28, 2015, from http://www.oncourse.com.au/articles/McKinsey%20On%20Performance%20Culture.pdf

Kotter, J. P. (1996). *Leading change*. Boston, MA: Harvard Business Review Press.

Kotter, J. P. (2012). *Leading change*. Boston, MA: Harvard Business Review Press.

Kouzes, J., & Posner, B. (2012). *The leadership challenge: How to make extraordinary things happen in organizations*. San Francisco, CA: Jossey-Bass.

Kriegel, R. J., & Brandt, D. (1996). *Sacred cows make the best burgers*. New York, NY: Warner Books, Inc.

Laloux, F. (2014). *Reinventing organizations: A guide to creating organizations inspired by the next stage of human consciousness*. Brussel, BE: Nelson Parker.

Langley, G. J., Moen, R., Nolan, K. M., Nolan, T. W., Norman, C. L., & Provost, L. P. (2009). *The improvement guide: A practical approach to enhancing organizational performance*. San Francisco, CA: Jossey-Bass.

Larkin, T., & Larkin, S. (1994). *Communicating change: Winning employee support for new business goals*. New York, NY: McGraw-Hill.

Lawrence, P. R. (1954). How to deal with resistance to change. *Harvard Business Review, 32*(3), 49–57.

Lewis, L. K., Schmisseur, A. M., Stephens, K. K., & Weir, K. E. (2006). Advice on communicating during organizational change. The content of popular press books. *Journal of Business Communication, 43*(2), 113–137.

Lippitt, L. L. (1999). Preferred futuring: The power to change whole systems of any size. In P. Holman, & T. Devane (Eds.), *The change handbook* (pp. 159–174). San Francisco, CA: Berrett-Koehler.

Mario Andretti Quotes. (n.d.). In *BrainyQuote*. Retrieved December 18, 2015, from http://www.brainyquote.com/quotes/quotes/m/marioandre130613.html

Maurer, R. (2010). *Beyond the wall of resistance: Why 70% of all changes still fail—and what you can do about it*. Austin, TX: Bard Press.

Maxwell, J. C. (2013). *The 17 indisputable laws of teamwork: Embrace them and empower your team*. Nashville, TN: Thomas Nelson Inc.

Miller, K. (2002). *The change agent's guide to radical improvement*. Milwaukee, WI: American Society for Quality.

Mourier, P., & Smith, M. R. (2001). *Conquering organizational change. How to succeed where most companies fail*. Atlanta, GA: CEP Press.

Novak, D. (2012). *Taking people with you: The only way to make big things happen*. New York, NY: Portfolio and Penguin.

Richa. (2014, June 12). *Team structure: Creating and managing great teams*. Retrieved November 10, 2015, from https://blog.udemy.com/team-structure/

Robertson, B. J. (2015). *Holacracy: The new management system for a rapidly changing world*. New York, NY: Henry Holt and Company.

Schein, E. H. (2009). *The corporate culture survival guide*. San Francisco, CA: John Wiley & Sons.

Team based organization. (n.d.). In *BusinessDictionary.com*. Retrieved January 28, 2016, from http://www.businessdictionary.com/definition/team-based-organization-TBO.html

Ten Have, S., Ten Have, W. D., & Janssen, B. (2009). *Het Veranderboek: 70 vragen van managers over organisatieverandering*. Amsterdam, NL: Mediawerf.

Watkins, M. D. (2013). *The first 90 days: Proven strategies for getting up to speed faster and smarter, updated and expanded*. Boston, MA: Harvard Business Review Press.

White, J. (2011, March 17). *Born to run: Haile Gebrselassie interview*. Retrieved January 18, 2016, from http://www.telegraph.co.uk/sport/othersports/athletics/8373361/Born-to-run-Haile-Gebrselassie-interview.html

Zaffron, S., & Logan, D. (2009). *The three laws of performance: Rewriting the future of your organization and your life*. San Francisco, CA: Jossey-Bass.

4 Methodology

Summarizing Scientific Evidence

Evidence summaries come in many forms. One of the best known is the conventional literature review, which provides a general overview of the relevant scientific literature published on a given topic. However, a conventional literature review is not always entirely trustworthy: Studies are selected based on the researcher's individual preferences rather than on explicit and objective criteria, and the research results are generally not subject to critical appraisal (Antman, 1992; Bushman & Wells, 2001; Chalmers, Enkin, & Keirse, 1993; Fink, 1998). Most conventional literature reviews are therefore prone to severe bias and are considered to be unsuitable to answer questions about the effectiveness of strategies or interventions. This is why Rapid Evidence Assessments (REAs) are the preferred method for reviewing evidence in evidence-based management. Such reviews address a focused question through a methodology that identifies the most relevant studies and only includes those studies that meet explicit quality and relevance criteria as determined by several researchers (Higgins & Green, 2006; Petticrew & Roberts, 2006). Unlike a conventional literature review, an REA will be transparent, verifiable, reproducible, and, therefore, less biased and more relevant.

To examine the evidence base of the 18 assumptions in this book, we conducted a series of REAs that are presented here. Each of the REAs conducted involved the following 12 steps individually covered in each of the chapters of this book:

1 Background
2 Definition
3 Causal mechanism
4 Inclusion criteria
5 Search strategy
6 Study selection
7 Data extraction
8 Critical appraisal

Methodology 63

9 Main findings
10 Synthesis
11 Conclusion
12 Practical reflections

1 Background: What Is the Professional Context of the Assumption?

The background states the rationale for an REA and explains why the assumption being examined is important. It provides examples from the popular academic literature that illustrate the assumption and its underlying conventions. Chapter 3 provides a full explanation of how these examples were acquired. Some assumptions in this book occur in a specific context. When this is the case, the background section addresses this context.

2 Definition: What Is Meant by X?

Common to all the assumptions discussed in this book is that there are usually several definitions available of the key element in the assumption (e.g., *participation*, *commitment*, or *urgency*). This section provides an overview of the most common definition.

3 Assumed Causal Mechanism: How Does X Work?

A causal mechanism spells out the process by which the key elements of the assumption are expected to produce a positive change outcome (i.e., how does it work?). For example, it is explained in Chapter 6 how participation is assumed to have a positive effect on the outcome of the change process. The causal mechanism is indicative and leading in determining the relevant outcome measures, search terms, criteria for including or excluding studies, and framework for synthesizing the findings.

4 Inclusion: Which Studies to Include?

This section specifies the criteria and justification for the inclusion (or exclusion) of particular studies. In most cases these criteria will be determined by the definition and the assumed causal mechanism. The following generic inclusion criteria were applied for all REAs:

1 Type of publication: only articles published in peer-reviewed, scholarly journals
2 Language: only articles in English
3 Type of studies: quantitative studies and, if not available, qualitative
4 Measurement: only studies in which the effect of the assumption's key element was measured

5   Context: only studies related to workplace settings
6   Level of trustworthiness: only studies that were graded Level D or above (see 7).

5 Search Strategy: How Was the Research Evidence Sought?

Based on the definition and key elements of the assumption, a structured search using combinations of different search terms was conducted to identify peer-reviewed studies. When this yielded an insufficient number of studies to reach a conclusion, a second search was conducted for relevant studies in other management domains. In both cases the search was limited to the following three bibliographical databases:

- ABI/INFORM Global from ProQuest
- Business Source Premier from EBSCO
- PsycINFO from Ovid

If the second search again yielded an insufficient number of studies, a third search was carried out to find relevant studies in other disciplines in which using databases relevant to the discipline in question were searched, such as PubMed (health care) and ERIC (education), or generic databases, such as Google Scholar.

Finally, if the third search also failed to yield a sufficient number of studies, then studies indirectly related to the assumption, such as possible underlying psychological or sociological principles, were looked at. For example, an initial search for studies relevant to the assumption 'People will not change when there is no sense of urgency' resulted in a small number of studies. For this reason studies on related concepts such as time pressure and fear appeal were also sought. Figure 4.1 provides an overview of the search steps.

6 Study Selection: How Were the Studies to Be Included Selected?

In most cases the search yielded a large number of studies, sometimes several hundred. Some of the studies found were not directly relevant to the research question. Hence, two reviewers independently screened the titles and the abstracts of the studies identified for their relevance to the assumption. In the event of doubt, lack of information, or disagreement, the study was included. The remaining studies for inclusion were then selected based on the full text of the article. Studies were excluded where they failed to meet the inclusion criteria. Again, two reviewers worked independently to identify which studies were to be included or excluded. Where the two reviewers disagreed on inclusion, a third reviewer assessed whether the study was appropriate for inclusion with no prior knowledge of the initial reviewers' assessments. The decision of the third reviewer was final.

Methodology 65

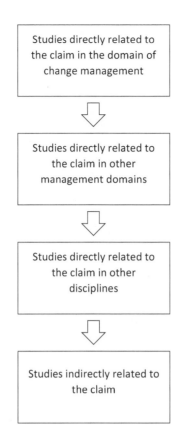

Figure 4.1 Overview of the Research Steps

7 Data Extraction

Data extraction involved the collation of the results of the studies included. In this phase relevant data was extracted from the final set of studies. Specifically, this was data on year of publication, research design, sample size, population (e.g., industry and type of employees), possible moderators or mediators, outcome measures, main findings, effect sizes, and limitations.

8 Critical Appraisal: How Was the Trustworthiness of the Evidence Appraised?

8.1 Methodological Appropriateness

A study's trustworthiness was first determined by its methodological appropriateness. The appropriateness was considered high when the research design reflected the best way to answer the research question. The trustworthiness of a study with poor methodological appropriateness was therefore low no matter how well the study was otherwise conducted.

Table 4.1 Six Levels to Determine the Methodological Appropriateness of the Research Design of the Studies Included

Design	Appropriateness	Level
Systematic review and meta-analysis of randomized controlled studies	Very high	A+
Systematic review and meta-analysis of controlled and/or before-after studies	High	A
Randomized controlled studies		
Systematic review and meta-analysis of cross-sectional studies	Moderate	B
Non-randomized controlled before-after studies		
Interrupted time series		
Controlled studies without a pretest and uncontrolled studies with a pretest	Limited	C
Cross-sectional studies	Low	D

For cause-and-effect claims (i.e., if I do A, will it result in B?), a study that used both a control group and random assignment was regarded as the gold standard. Non-randomized studies and before-after studies came next in terms of appropriateness. Cross-sectional studies (surveys) were regarded as having the greatest chance of showing bias in the outcome and therefore came lower down in the ranking in terms of appropriateness. Meta-analyses in which statistical analysis techniques were used to pool the results of controlled studies were therefore regarded as the most appropriate design.

The classification system of Shadish, Cook, and Campbell (2002) and Petticrew and Roberts (2006) was used to determine the methodological appropriateness of the research design of the studies included on the basis of a systematic assessment. Any discrepancies were resolved through discussion or by consulting a third party where necessary. The following four levels of appropriateness were used for the classification (see Table 4.1):

8.2 Methodological Quality

The trustworthiness of a study, however, is also affected by its methodological quality, that is, how it was conducted. To determine methodological quality all the studies included were systematically assessed based on explicit quality criteria, such as the PRISMA (Moher, Liberati, Tetzlaff, & Altman, 2009) and CONSORT statement (Moher, Schulz, & Altman, 2001), the CASP checklists (Critical Appraisal Skills Programme, n.d.), the checklists of the EPPI-Centre (Newman & Elbourne, 2005), and the critical appraisal criteria developed by the CEBMa (Center for Evidence-Based Management, n.d.). Based on a tally of the number of weaknesses, the trustworthiness was downgraded, and the final level was determined as follows: downgrade one level if two weaknesses were identified, downgrade two levels if four weaknesses were identified, and so on.

8.3 Impact: Effect Sizes

An effect (association or difference) can be statistically significant but may not necessarily be of practical relevance: Even a trivial effect can be statistically significant if the sample size is big enough. For this reason the effect size—a standard measure of the magnitude (strength) of the effect—of the studies included was assessed. To determine the magnitude of an effect Cohen's rule of thumb (Cohen, 1988) was applied. According to Cohen (1988) a *small* effect is an effect that is only visible through careful examination. A *medium* effect, however, is one that is 'visible to the naked eye of the careful observer.' Finally, a *large* effect is an effect that anyone can easily see because it is substantial.

9 Main Findings: What Was Found?

This section provides an overview of the main findings relevant to the assumption. The main evidence from the REA is presented for each finding, together with the level of trustworthiness and the effect size.

10 Synthesis of Evidence: What Does This Mean?

To draw conclusions from the study results, this section provides a summary of the main findings. In addition, the evidence base supporting (or contradicting) the assumption is described. For example, the effects found may be large, but the evidence base may be small due to its limited volume, a low overall level of trustworthiness, or significant gaps in the literature that leave key questions unanswered. The evidence may also be contradictory or simply absent.

11 Conclusion: What Is the Evidence for the Assumption?

This section presents the final conclusions. These are based on the overall methodological appropriateness and quality of the studies that were included and the practical relevance of the effect sizes found. The final conclusion is expressed in terms of the degree of likelihood that the assumption may be true based on the evidence found in terms of: very likely, likely, neutral, unlikely, and very unlikely.

12 Practical Reflections

As stated in Chapter 1, EBP is based on different sources of evidence. Evidence in the scientific literature alone is insufficient—we need the experience and expertise of practitioners to be able to determine whether the research findings will apply in a particular situation or how likely it is that an 'evidence-based' assumption will work in a given context. Practitioner expertise is also necessary when the evidence is contradictory or lacking. This section therefore shows how the findings of the REA relate to the daily practice of change managers and discusses their implications in practice.

Limitations

An REA provides a balanced assessment of what is known in the scientific literature about an intervention, claim, or practical issue by applying a systematic review method to search and critically appraise primary studies. However, for it to be 'rapid,' concessions have been made in terms of the breadth and depth of the search process for the REAs in this book. These include the exclusion of unpublished research, the use of a limited number of databases, and a main focus on meta-analyses and primary studies published over the past 20 years. As a consequence, some relevant studies may have been omitted. The critical appraisal also did not always include a comprehensive review of the psychometric properties of the tests, scales, and questionnaires used in the studies included. Given these limitations, care must be taken to present the findings in this book as conclusive.

References

Antman, E. M. (1992). A comparison of results of meta-analyses of randomized controlled trials and recommendations of clinical experts. *Journal of the American Medical Association*, 286(2), 240–248.

Bushman, B. J., & Wells, G. L. (2001). Narrative impressions of literature: The availability bias and the corrective properties of meta-analytic approaches. *Personality and Social Psychology Bulletin*, 27(9), 1123–1130.

Center for Evidence-Based Management (CEBMa). (n.d.). *Resources and tools*. Retrieved January 14, 2016, from http://www.cebma.org/resources-and-tools/

Chalmers, I., Enkin, M., & Keirse, M. J. (1993). Preparing and updating systematic reviews of randomized controlled trials of health care. *The Milbank Quarterly*, 71(3), 411–437.

Cohen, J. (1988). *Statistical power analysis for the behavioral sciences* (2nd ed.). New York, NY: Routledge.

Critical Appraisal Skills Programme (CASP) (n.d.). *CASP checklists*. Retrieved January 29, 2015, from http://www.casp-uk.net/#!casp-tools-checklists/c18f8

Fink, A. (1998). *Conducting research literature reviews: From the Internet to paper*. London, UK: Sage Publications.

Higgins, J. P. T., & Green, S. (2006). *Cochrane handbook for systematic reviews of interventions* 4.2.6 [updated September 2006]. Retrieved September 1, 2015, from http://community.cochrane.org/sites/default/files/uploads/Handbook4.2.6Sep2006.pdf

Moher, D., Liberati, A., Tetzlaff, J., Altman, D. G., & PRISMA Group. (2009). Reprint—Preferred reporting items for systematic reviews and meta-analyses: The PRISMA statement. *Physical Therapy, 89*(9), 873–880.

Moher, D., Schulz, K. F., & Altman, D. G. (2001). The CONSORT statement: Revised recommendations for improving the quality of reports of parallel-group randomized trials. *The Lancet, 357*(9263), 1191–1194.

Newman, M., & Elbourne, D. (2005). Improving the usability of educational research: Guidelines for the reporting of primary empirical research Studies in Education (the REPOSE guidelines). *Evaluation and Research in Education, 18*(4), 201–212.

Petticrew, M., & Roberts, H. (2006). *Systematic reviews in the social sciences: A practical guide*. Malden, MA: Blackwell.

Shadish, W. R., Cook, T. D., & Campbell, D. T. (2002). *Experimental and quasi-experimental designs for generalized causal inference*. Boston, MA: Wadsworth Cengage Learning.

5 Examining the Story of Change
Part I

Introduction

The 'Story of Change' is composed of assumptions grounded in the popular management books and the practice of today's consultants. They have been subjected to our evidence-based management approach, as described in the previous chapters. The evidence base of these assumptions is presented in the three following chapters. This chapter discusses the examination of the first six claims, as mentioned in the 'Story of Change':

> Given the fact that 70 percent of all change initiatives fail, we clearly need an effective professional framework to manage change. Because it's important to know where we are heading, there must be a clear vision. Another prerequisite is to establish a sense of urgency to fuel change and motivate people. Leaders are immensely important in implementing change, and trust is essential. When managing change, a transformational leadership style is more effective than a transactional one. Organizational change also requires leaders with strong emotional intelligence (EI).

'70 Percent of All Change Initiatives Fail'

Introduction

In the field of change management there is a persistent, pervasive claim about how many change initiatives fail. Numerous change experts, reputed consulting firms, and even highly esteemed academics claim that as many as 70 percent of all change initiatives never meet their goals. For example, Michael Beer and Nitin Nohria, authors of the best-selling book *Cracking the Code of Change*, state: "The brutal fact is that about 70% of all change initiatives fail" (Beer & Nohria, 2000). Harvard Professor John Kotter confirms: "I estimate that today more than 70 percent of needed change either fails to be launched, even though some people clearly see the need, fails to be completed even though some people exhaust themselves trying, or finishes over budget, late and with initial aspirations unmet" (Kotter, 2008, p. 12). Even McKinsey & Company, one of the world's most reputed and influential consulting firms, claim on their Web site: "Change management as it is traditionally applied is outdated. We know, for example, that 70 percent of change programs fail to achieve their goals . . ." (Ewenstein, Smith, & Sologar, 2015, para 1). The question is, however: How accurate is this number? In the past century we have seen a huge number of innovative breakthroughs in management and business that have radically transformed productive activity and spurred the growth of the economy. If 70 percent of all change initiatives fail, how would such innovation and economic growth be possible? When reading through the books and articles that mention the assumption, it quickly becomes clear that most authors fail to provide empirical evidence, lump together different types of change, and use different criteria to define success. So where does this number come from? And is it evidence based?

What Is Meant by the Claim That 70 Percent of All Change Initiatives Fail?

One of the earliest reports of the assumption stems from Hammer and Champy (1993), founders of the management theory of business process reengineering. In their best-selling book *Reengineering the Corporation* they state: "Our unscientific estimate is that as many as 50 to 70 percent of the organizations that undertake a reengineering effort do not achieve the dramatic results they intended" (Hammer & Champy, 1993, p. 200). Note that their claim was based on their own 'unscientific estimate' and did not relate to 'all change initiatives.' In subsequent years the claim was widely referred to, both in the popular and in the academic literature, and it was embraced by several leading international consulting firms. The widespread dissemination of Hammer and Champy's (1993) quote, however, led to gross misinterpretation and went further and further away from its original and intended essence: a personal, highly subjective estimate regarding the success rate of reengineering. Hammer and Stanton themselves made an attempt to correct this: "Unfortunately, this simple descriptive observation has been widely misrepresented and transmogrified and distorted into a normative statement . . ." (Hammer & Stanton, 1995, p. 14, as cited in Hughes, 2011). In the following decade, however, their quote has been transformed into a universal truth that was reported in numerous management articles and business books. Despite the fact that several studies have recently questioned the validity of the assumption (e.g., Cândido & Santos, 2015; Hughes, 2011; Slater, 2015), it has become ubiquitous among both academics and practitioners.

Search Strategy

Our search for relevant studies took place in two phases. First, databases were searched using key words such as *change, intervention, fail*, and *success rate*. This yielded more than 200 studies published in peer-reviewed journals. After screening the abstracts for relevance, all studies were excluded. Second, the references listed in popular management literature that reported the claim were screened. This second search yielded two relevant studies: a meta-analytical review and a cross-sectional study.

Assessing Quality and Relevance

After critical appraisal of the remaining two articles, both were excluded due to serious methodological concerns.

Main Finding

1 There is no valid and reliable empirical evidence available supporting the claim that 70 percent of all initiatives fail.

The few empirical studies supporting the assumption suffer from serious methodological limitations and shortcomings that compromise the findings. For instance, the meta-analytical review that was excluded reports success rates for different types of organizational change (Smith, 2002). After comparing the outcomes of 49 studies on topics ranging from mergers and acquisitions to culture change and implementing new IT systems, the author concludes that the median success rate was a mere 33 percent. However, the author failed to describe how the studies included were selected, their methodological quality was not assessed, and no valid and reliable outcome measures were used. In addition, a total success score was calculated on the basis of the unweighted mean average of all individual studies. This appears to be a way of combining the outcome of different studies but is in fact a subjective form of 'vote counting' and widely regarded as unreliable (Hedges & Olkin, 1980; Hunter & Schmidt, 1990). Finally, the author himself suggests that his data may well be outdated.

Synthesis of Evidence

Over the past decades there have been numerous publications reporting the high failure rates of change initiatives. None of them, however, provides any valid, reliable scientific evidence supporting the assumption. This suggests that it was mainly informed by popular magazines and business books lacking any reference to scientific research—and may have been deliberately emphasized by opportunistic management consultants and business school professors as a means to market their services (Hughes, 2011).

Conclusion

The scientific research literature does not support the assumption that 70 percent of all change initiatives fail. We therefore conclude that this claim is very unlikely to be true.

Practical Reflections

Although we recognize that managing change can be difficult, there is no reliable evidence that most change initiatives are doomed to fail—in fact, based on our own practical experience, we would claim that most change efforts actually succeed. However, the prevailing idea that 70 percent of all change initiatives fail can be explained. We detect a kind of coping mechanism to compensate for the heavy responsibility that organizational change represents. It is a bit like a profit warning, legitimizing not only potential failure up front but also justifying the involvement of other parties (such as external consultants) who will supposedly help to reduce uncertainty and make the change process a success. Therefore, from a practical point of view, managers should clearly reconsider involving consultants. Blindly assuming that without them change has a high risk of failure is extremely misleading and can potentially be harmful. Besides, the idea that change is highly likely to fail may seriously hinder the change process itself by creating uncertainty, inhibiting innovation, and affecting organizational learning. As a result it can have real, negative, self-fulfilling consequences.

'A Clear Vision Is Essential for Successful Change'

"The underpinning theory being that achieving shared vision would allow for more effective facilitation of the change process ultimately leading to attaining goals set forth in this system's master plan" (Barnett, 2011, p. 131).

Introduction

After creating a sense of urgency and forming a guiding coalition, Step 3 in Kotter's eight-step change model is creating a vision for change (Kotter, 1996). In Step 4, this vision then has to be communicated in such a way that everybody understands, knows, and even more important, *feels* that vision. A shared vision is often seen as a prerequisite for successful change (Barnett, 2011). A vision is not only meant to energize and inspire in some abstract fashion, but it must also be practical and lead to concrete results. It must help to steer the change process. And to be aligned with Step 4, the vision must be clear and concise so that it can be communicated easily. And as Kotter, writing in Forbes (2011), recommends:

> If you are part of an organization that is trying to drive a large change, whether that's implementing a new IT system or moving to a new go-to-market strategy, you need to have a change vision. This is a picture for people of what the organization will look like after they have made significant changes, and it also shows them the opportunities they can take advantage of once they do that. It serves to motivate people, and it's essential to any successful change you're trying to make.
>
> (Kotter, 2011a, para 1)

He also states:

> A great change vision is something that is easy for people to understand. It can be written usually in a half page, communicated in 60 seconds, is both intellectually solid but has emotional appeal, and it's something that can be understood by the broad range of people that are ultimately going to have to change—and that could be a secretary or an executive, it could be somebody from Germany or from the United States. Which makes it easy to communicate and to communicate it in a way that people will 'get it,' if you will, and will, if you do it right, buy into it.
>
> (Kotter, 2011a, para 5)

What Do We Mean by Vision?

A change vision is not the same as a general or corporate vision (Kotter, 2011a). However, it makes sense to explore definitions and concepts related to vision in general and corporate vision in particular. A dictionary definition of vision (Vision, n.d.) is that it is "a vivid, imaginative conception or anticipation." It is a look into the future—hopeful and inspiring, but in the context of organizations it must also be realistic and lead to tangible results (e.g., Robbins & Duncan, 1988). A vision statement can be general (or organization-wide, timeless, etc.), as most corporate vision statements, or more specifically related to change initiatives, a vision for change.

In the academic literature, vision is sometimes loosely defined as a 'roadmap' (Barge, 1994, p. 183), an 'agenda' (Kotter, 1982, p. 60), or as "a set of blueprints for what the organization will be in the future" (Tichy & DeVanna, 1986, p. 128). We also find more detailed definitions of vision as ". . . a statement of purpose determined by management based on the organization's core values and beliefs that defines the organization's identity and combines an ideal manifestation of its direction together with a tangible prescription for realizing its goals" (Landau, Drori, & Porras, 2006, p. 147) or as ". . . an idea of a valued outcome which represents a higher order goal and motivating force at work" (West, 1990, p. 310).

There are also some derivative concepts, such as leader vision and vision clarity. According to Barratt-Pugh, Bahn, and Gakere (2013) leader vision is particularly relevant to change management as it is defined as the leader's capacity to communicate the strategic vision of the organization. Vision clarity is similarly related to communication but focuses more on the intelligibility of the message or statement itself. As already stated, a vision must contribute to tangible results. And it can only do so if it is sensible and properly understood (Kotter, 1995).

Vision is related to the quality and achievement of goals. Goal setting and goal clarity are related and (partly) overlapping constructs in this regard. Tentatively we can argue that vision is about goal setting, with the added intent of aligning those goals with the company's values at a higher level of abstraction.

Collins and Porras (1996) focus on 'visionary companies,' having 'big, hairy, audacious goals' (BHAGs) that are clear and compelling. These BHAGs serve as a unifying focal point of effort and act as catalysts for team spirit. Collins and Porras plead for a clear finish line because "people like to shoot for finish lines" (Collins & Porras, 1996, p 73). For a change vision it is important to be logical, concrete, specific, and correct. But affective dimensions must also be taken into consideration (e.g., Adamson, Pine, Van Steenhoven, & Kroupa, 2006); a change vision also has to be emotionally appealing, attractive, resonant, and touching (Ten Have, Ten Have, Huijsmans, & Van der Eng, 2015).

How Does It Work?

The assumption underlying the importance and presumed effectiveness of vision can be summarized in the following quote:

> The perspective regarding vision as a crucial element in successful change and a powerful tool for inducing desirable developments within an organization rests on the assumption that organizational members tend to be confused by competing agendas and multiple directions for change that often emanate from different levels or units in the organization. Hence, strong motivation and guidance is required to grasp and adopt a coherent agenda for change.
> (Landau et al., 2006, p. 148)

A shared vision can contribute to increased commitment and social cohesion (Oswald, Mossholder, & Harris, 1997; Zuckerman, Kaluzny, & Ricketts, 1995). It was also observed that when team members did not attempt to develop a shared understanding of the team's purpose, there was a risk that they would become ineffective (Gersick, 1988).

As plausible as this all seems, however, with regard to values (which are supposed to underscore a vision statement) sociologist Herbert Blumer noted back in 1969:

> [People] may fit their acts to one another on orderly joint actions on the basis of compromise, out of duress, because they may use one another, or out of sheer necessity in achieving their respective ends, because it is the sensible thing to do.
> (Blumer, 1969, p. 76)

In other words, a strong focus on workable relationships may be more effective than on attempting to create a set of shared abstract values, a vision, and the like.

Search Strategy

Relevant databases were searched using the keywords *vision* and *change vision*.

Assessing Quality and Relevance

Our initial search yielded a total of 366 studies. After screening the abstracts for relevance, 341 studies were excluded. Full-text screening of the articles resulted in the exclusion of another 17 studies. This resulted in eight articles, of which not a single one was a meta-analysis or systematic review. The overall quality of the studies that were reviewed was low. The studies were published between 1995 and 2015, with half of them published after 2010.

Via a literature search called snowballing and a rough search for adjacent constructs such as goal setting and goal clarity, another eight relevant studies were included, of which three are meta-analyses.

Findings

1   Companies with a clear vision tend to perform better than those without them (Level D).

Several studies suggest that companies with a clear vision tend to perform better than those without them. For instance, it was found that growth-oriented visions and strong vision communication produced higher growth rates (Baum, Locke, & Kirkpatrick, 1998). In addition it was found that 93 percent of the most successful software firms had clear and ambitious visions, as compared with 25 percent of the least successful (Hoch, Roeding, Purkert, & Lindner, 1999). Finally, the importance of having a 'product vision' for successful product development has also been reviewed (Brown & Eisenhardt, 1995).

2   Groups with clear shared goals outperform those without these (Level B).

In their meta-analysis of the effects of group goals on group performance done more than 20 years ago, O'Leary-Kelly, Martocchio, and Frink (1994) found that groups with clear shared goals outperformed those without them. A more recent meta-analysis of 17 studies by Hülsheger, Anderson, and Salgado (2009) confirms this positive relationship and indicated that compared to other team process variables such as communication, support for innovation, and task orientation, vision tends to have the highest impact.

3   *Specific difficult goals are related to stronger performance (Level A).*

Goal-setting theory proposes that setting specific difficult goals leads to better performance than setting specific but easy goals or vaguely formulated goals (Locke & Latham, 1990). This theory is well established as an individual motivation theory but has proven to be valid for groups in organizations as well (e.g., O'Leary-Kelly et al., 1994). Seventeen years after O'Leary-Kelly et al.'s (1994) meta-analysis, these results were in large part confirmed in the meta-analysis of Kleingeld, Van Mierlo & Arends (2011). They further found evidence that goals aimed at maximizing individual performance can undermine group performance in interdependent groups and that goals aimed at maximizing the individual contribution to the group can increase performance. Reflecting on the relationship with vision, in general vision statements are on a higher abstraction level and harmonize abstract values with concrete goals. A corporate vision statement is never an isolated statement, however; it is aligned with a mission statement and strategic goals. Similarly a clear *change vision* implies both the rationale for and intended effects of a change initiative (Ten Have et al., 2015). From this finding we may tentatively conclude that the intended effects must be specific, concisely described, and challenging enough to have a motivating effect.

4   *The way a vision is communicated is related to several indicators for successful change (Level C).*

Luo and Jiang (2014) found that creating a shared vision that is communicated in a charismatic way is related to more positive emotional responses and commitment to organizational change. Earlier Farmer, Slater, and Wright (1998) reported that it was the effective communication of the vision that made members more likely to agree with that vision.

Synthesis of Evidence

Change vision is considered to be one of the most attractive topics in change management, as shown by enthusiastic coverage, in particular in the popular management literature. In academic publications we are confronted with an abundance of references to (change) vision, but the evidence is of a relatively low level. The level of evidence improves when vision is considered as, for example, goal setting. The emphasis then is on clarity and the effect of clear goals. Notwithstanding the fact that Kotter (1996) conceptualizes change vision as something specific and concrete (a subject-related end state), one has to realize that vision in most cases is seen as something on a level above goals (such as specific, measurable, achievable, relevant, time-bound [SMART] goals). It is (also) overarching, compelling and inspiring on a more affective, emotional dimension. Vision has proven to positively

Conclusion

The academic research literature does support the claim that a clear vision is needed for successful change. We therefore conclude that, based on the evidence found, this claim is likely to be true. A change vision provides people with a perspective and some kind of direction in the uncertain and demanding circumstances related to a serious change. If *clear* is defined in alignment with this, and if a change vision is also compelling and not hermetic, it contributes in a positive way to change management and to accomplishing the goals related to change.

Practical Reflections

As a manager, do you need to provide people with a change vision to create successful change? Clearly, providing a change vision can contribute to successful change. When designed in the right way, such a vision meets essential psychological needs, such as providing clarity about the goals of change and creating confidence in them, as well as inspiration, motivation, and intellectual stimulation. Putting effort into envisioning the change—defining and communicating the reason or purpose of the change—is recommended when managing change. The outcome of such effort is not fully predictable, however, as the manager cannot control how employees will make sense of what happens around them. Qualitative findings have indeed revealed that the members of an organization tend not to adhere to a single shared vision but rather to construct their own visions (Barnett, 2011). However, the most important function of a (change) vision is to set people in motion, to activate or trigger them. And, to quote the words of organizational psychologist Karl Weick (1995): "Once set in motion, sense making tends to confirm the faith through its effect on actions that make material that (which) previously had been merely envisioned" (p. 55).

'People Will Not Change If There Is No Sense of Urgency'

Introduction

The term *sense of urgency* in relation to change was officiously introduced in John Kotter's book *Leading Change* (1996) and in his preceding article in *Harvard Business Review* (Kotter, 1995). Establishing a sense of urgency about the need to change is the first step in Kotter's eight-step change model, basically setting the premise of this chapter: People will not change if there is no sense of urgency (Kotter, 1996).

Besides Kotter's (1995) model for change that addresses the need for a sense of urgency, the term is also commonly used in practice. Students often stress their sense of urgency as a critical factor to success, as their productivity boosts just a few days before their assignments are due. In his book *The Road Ahead*, Bill Gates (1995) moreover assigns the secret of Microsoft's success to the fact that the company always envisions being on the losing side. That feeling continuously creates a sense of urgency that causes employees to work harder to survive in the complex and highly competitive environment of the IT industry.

A sense of urgency seems to be an important factor in change management and is often presented in such an appealing way that questioning it may seem rather superfluous. At face value, indeed, a sense of urgency seems perfectly logical. Kotter (1996, p. 42) bluntly states that it is simply human nature, in the sense that humans don't like change if it is not really necessary. Humans prefer to stick with the status quo and usually deny the first signs that something is amiss and that this could lead to change. However, some critical questions need to be raised. Are humans not in a constant state of flux? Is it not human nature to constantly change and adapt to the environment? Is it really true that we are only ready to change when we are on the verge of a crisis or when our very existence or survival is at stake?

What Is Meant by a Sense of Urgency?

Urgency is defined as the "condition of being urgent" (Urgency, n.d.), with *urgent* meaning compelling immediate action or attention (Urgent, n.d.). To increase understanding of what is implied by a sense of urgency, Kotter (2008) describes the antonym of a sense of urgency: *complacency*. For complacency, he cites a dictionary definition: "a feeling of contentment or self-satisfaction, especially when coupled with an unawareness of danger or trouble" (p. 19). Although the Kotter definition of creating a sense of urgency is most often referred to, authors have also defined the concept in various overlapping terms (Ahmad & Jalil, 2013):

- Business as usual as being unacceptable (Kotter, 1995, 1996).
- Shaking people out of their comfort zone (Harari, 1995).
- One's personal interests to take on the challenges suggested by change (Belasco, 1990).
- The wide spread belief that if we do not quickly change our ways, we may die (Covington, 2001).

How does It Work?

In the domain of change management, the framework set out by Kotter (1995) is widely accepted and used in practice. The framework is quite simple. Where complacency is high, the sense of urgency will be low, and consequently, change initiatives will fail. In his own words, "With urgency low, it's difficult to put together a group with enough power and credibility to guide the effort or to convince key individuals to spend the time necessary to create and communicate a change vision" (Kotter, 1996, p. 38). He relates cautiousness to complacency and risk taking to being proactive, which is perceived to be good leadership.

"Real leaders often create these sorts of artificial crises rather than waiting for something to happen" (Kotter, 1996, p. 48). Kotter subsequently makes nine recommendations (Kotter, 1996) to raise the level of urgency, the following three of which stand out:

- Create a crisis by allowing a financial loss, exposing managers to major weaknesses vis-à-vis competitors, or allowing errors to blow up instead of being corrected at the last minute.
- Set revenue, income, productivity, customer satisfaction, and cycle-time targets so high that they can't be reached by conducting business as usual.
- Encourage consultants and other means to force more relevant data and honest discussion into management meetings. (p. 46)

Search Strategy

Initially, we searched relevant databases using the term *sense of urgency*. Due to the small number of search results that this yielded, the related terms *increasing urgency*, *urgent*, *major/great opportunity*, *need for change*, *potential crises*, and *problem awareness* were added to our search string. Inherent to the concept of a sense of urgency are the factors: time (i.e., feeling that something is at stake and that time is running out) and fear (i.e., the notion that there is something at stake that if not dealt with properly, could have disastrous consequences). Hence, we also included the more thoroughly researched concepts of *time pressure* and *fear appeal* in the searches to gain more insight into the assumed mechanisms surrounding sense of urgency.

Assessing Quality and Relevance

Our initial search specifically directed toward sense of urgency yielded a total of 72 studies. After screening the abstracts for relevance, 59 studies were excluded. Full-text screening of the articles resulted in the exclusion of another seven studies. The remaining six studies matched our criteria for relevance; most were cross-sectional in nature. An additional broad search using additional terms in other domains (e.g., time pressure and fear appeal) was carried out, which resulted in inclusion of another 15 relevant articles (three meta-analyses and 12 studies).

Examining the Story of Change 81

Main Findings

1 *A sense of urgency is related to change, although not necessarily as a precondition (Level D)*

It was found that a lack of sense of urgency is a barrier to successful change implementation (Bokhoven et al., 2008). It was further found that team crisis is positively related to team unlearning, that is, changing the habitual routines that team members share (Akgün, Lynn, & Byrne, 2006). It was also found, however, that a sense of urgency is *not always necessary for far-reaching change to start*. Change processes can start for many reasons, a sense of urgency being just one of them (Bennebroek Gravenhorst, Werkman, & Boonstra, 2003).

Adjacent Research on the Concepts of Time Pressure and Fear Appeal

2 *Time pressure is positively related to making concessions and cooperation in decision-making processes and increases performance in experimental settings (Level A).*

There is strong evidence indicating that acute time pressure in decision-making processes leads to increased negotiator concession making and cooperation, as well as making it more likely that agreements will be achieved (Stuhlmacher, Gillespie, & Champagne, 1998). This effect was stronger when deadlines were closer. It was also found that time pressure did not systematically impair performance. In fact, under some conditions, time pressure increased performance (Goodie & Crooks, 2004).

3 *Raising fear leads employees to engage in short-term thinking (Level A).*

Fear can be aroused in people with a specific goal in mind: to avoid danger, to take preventive measures, or to stimulate proactive behavior. However, there is strong evidence indicating that fear tends to lead people to engage in short-term thinking, favoring immediate consequences (Gray, 1999). This suggests that if a change agent appeals to an employee's fear, for example, by pointing out the possibility of job loss, he or she may be priming that employee for short-term thinking. It should be noted, however, that this particular study concerned students in an artificial setting, so the generality of the findings may be limited.

4 *When appealing to employee fear, self-efficacy* needs to be taken into account (Level A)*

Within the theory of fear appeal and attitude change, Rogers (1975) identifies three factors that determine people's reaction: the probability of occurrence, the magnitude of the negative consequences, and the efficacy of the response. This suggests that an employee must: (1) make an assessment of the likelihood that a certain adverse outcome will occur; (2) consider the outcome bad enough to motivate him or her; and (3) feel capable of effectively being able to do something about it. This theory was confirmed by a recent high-quality meta-analysis demonstrating that a perceived threat only has an effect if a person's self-efficacy is also high (Peters, Ruiter, & Kok, 2013). This result suggests that creating a sense of urgency only works when the employees concerned have a high degree of self-efficacy.

Synthesis of Evidence

There are few published research papers specifically dealing with a sense of urgency. The studies included here did not present clear support for the assumption that people will *not* change if there is no sense of urgency. However, these studies did moderately support a more subtle claim that a sense of urgency is a factor or driver of behavior, although not a prerequisite as such. Adjacent research further identified several factors that need to be taken into account when an artificial crisis is instigated. Time pressure was found to have a positive effect on cooperation and performance. However, when time pressure is combined with a change agent appealing to an employee's fear, this may have the effect of driving the employee toward short-term thinking. In addition, creating a crisis or appealing to fear seems to work only when those to whom the intervention applies also have a high level of self-efficacy.

Conclusion

The scientific research literature does not support the claim that a sense of urgency is crucial to successful organizational change. Moderate support was found for a more modest claim that creating a sense of urgency is a driver of change, although not a prerequisite per se. Moreover, high-quality studies from other disciplines suggest that establishing a sense of urgency by instigating an artificial crisis can lead to short-term thinking and is effective only when the self-efficacy of those affected by the intervention is also high. Based on the evidence, we therefore conclude that the assumption that creating some degree of a sense of urgency contributes to successful change is somewhat likely to be true. However, if one creates a sense of urgency by instigating a crisis (including increasing fear), the resulting sense of urgency is unlikely to contribute to successful change.

Practical Reflections

Based on the available scientific evidence, practitioners need to be aware of the fact that creating a sense of urgency among employees is not a critical requirement for successful change. In fact, change initiatives may start for many reasons and should be initiated in a way that is appropriate, given the context. Creating some sense of urgency can contribute to successful change when there is real urgency and not all those involved in the change process are convinced of the inevitability of change. For instance, creating a sense of urgency by instigating a crisis (including applying the fear factor), might in the short term contribute to desired behavior. However, when people do not feel capable of being able to do something about it, it may lead to unintended consequences. When establishing an artificial crisis, managers should therefore take into account its likely influence on short-term thinking and employees' sense of self-efficacy. Only when framed effectively can it perhaps enforce what is in fact a questionable way to bring about successful change.

'Trust in the Leader Is Needed for Successful Change'

Introduction

It can hardly be considered as a definition, but the often-heard saying 'Trust is everything' underscores the importance given to the notion of trust. The following quote, attributed to Albert Einstein, illustrates the phenomenon that as the stakes get higher, trust seems to become increasingly important: "Whoever is careless with the truth in small matters cannot be trusted with important matters" (Albert Einstein Quotes, n.d.).

Leaders are responsible for dealing with important issues. And successful leadership is, at least in part, determined by the faith followers place in leaders. Management guru Drucker (1996) defines *leadership* simply as having followers. And faith or trust is the glue that binds the two. Leaders themselves subscribe to this idea, exemplified for example by the following quote from Jim Dougherty (2013): "In leading various companies over the years, one of the most valuable lessons I've learned is that establishing trust is *the* top priority" (para 4).

For at least half a century, the apparent significance of trust in leadership has also attracted scientific interest (Dirks & Ferrin, 2002), for example, in books such as *Interpersonal Competence and Organizational Effectiveness* (Argyris, 1962), *The Professional Manager* (McGregor, 1967), and *On Leadership* (Gardner, 1993).

What Is Meant by Trust?

There are numerous definitions of trust that sometimes overlap or even imply very different things. For example, Colquitt, Scott, and LePine (2007), in their review of the trust literature, note that trust is sometimes viewed by scholars as a behavioral intention, a cognitive action, a personality trait, or as a synonym for a variety of concepts such as trustworthiness, cooperation, or risk taking. Mayer, Davis, and Schoorman (1995) define trust "as the willingness of a trustor to be vulnerable to the actions of a trustee, based on the expectation that the trustee will perform a particular action" (Colquitt, Scott, & LePine, 2007, p. 909). Colquitt et al. point out that trust therefore has two primary components: the acceptance of vulnerability and positive expectations. Conceptually, trust is distinguished from the supposed antecedents of trust, namely trustworthiness and trust propensity. Trustworthiness focuses on certain characteristics of the trustee, as perceived by the trustor. Mayer, Davis, and Schoorman (1995) identify ability, benevolence, and integrity as characteristics with a unique impact on trust. *Ability* is the assumed knowledge and skills of the trustee to perform expected behavior. *Benevolence* is the assumed intention of the trustee to do good toward the trustor. And *integrity* is the extent to which the trustee is believed to be fair and to adhere to moral and ethical principles. Ability and integrity are considered to be cognition-based sources of trust, implying rational decision making, and benevolence is considered to be more an affect-based source of trust, implying care and supportiveness.

Trust propensity focuses on the trustor. It is considered to be a stable characteristic or personality trait that also influences how someone interprets the environment and makes sense of events and what triggers are paid attention to. In other words, people who score higher on trust propensity are more readily inclined to trust and interpret cues about someone's trustworthiness more positively.

What is implied with trust, Colquitt et al. (2007) point out, has consequences for how the construct is operationalized and measured. Some questionnaires focus more on the vulnerability component, whereas others refer to the positive expectation component. They also distinguish direct measures that simply ask respondents to rate the extent to which they trust someone (e.g., their CEO, supervisor or coworker, organization, or board).

How Does Trust Work?

Several researchers have come up with models (and have empirically tested them) for the underlying mechanisms by which trust influences organizational outcomes. In line with the proposed definition and the corresponding antecedents of trust, the mechanism in place can be depicted graphically (see Figure 5.1). Trust can have different referents, such as leadership or coworkers. Organizational outcome also can refer to a wide variety of variables, such as job satisfaction, task performance, organizational citizenship behavior, and so on. This model is very basic, and there are many ways in which trust and its effects can be conceptualized. However, the model captures most of these ways in an integrative manner.

Search Strategy

Our specific focus is on finding scientific evidence for the effect of trust in leadership during organizational change or on other organizational outcomes

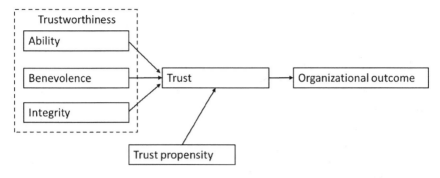

Figure 5.1 A Simplified Version of the Model of Organizational Trust, Based on Mayer et al. (1995)

that might be directly or indirectly related to the success of an organizational change initiative, such as organizational citizenship behavior or performance in general. Relevant databases were searched by combining the key words *trust*—and possible related key words such as *confidence* and *faith*—with key words related to leadership, such as *supervisor*, *CEO*, *board*, *management*, and *leader*.

Assessing Quality and Relevance

Our initial search yielded a total of 122 studies. After screening the abstracts for relevance, 112 studies were excluded. Full-text screening of the articles resulted in the exclusion of another 3 studies. Finally, after critical appraisal of the remaining 7 articles, a total of four meta-analyses—representing results from more than 428 single studies—were included. All four meta-analyses, which have a level of evidence of B, were published between 2007 and 2013.

Especially insightful and relevant to our assumption was the thorough meta-analysis by Colquitt et al. (2007), which builds on, refines, and complements Dirks and Ferrin's (2002) earlier work on the effects of trust in leadership and Mayers et al.'s (1995) model of organizational trust.

Main Findings

1 *Dispositional trust (trust propensity) and positive expectations have a positive effect on cooperation (Level B).*

Overall, dispositional trust (trust propensity, see Figure 5.1) had a small effect on cooperation. However, positive expectations of the trustee's behavior toward the trustor had a strong effect on cooperation. It is also found that trust has a stronger relationship with cooperation during situations with stronger conflicts of interests. In other words, when the stakes are higher, trust matters more (Balliet & Van Lange, 2013).

2   *Trust has medium positive (and beneficial) effects on process and outcome-related variables of negotiations (Level B).*

Trust has medium positive effects on integrative behaviors (enlarging the pie or creating a win-win situation), the trustor's outcome, the joint outcome, and outcome satisfaction during and following negotiations (Kong, Dirks, & Ferrin, 2014).

3   *Trust in leadership as well as organizational trust in general have small to medium beneficial effects on a wide variety of organizational outcomes (Level B).*

These two findings are based on meta-analyses that focus on studies on the role of trust in the resolution of conflicts and negotiations, respectively. More relevant to our assumption are the results found by Dirks and Ferrin (2002), who specifically focus on the effect of trust in leadership on a wide variety of outcome variables such as job satisfaction, organizational commitment, intent to quit, belief in information, decision commitment, organizational citizenship behavior, and job performance. The effects were small to medium, and they were all in a beneficial direction. Colquitt et al. (2007) found that trust, both with leadership and coworkers as referents, was moderately related to organizational outcomes such as risk taking, task performance, organizational citizenship behavior, and counterproductive behavior. Again, all effects were in a beneficial direction, implying that counterproductive behavior was negatively related and organizational citizenship behavior positively related to trust.

4   *Several variables with small to medium effects on trust (so-called antecedents of trust) have been identified (Level B).*

Transformational leadership, transactional leadership, interactional justice, procedural justice, distributive justice, participative decision making, and perceived organizational support all have small to medium positive effects on trust. Unfulfilled expectations have a medium negative effect on trust (Dirks & Ferrin, 2002). Ability, benevolence, integrity, and trust propensity all have small to medium positive effects on trust (Colquitt et al., 2007).

Synthesis of Evidence

Trust, as a scientific construct, is operationalized in a variety of ways, depending on how it is defined. The four meta-analyses included in our search represented at least more than 119 studies. This number is a minimum based on the number of included studies in the meta-analysis of Colquitt et al. (2007). Overall, based on a large number of studies included in the meta-analyses, and irrespective of how the construct was defined, small to medium effects of trust on organizational outcomes were found.

The meta-analyses were conducted thoroughly, and studies were carefully screened for relevance and method. The model of organizational trust as proposed by Mayer et al. (1995) proved to be a useful framework, integrating the many existing approaches. Besides, it could be used by others as a basic nomological network of the trust construct. However, the version depicted in Figure 5.1 is an oversimplified model, and many nuances can be made. Trust propensity, for example, is not only related to trust but also directly related to at least some organizational outcomes (Colquitt et al., 2007), without being mediated by the trust construct. And trust propensity influences the way someone perceives or filters cues about trustworthiness of the leader. All these possible effects and nuances are not visible in the initial model or organizational trust as depicted in Figure 5.1.

Conclusion

The scientific research literature supports the claim that trust in a leader is needed for successful change. Given the consistent effects it has on a wide variety of organizational outcomes that might be relevant to organizational change, we therefore conclude that this claim is likely to be true.

Practical Reflections

Fostering trust has many benefits. Trust in a leader has an effect on attitudinal, behavioral, and performance outcomes. Trust in general, also among employees, is a vital component of effective working relations. The model of organizational trust proposed by Mayer et al. (1995) identifies some levers that enable leaders to increase trust in them, in their organization, and in each other. Because the propensity to trust is mostly considered to be a stable personality trait of the trustor, this will be hard for the leader to influence. Besides, testing for trust propensity as a standard hiring procedure might be a bit far-fetched. Although trust isn't a one-way process, leaders do have considerable influence on the characteristics of trustworthiness, the other antecedent of trust, as these are the characteristics that leaders display to their followers. As long as a leader is authentic and consistent in displaying integrity, is honest about his or her abilities and capabilities, and shows a genuine interest in employees, trust is likely to increase. Consequently, trust will result in better overall performance and a more pleasant working environment.

'When Managing Change, a Transformational Leadership Style Is More Effective Than a Transactional One'

Introduction

In the management literature, organizational change and leadership are inextricably linked. In both popular books and scientific literature, the effect of leadership on change outcomes is widely discussed and studied. Amazon offers thousands of books with *change* and *leadership* in the title, and the research database ABI/INFORM contains more than 250 scientific papers on this topic. It is argued, however, that when it comes to organizational change, it is not just any kind of leadership that matters but rather leaders with a 'transformational leadership style.' Whereas transactional leadership is seen as the appropriate leadership style for day-to-day business ('keeping the ship afloat'), transformational leadership drives forces, visions, and processes that fuel large-scale, transformational change (Kotter, 2011b). In this light, the business dictionary defines *transformational leadership* as "[s]tyle of leadership in which the leader identifies the needed change, creates a vision to guide the change through inspiration, and executes the change with the commitment of the members of the group" (Transformational leadership, n.d.). As many organizations are currently subject to continuous change and employee motivation is becoming increasingly important, the transformational leadership style seems to be preferable in many situations involving change. This is clearly illustrated by the following quote: "Working for a transformational leader can be a wonderful and uplifting experience. They put passion and energy into everything. They care about you and want you to succeed" (Changing minds, n.d.). This all supports the claim that when managing change, a transformational leadership style will be more effective than a transactional one. But the question is, does this assumption also stand up to scientific scrutiny?

What Kinds of Leadership Styles Are There?

One of the first studies on leadership style was conducted by Lewin, Lippitt, and White (1938). In this early study, schoolchildren were assigned to one of three groups, each with a teacher who used a different leadership style. When Lewin et al. observed the behavior of the children in response to the different styles of leadership, they identified three styles:

1. Authoritarian or autocratic—telling people what to do and how to do it without listening to their advice.
2. Participative or democratic—involving people in the decision-making process but maintaining the final decision-making authority.
3. Delegative or laissez-faire—allowing people to make decisions but maintaining responsibility for the decisions that are made.

Since Lewin and colleagues' identification of these three leadership styles, numerous studies have been conducted on this subject, and as a result, many different leadership styles have been discussed in both the scientific and popular literature. A landmark date for this area of study was 1978, when James MacGregor Burns, an American historian and political scientist, introduced two contrasting styles of leadership: transactional and transformational (Burns, 1978).

It should be noted that leadership style does not only refer to the style of a single leader but can also relate to the overall leadership style of an organization.

What Is Meant by Transformational and Transactional Leadership?

Transactional leadership is based on exchanges between a leader and his or her employees, with rewards and punishments as key motivators. Transactional leaders, who focus their attention on achieving agreed standards, intervene when mistakes are made or performance is poor. In contrast, transformational leadership is based on the creation of a shared vision that employees are encouraged and empowered to pursue. Leaders who favor this style focus on the organization's higher-order goals and look "for potential motives in followers, seek to satisfy higher needs, and engage the full person of the follower" (Burns, 1978, p. 4). According to Bernard Bass, a pioneer in leadership research, the concept of transformational leadership consists of four dimensions: (1) charisma or idealized influence; (2) inspirational motivation; (3) intellectual stimulation; and (4) individualized consideration. Additionally, Bass operationalizes transactional leadership in three dimensions: (1) contingent reward; (2) management by exception—active; and (3) management by exception—passive (Bass, 1985). These various dimensions are still widely used to study both styles.

The concept of transactional versus transformational leadership styles has resulted in more than 1,000 empirical studies in peer-reviewed journals. Since the publication in 1978 of Burns's findings, many comparable leadership styles have been introduced (e.g., task versus people oriented), but Burns's theory on leadership style is still the one that is based on the best available evidence.

How Does It Work?

The effectiveness of transformational and transactional leadership styles is studied in numerous ways. Different aspects of performance are defined to investigate the impact of both styles. Performance outcomes are typified as either change oriented or non-change oriented (Chiaburu, Smith, Wang, & Zimmerman, 2015). Change-oriented performance is linked, for instance, to proactive and contextual behavior (behavior that is self-directed and future-focused) or creative performance. This type of performance is characterized by motivated behaviors that go beyond employees' prescribed job roles and tasks. To the contrary, non-change-oriented performance include prosocial behaviors (actions designed to maintain the organization's social system) and task performances (successful completion of the formal job description). This type of performance is characterized by behaviors that are predominantly restricted to the formal job description. It is assumed that the underlying mechanism behind transformational leadership is based on a leader's capacity to motivate employees, make them aware of the consequences of their tasks, help them to align their personal goals and needs with those of the organization, and therefore motivate them to perform beyond expectations. For this reason transformational leadership is assumed to positively influence change-oriented outcomes, whereas a transactional leadership style is expected to have a larger impact on non-change-oriented outcomes.

Search Strategy

Relevant databases were searched thoroughly to find meta-analyses using the following key words: *transformational leadership, people-oriented leadership, relationship-oriented leadership, transactional leadership,* and *task-oriented leadership.* Thereafter, single studies were sought using the same key words, yet combined with the following key words: *organizational change, change,* and *change management.* Studies were included for further analysis if they were related to organizational or behavioral components such as performance, effectiveness, or motivation.

Assessing Quality and Relevance

Our initial search yielded a total of 350 studies. After screening the abstracts for relevance, 303 studies were excluded. After critical appraisal of the remaining 47 articles, a total of five meta-analyses and 23 single studies were included. The meta-analyses represented results from more than 200 single studies. The methodological quality of the four meta-analyses was moderate, and they were all published between 2000 and 2014. The quality of the remaining meta-analysis was limited and was published 20 years ago. The methodological quality of the 23 single studies varied from high (randomized controlled studies) to low (cross-sectional studies).

Main Findings

1 *Transformational and transactional leadership are both moderately positively related to change-oriented and non-change-oriented outcomes (Level A).*

There is strong and consistent evidence that both leadership styles have a moderate positive effect on performance outcomes that are change oriented as well as non-change oriented (Chiaburu et al., 2015; Herrmann & Felfe, 2013; Lowe, Kroeck, & Sivasubramaniam, 1996; Wang, Courtright, & Colbert, 2011). Hence, both leadership styles positively relate to proactive contextual performance (actions beyond job description and contributing to the social context around the job), prosocial performance (actions to maintain the organization), and task performance (actions relating to formal job description). Results show that transformational leadership is the strongest predictor for change-oriented outcomes, whereas transactional leadership appears to be the strongest in predicting non-change-oriented outcomes. However, differences between these relationships are small and of limited practical relevance.

2   *Transformational leadership has a moderate positive effect on an individual's creative performance (Level B).*

It was found that transformational leadership is moderately positively related to the creativity of employees—they tend to learn from their mistakes and dare to experiment with various options without fear for failure (Wang et al., 2011).

3   *The positive relationship between transformational leadership and performance holds across organizational type, leader level, and geographic region (Level B).*

Findings relating to the positive relationship between transformational leadership and performance did not show any differences across type of organization, leader level, or geographic region (Wang et al., 2011).

4   *The strongest relationship between transformational leadership and performance occurred at team level. Additionally, charismatic leadership (which is part of transformational leadership) also seems more effective at increasing group performance rather than increasing individual performance (Level B).*

There is strong evidence that the effect of transformational leadership is strongest at group or team level. A possible explanation for this finding is that at group level a leader will, in general, demonstrate only one style of leadership behavior in his or her interaction with the members of a group, which strengthens its effect (DeGroot, Kiker, & Cross, 2000). In addition, leaders tend to function as role models, which in the case of a transformational leader may result in higher team commitment, cooperation, and therefore performance among team members (Wang et al., 2011).

Synthesis of Evidence

Over the last 50 years, there have been a considerable number of studies on the relationship between transactional leadership and (change) performance. After critically selecting and assessing the available scientific evidence, the main findings are mainly based on well-designed meta-analyses and randomized controlled studies. It appears that, contrary to most expectations, both transformational leadership and transactional leadership have a moderate positive effect on change-oriented performance, showing the importance of both leadership styles when implying change. The latter is also suggested in various single studies that are not included in the meta-analyses, in which transactional leadership (besides transformational leadership) is also found to positively influence specific organizational change outcomes (Burpitt, 2009; Diab, 2014; Vaccaro, Jansen, Van Den Bosch, & Volberda, 2012; Zagoršek, Dimovski, & Škerlavaj, 2009). However, besides this effect, the scientific evidence also reveals several differences. It appears that transformational leadership also positively influences employees' creative performances and has its strongest effect on the group or team level. Transactional leadership, on the other hand, has been shown to be more effective when individual task performance is the predominant outcome of interest.

Conclusion

The scientific research literature does not support the claim that transformational leaders are more likely to be effective than transactional ones in realizing change. The scientific evidence demonstrates the importance of both leadership styles for different areas of organizational change. We therefore conclude that, based on the evidence found, this claim is very unlikely to be true.

Practical Reflections

Transformational leaders can indeed positively affect organizational change. However, transformational leadership is not the only solution, as transactional leaders could also be of value. It should be clear what kind of performance outcomes will determine the success of change as this will be indicative for the kind of leadership style that will be more likely to be successful. When group performance or employees creativity is the key to success, the transformational leadership style is indeed preferable. In contrast, transactional leadership is preferable when individual task performance is critical to the organization's change goals. Although this latter one seems less socially acceptable within many organizations, implying hard interventions such as rewards and punishments, both styles are needed for change processes to be successful. Keeping in mind that 'the ship needs to float, while it is being rebuilt,' it might be most effective to balance transformational and transactional leadership styles.

'Organizational Change Requires Leaders With Strong Emotional Intelligence'

Introduction

EI is widely believed to be a crucial part of a manager's—or leader's—repertoire. In fact, well-known consultancy firms such as Hay Group sell training courses that are supposed to develop your EI, claiming, "EI can make the difference between a highly effective and an average professional contributor" (Hay Group, n.d.). The concept of EI was introduced in 1990 by Salovey and Mayer (1990). In the domain of business and management, however, EI became widely popular when *New York Times* journalist Daniel Goleman released his best-selling book *Emotional Intelligence: Why It Can Matter More Than IQ* in 1995. Since then EI has grown to become one of the hottest buzzwords today, claiming to provide all kinds of benefits such as lower stress levels, increased self-confidence, and personal happiness. Even Goleman (n.d.) himself has been surprised by the massive uptake and popularization of EI:

> The phrase *emotional intelligence*, or its casual shorthand EQ, has become ubiquitous, showing up in settings as unlikely as the cartoon strips *Dilbert* and *Zippy the Pinhead* and in Roz Chast's sequential art in *The New Yorker*. I've seen boxes of toys that claim to boost a child's EQ; lovelorn personal ads sometimes trumpet it in those seeking prospective mates. I once found a quip about EQ printed on a shampoo bottle in my hotel room. (para 4)

As a result, today EI is widely accepted as the sine qua non of effective leadership.

What Is Meant by Emotional Intelligence?

EI refers to a form of intelligence that is not about how we process information or think but instead relates to the emotional side of life, such as the ability to recognize and effectively deal with one's own and others' emotions. There are numerous definitions of EI, most of them addressing three types of skills: the identification of specific emotions in oneself and others, using emotion to guide thought, and regulating emotion. In the scientific literature, the research on EI can be divided into three schools of thought. The first school regards EI as an ability-based construct determined by a person's ability to perceive, reason with, understand, and regulate emotions (Joseph & Newman, 2010). In this school EI is considered to be a special form of intelligence that partly overlaps with conventional intelligence (IQ) and that can be measured with a standardized test, such as the Mayer-Salovey-Caruso Emotional Intelligence Test (Mayer, Caruso, & Salovey, 2000).

The second school regards EI as a trait-based construct that is determined by a person's self-perceived, emotion-related personality traits. In this school EI is considered to be a form of intelligence that is different from IQ and that can be measured by means of a self-report questionnaire.

The third school regards EI as a mixed construct determined by a wide array of competencies and skills. This school builds on the work of Goleman (2015), who distinguishes five components that determine a person's

EI: (1) self-awareness, (2) self-regulation, (3) motivation, (4) empathy, and (5) social skills. This school does not consider EI to be a form of intelligence but rather a mix of intellect, personality traits, and affect.

All three schools have been subjected to serious criticism by the academic community. The ability-based construct of EI has been criticized for lacking predictive validity in the workplace and for measuring conformity and knowledge of emotions instead of ability. The trait-based construct has been criticized for its use of self-report questionnaires, which are known to be biased by socially desirable responding. Finally, the mixed construct has been criticized for defining EI "by exclusion as any desirable characteristic not represented by cognitive ability" (Joseph & Newman, 2010, p. 55).

How Does It Work?

EI is said to be a much better predictor of success than 'normal' intelligence and the big five personality traits, especially in domains such as academic performance, job performance, negotiation, leadership, emotional labor, trust, work-family conflict, and stress (O'Boyle, Humphrey, Pollack, Hawver, & Story, 2011). It is widely assumed that being aware of your own emotions and being able to recognize and understand the emotions of others provide you the opportunity to influence those emotions in a productive way, which makes you more successful. For a change manager, helping people to deal with their emotions—being able to recognize, understand, and successfully manage their confusion and uncertainty as the organization adapts to changes—is considered to be a critical component of successful change. Thus, organizational change requires leaders who score high on EI (Smollan & Parry, 2011). This assumption obviously appeals to the common sense, but whether it makes academic sense is another question.

Search Strategy

Relevant databases were searched using the key words *emotional intelligence* or *emotional quotient*. The search yielded more than 4,000 studies published in peer-reviewed journals.

Assessing Quality and Relevance

Focusing on meta-analysis and systematic reviews yielded 38 results. After screening the titles and abstracts for relevance, 33 articles were excluded. Full-text screening and critical appraisal of the remaining articles did not result in further exclusions. The five meta-analyses that met the appraisal criteria represent results from more than 150 single studies. The overall quality of the meta-analyses included was moderate: Most of them were based on cross-sectional studies, and only one meta-analysis evaluated the methodological quality of the studies included.

Main Findings

1 *Emotional intelligence is weakly correlated with transformational leadership (Level B).*

EI was found to be moderately correlated with transformational leadership (Harms & Credé, 2010). However, this was only present in studies where results may have been inflated due to methodological flaws and socially desirable responding. The more rigorous studies revealed a weak correlation. Lower estimates were found for transactional and laissez-faire leadership.

2 *Emotional intelligence correlates moderately with job performance but only because the construct overlaps with other, well-established psychological constructs (Level B).*

The three different constructs of EI in the scientific literature (ability based, trait based, and mixed) were examined. All constructs were found to be moderately correlated with job performance (O'Boyle et al., 2011). It should be noted, however, that one meta-analysis (Level C) found that only a small part of job performance can be explained by EI (Van Rooy & Viswesvaran, 2004). Moreover, a wide number of studies indicate that the active ingredients of EI include well-established psychological constructs, such as conscientiousness, self-efficacy, self-rated performance, and extraversion, which all have been shown to correlate with job performance (Joseph, Jin, Newman, & O'Boyle, 2015).

3 *Emotional intelligence is not much more important than 'normal' intelligence (Level B).*

Goleman claims that "for star performance in all jobs, in every field, emotional competence is twice as important as purely cognitive abilities" (Goleman, 1998, p. 34). However, the scientific evidence does not support this claim. At best, only the mixed model of EI has some added value over 'normal' intelligence (cognitive ability) and the big five personality traits. At worst, EI has close to zero added value (Joseph & Newman, 2010).

Synthesis of Evidence

In the past two decades, hundreds of studies have been published on the topic of EI. The resulting evidence for EI being an important factor for organizational change is weak and divergent. The added value of EI over cognitive abilities and the big five personality traits is at best questionable. Although EI does have an effect on job performance, this effect is rather small. In addition, there is strong evidence that the construct of EI largely overlaps with other well-established psychological constructs.

Conclusion

The scientific research literature does not support the claim that organizational change requires leaders with strong EI. We therefore conclude that, based on the evidence found, this claim is unlikely to be true.

Practical Reflections

Caution is advised when idealizing EI in an organizational setting. EI is not a radical new construct that will revise or redefine change. EI is nevertheless positively linked with variables such as job performance and work climate. Even though EI has some positive effects, the effects of EI may well overlap with those of other psychological constructs. The question then for practitioners is to what extent investing in EI leaders is worthwhile? Promoting emotionally intelligent leaders might have a positive influence on the change process, but it is not a revolutionary solution that can be added to the evidence-based tool kit for achieving successful change.

Note

* *Self-efficacy* is defined as people's beliefs about their capabilities to produce designated levels of performance that exercise influence over events that affect their lives.

References

Adamson, G., Pine, J., Van Steenhoven, T., & Kroupa, J. (2006). How storytelling can drive strategic change. *Strategy & Leadership, 34*(1), 36–41.

Ahmad, H., & Jalil, J. (2013). Relationship between personality traits and sense of urgency: A study of Repso Malaysia. *IBIMA Business Review, 2013*, 1–22.

Akgün, A. E., Lynn, G. S., & Byrne, J. C. (2006). Antecedents and consequences of unlearning in new product development teams. *The Journal of Product Innovation Management, 23*, 73–88.

Albert Einstein Quotes. (n.d.). In *BrainyQuote*. Retrieved December 20, 2015, from http://www.brainyquote.com/quotes/quotes/a/alberteins125154.html

Argyris, C. (1962). *Interpersonal competence and organizational effectiveness.* Homewood, IL: Dorsey Press.

Balliet, D., & Van Lange, P. A.M. (2013). Trust, conflict, and cooperation: A meta-analysis. *Psychological Bulletin, 139*(5), 1090–1112.

Barge, J. K. (1994). *Leadership: Communication skills for organizations and groups.* New York, NY: St. Martin's Press.

Barnett, K. (2011). System members at odds: Managing divergent perspectives in the higher education change process. *Journal of Higher Education Policy and Management, 33*(2), 131–140.

Barratt-Pugh, L., Bahn, S., & Gakere, E. (2013). Managers as change agents. *Journal of Organizational Change Management, 26*(4), 748–764.

Bass, B. M. (1985). *Leadership and performance beyond expectations.* New York, NY: The Free Press.

Baum, J. R., Locke, E. A., & Kirkpatrick, S. A. A. (1998). Longitudinal study of the relation of vision and vision communication to venture growth in entrepreneurial firms. *Journal of Applied Psychology, 83*(1), 43–54.

Beer, M., & Nohria, N. (2000). Cracking the code of change. *Harvard Business Review, 78*(3), 133–141.

Belasco, J. A. (1990). *Teaching the elephant to dance. Empowering change in your organization.* New York, NY: Crown Publishers.

Bennebroek Gravenhorst, K. M., Werkman, R. A., & Boonstra, J. J. (2003). The change capacity of organisations: General assessment and five configurations. *Applied Psychology, 52*(1), 3–105.

Blumer, H. (1969). *Symbolic interactionism: Perspective and method.* Englewood Cliffs, NJ: Prentice-Hall.

Bokhoven, Van M. A., Koch, H., Dinant, G. J., Bindels, P. J. E., Grol, R. P. T. M., & Weijden, Van der T. (2008). Exploring the black box of change in improving test-ordering routines. *Family Practice, 25*(3), 139–145.

Brown, S., & Eisenhardt, K. (1995). Product development: Past research, present findings, and future directions. *The Academy of Management Review, 20*(2), 343–378.

Burns, J. M. (1978). *Leadership.* New York, NY: Harper & Row.

Burpitt, W. (2009). Exploration versus exploitation: Leadership and the paradox of administration. *Journal of Behavioral and Applied Management, 10*(2), 227–246.

Cândido, C. J. F., & Santos, P. (2015). Strategy implementation: What is the failure rate? *Journal of Management & Organization, 21*(2), 237–262.

Changing Minds. (n.d.). *Transformational leadership.* Retrieved November 20, 2015, from http://changingminds.org/disciplines/leadership/styles/transformational_leadership.htm

Chiaburu, D. S., Smith, T. A., Wang, J., & Zimmerman, R. D. (2015). Relative importance of leader influences for subordinates' proactive behaviors, prosocial behaviors, and task performance. *Journal of Personnel Psychology, 13*(2), 70–86.

Collins, J. C., & Porras, J. I. (1996). Building your company's vision. *Harvard Business Review, 74*(5), 65–77.

Colquitt, J. A., Scott, B. A., & LePine, J. A. (2007). Trust, trustworthiness, and trust propensity: A meta-analytic test of their unique relationships with risk taking and job performance. *Journal of Applied Psychology, 92*(4), 909–927.

Covington, J. (2001). Leading successful, sustainable change. *Executive Excellence, 18*(12), 15–16.

DeGroot, T., Kiker, D. S., & Cross, T. C. (2000). A meta-analysis to review organizational outcomes related to charismatic leadership. *Canadian Journal of Administrative Sciences, 17*(4), 356–372.

Diab, S. M. (2014). The impact of leadership styles on selection the areas of organizational change (An empirical study on the Jordanian pharmaceutical companies). *International Journal of Business and Management, 9*(8), 140–154.

Dirks, K. T., & Ferrin, D. L. (2002). Trust in leadership: Meta-analytic findings and implications for research and practice. *Journal of Applied Psychology, 87*(4), 611–628.

Dougherty, J. (2013, December 3). *The best way for new leaders to build trust.* Retrieved November 11, 2015, from https://hbr.org/2013/12/the-best-way-for-new-leaders-to-build-trust/

Drucker, P. F. (1996). *Your leadership is unique. Good news: There is no one "leadership personality"*. Retrieved December 12, 2015, from http://boston.goarch.org/assets/files/your%20leadership%20is%20unique.pdf

Ewenstein, B., Smith, W., & Sologar, A. (2015, July). *Changing change management*. Retrieved January 1, 2016, from http://www.mckinsey.com/insights/leading_in_the_21st_century/changing_change_management?cid=other-eml-ttn-mip-mck-oth-1512.

Farmer, B. A., Slater, J. W., & Wright, K. S. (1998). The role of communication in achieving shared vision under new organizational leadership. *Journal of Public Relations Research*, 10(4), 219–235.

Gardner, J. W. (1993). *On leadership*. New York, NY: Free Press.

Gates, B. (1995). *The road ahead*. New York, NY: Viking Press.

Gersick, C. J. (1988). Time and transition in work teams: Toward a new model of group development. *Academy of Management Journal*, 31(1), 9–41.

Goleman, D. (1995). *Emotional intelligence: Why it can matter more than IQ*. New York, NY: Bantam Dell.

Goleman, D. (1998). *Working with emotional intelligence*. New York, NY: Bantam Dell.

Goleman, D. (2015). *On emotional intelligence*. Boston, MA: Harvard Business Review Press.

Goleman, D. (n.d.). *Emotional intelligence*. Retrieved January 14, 2016, from http://www.danielgoleman.info/topics/emotional-intelligence/

Goodie, A. S., & Crooks, C. L. (2004). Time-pressure effects on performance in a base-rate task. *The Journal of General Psychology*, 131(1), 18–28.

Gravenhorst, Bennebroek K. M., Werkman, R. A., & Boonstra, J. J. (2003). The change capacity of organisations: General assessment and five configurations. *Applied Psychology*, 52(1), 3–105.

Gray, J. R. (1999). A bias toward short-term thinking in threat-related negative emotional states. *Personality and Social Psychology Bulletin*, 25(1), 65–75.

Hammer, M., & Champy, J. (1993). *Reengineering the corporation: A manifesto for business revolution*. London, UK: Nicholas Brearly.

Hammer, M., & Stanton, S. A. (1995). *The reengineering revolution: A handbook*. New York, NY: HarperCollins.

Harari, O. (1995). U2D2: The Rx for leadership blues. *Management Review*, 84(8), 34–36.

Harms, P. D., & Credé, M. (2010). Emotional intelligence and transformational and transactional leadership: A meta-analysis. *Journal of Leadership & Organizational Studies*, 17(1), 5–17.

Hay Group. (n.d.). *Emotional intelligence training*. Retrieved January 14, 2016, from http://www.haygroup.com/leadershipandtalentondemand/your-challenges/emotional-intelligence/index.aspx

Hedges, L., & Olkin, I. (1980). Vote-counting methods in research synthesis. *Psychological Bulletin*, 88(2), 359–369.

Herrmann, D., & Felfe, J. (2013). Moderators of the relationship between leadership style and employee creativity: The role of task novelty and personal initiative. *Creativity Research Journal*, 25(2), 172–181.

Hoch, D. J., Roeding, C., Purkert, G., & Lindner, S. K. (1999). *Secrets of software success: Management insights from 100 software firms around the world*. Boston, MA: Harvard Business Review Press.

Hughes, M. (2011). Do 70 per cent of all organizational change initiatives really fail? *Journal of Change Management*, *11*(4), 451–464.

Hülsheger, U. R., Anderson, N., & Salgado, J. F. (2009). Team-level predictors of innovation at work: A comprehensive meta-analysis spanning three decades of research. *Journal of Applied Psychology*, *94*(5), 1128–1145.

Hunter, J., & Schmidt, F. (1990). *Methods of meta-analysis: Correcting error and bias in research findings*. Thousand Oaks, CA: Sage Publications.

Joseph, D. L., & Newman, D. A. (2010). Emotional intelligence: An integrative meta-analysis and cascading model. *Journal of Applied Psychology*, *95*(1), 54–78.

Joseph, D. L., Jin, J., Newman, A., & O'Boyle, E. H. (2015). Why does self-reported emotional intelligence predict job performance? A meta-analytic investigation of mixed EI. *Journal of Applied Psychology*, *100*(2), 298–342.

Kleingeld, A., Van Mierlo, H., & Arenas, L. (2011). The effect of goal setting on group performance: A meta-analysis. *Journal of Applied Psychology*, *96*(6), 1289–1304.

Kong, D. T., Dirks, K. T., & Ferrin, D. L. (2014). Interpersonal trust within negotiations: Meta-analytic directions, critical contingencies, and directions for future research. *Academy of Management Journal*, *57*(5), 1235–1255.

Kotter, J. P. (1982). *The general managers*. New York, NY: Free Press.

Kotter, J. P. (1995). Leading change: Why transformation efforts fail. *Harvard Business Review*, *73*(2), 59–67.

Kotter, J. P. (1996). *Leading change*. Boston, MA: Harvard Business Review Press.

Kotter, J. P. (2008). *A sense of urgency*. Boston, MA: Harvard Business Review Press.

Kotter, J. P. (2011a, June 7). *How to create a powerful vision for change*. Retrieved October 14, 2015, from http://www.forbes.com/sites/johnkotter/2011/06/07/how-to-create-a-powerful-vision-for-change/#14c411932a3c

Kotter, J. P. (2011b, July 12). *Change management vs. change leadership—What's the difference?* Retrieved November 20, 2015, from http://www.forbes.com/sites/johnkotter/2011/07/12/change-management-vs-change-leadership-whats-the-difference/#45ed310618ec

Landau, D., Drori, I., & Porras, J. (2006). Vision change in a governmental R&D organization. *The Journal of Applied Behavioral Science*, *42*(2), 145–171.

Lewin, K., Lippitt, R., & White, R. K. (1938). Patterns of aggressive behavior in experimentally created "social climates". *The Journal of Social Psychology*, *10*(2), 271–299.

Locke, E. A., & Latham, G. P. (1990). *A theory of goal setting and task performance*. Upper Saddle River, NJ: Prentice Hall.

Lowe, K. B., Kroeck, K. G., & Sivasubramaniam, N. (1996). Effectiveness correlates of transformational and transactional leadership: A meta-analytic review of the MLQ literature. *The Leadership Quarterly*, *7*(3), 385–425.

Luo, Y., & Jiang, H. (2014). Effective public relations leadership in organizational change: A study of multinationals in mainland China. *Journal of Public Relations Research*, *26*(2), 134–160.

Mayer, J. D., Caruso, D. R., & Salovey, P. (2000). Selecting a measure of emotional intelligence: The case for ability scales. In R. Bar-On, & J. D. A. Parker (Eds.), *The handbook of emotional intelligence* (pp. 320–342). New York, NY: Jossey-Bass.

Mayer, R. C., Davis, J. H., & Schoorman, F. D. (1995). An integrative model of organizational trust. *Academy of Management Review*, *20*, 709–734.

McGregor, D. (1967). *The professional manager*. New York, NY: McGraw-Hill.

O'Boyle, E. H., Humphrey, R. H., Pollack, J. M., Hawver, T. H., & Story, P. A. (2011). The relation between emotional intelligence and job performance: A meta-analysis. *Journal of Organizational Behavior, 32*(5), 788–818.

O'Leary-Kelly, A. M., Martocchio, J. J., & Frink, D. D. (1994). A review of the influence of group goals on group performance. *Academy of Management Journal, 37*(5), 1285–1301.

Oswald, S. L., Mossholder, K. W., & Harris, S. G. (1997). Relations between strategic involvement and managers' perceptions of environment and competitive strengths: The effect of vision salience. *Group and Organization Management, 22*(3), 343–365.

Peters, G. J. Y., Ruiter, R. A., & Kok, G. (2013). Threatening communication: A critical re-analysis and a revised meta-analytic test of fear appeal theory. *Health Psychology Review, 7*(1), 8–31.

Robbins, S. R., & Duncan, R. B. (1988). The role of the CEO and top management in the creation and implementation of strategic vision. *The Executive Effect: Concepts and Methods for Studying Top Managers, 2*, 205–236.

Rogers, R. W. (1975). A protection motivation theory of fear appeals and attitude change. *Journal of Psychology, 91*(1), 93–114.

Rooy, Van D. L., & Viswesvaran, C. (2004). Emotional intelligence: A meta-analytic investigation of predictive validity and nomological net. *Journal of Vocational Behavior, 65*(1), 71–95.

Salovey, P., & Mayer, J. D. (1990). Emotional intelligence. *Imagination, Cognition and Personality, 9*(3), 185–211.

Slater, R. (2015). *Leadership genius: 40 insights from the science of leading*. Abingdon, UK: Teach Yourself.

Smith, M. E. (2002). Success rates for different types of organizational change. *Performance Improvement, 41*(1), 26–33.

Smollan, R., & Parry, K. (2011). Follower perception of the emotional intelligence of change leaders: A qualitative study. *Leadership, 7*(4), 435–462.

Stuhlmacher, A. F., Gillespie, T. L., & Champagne, M. V. (1998). The impact of time pressure in negotiation: A meta-analysis. *The International Journal of Conflict Management, 9*(2), 97–116.

Ten Have, S., Ten Have, W. D., Huijsmans, A. B., & Van der Eng, N. (2015). *Change competence: Implementing effective change*. New York, NY: Routledge.

Tichy, N. M., & DeVanna, M. A. (1986). *The transformational leader*. New York, NY: John Wiley & Sons.

Transformational leadership. (n.d.). In *BusinessDictionairy.com*. Retrieved January 30, 2016, from http://www.businessdictionary.com/definition/transformational-leadership.html

Urgency. (n.d.). In *American heritage® dictionary of the English language, fifth edition*. Retrieved January 30, 2016, from http://www.thefreedictionary.com/urgency

Vaccaro, I. G., Jansen, J. J., Van den Bosch, F. A., & Volberda, H. W. (2012). Management innovation and leadership: The moderating role of organizational size. *Journal of Management Studies, 49*(1), 28–51.

Van Bokhoven, M. A., Koch, H., Dinant, G. J., Bindels, P. J. E., Grol, R. P. T. M., & Van der Weijden, T. (2008). Exploring the black box of change in improving test-ordering routines. *Family Practice, 25*(3), 139–145.

Van Rooy, D. L., & Viswesvaran, C. (2004). Emotional intelligence: A meta-analytic investigation of predictive validity and nomological net. *Journal of Vocational Behavior, 65*(1), 71–95.

Vision. (n.d.). In *Dictionary.com*. Retrieved January 30, 2016, from http://dictionary.reference.com/browse/vision?s=t

Wang, G., Oh, I. S., Courtright, S. H., & Colbert, A. E. (2011). Transformational leadership and performance across criteria and levels: A meta-analytic review of 25 years of research. *Group & Organization Management*, 36(2), 223–270.

Weick, K. E. (1995). *Sensemaking in organizations*. Thousand Oaks, CA: Sage Publications.

West, M. A. (1990). The social psychology of innovation in groups. In M. A. West, & J. L. Farr (Eds.), *Innovation and creativity at work* (pp. 309–333). Chichester, UK: Wiley.

Zagoršek, H., Dimovski, V., & Škerlavaj, M. (2009). Transactional and transformational leadership impacts on organizational learning. *Journal for East European Management Studies*, 14(2), 144–165.

Zuckerman, H. S., Kaluzny, A. D., & Ricketts, T. C. (1995). Alliances in health care: What we know, what we think we know, and what we should know. *Health Care Management Review*, 20(1), 54–64.

6 Examining the Story of Change
Part II

Introduction

This chapter discusses the second part of the 'Story of Change,' presenting the evidence base of another six assumptions:

> "Supervisory support is critical for the success of change. A leader cannot succeed on his or her own—a powerful guiding coalition is needed. Furthermore, employees' capabilities to change determine the organization's capacity to change. Also, participation is key to successful change. Resistance to change is detrimental to the success of change. A fair change process is important in achieving successful change."

'Supervisory Support Is Critical for the Success of Change'

Introduction

There are many popular books, articles, and blogs that prescribe what steps a manager should take to improve performance. One of the recurring themes is that managers should support their employees in various ways. The term *supervisory support* is used mainly in scientific research and seldom in popular sources. Nonetheless, the importance of supervisory support, although not specifically mentioned, is widely recognized in popular sources.

For example, on the Forbes Web site the blog titled "Six Things That Will Make You (and Your Manager) a Better Leader" states:

> In strengthening your people skills, remember that the best leaders are always mindful of what matters most to those they lead. They believe that the goals of others are as important as their own. As such, make the time for others—you will be building meaningful relationships that can then serve to achieve results together.
>
> (Llopis, 2012, para 5)

Another example is provided by the Web site Inc., where the author of the article "How to Support Your Staff: You Can Get the Most Out of Your Staff by Cultivating a Creative, Friendly Environment Where Employees Feel Engaged and Challenged" writes:

> The best businesses invariably have the strongest employees. A company, as they say, is only as good as the company it keeps. That's precisely why supporting your staff—all the way from the top managers to the greenest new hires—should be a business leader's top priority. . . . Whether it is encouraging extra vacation days, scheduling additional time to talk to your staff, or even offering up midday yoga lessons, as a leader it is your job to build and maintain morale in your organization.
> (Klonsky, 2010)

The common popular belief is clear: Supervisory support is a vital determinant of organizational outcomes. But what does the research evidence tell us?

What Is Meant by Supervisory Support?

When employees receive feedback from and interact with their supervisor, they form perceptions of how the supervisor supports them. This may manifest itself based on how employees feel the supervisor helps them in times of need, praises them for a job well done, or recognizes them for extra effort. This is known as *perceived supervisory support*, a scientific construct that has been defined as: "employees' beliefs concerning the extent to which the supervisor values their contribution and cares about their well-being" (Edmondson & Boyer, 2013). Supervisory support, or to be more precise, the subordinate's perception of the degree of support given by the supervisor, is an element of the larger construct of perceived social support. Perceived supervisory support can take the form of instrumental support (e.g., providing work-related information or feedback) as well as emotional support (e.g., sympathy, praise, or encouragement) (Ng & Sorensen, 2008). Supervisory support is believed to be particularly important in organizations because the behavior of supervisors is often interpreted by employees as a representation of the organization (Stinglhamber & Vandenberghe, 2003).

How Does It Work?

Supervisory support is based on the principles of social exchange theory and the notion of reciprocity. *Social exchange theory* is a motivational theory that "posits that all relationships between individuals and supervisors are formed based on a subjective cost-benefit analysis. If the benefits received from the relationship exceed the costs incurred, then the employee will opt to remain in the relationship" (Edmondson & Boyer, 2013, p. 2187).

Besides this, the notion of reciprocity creates a sense of obligation on the part of the employee when the supervisor has given him or her support.

This will make the employee behave in a way that adds value to the supervisor and to the organization, presuming that the goals of the supervisor are aligned with the goals of the organization. Conversely, if supervisory support is less than expected, the employee may reciprocate negatively, such that commitment to the organization and job performance may decline (Mor Barak, Travis, Pyun, & Xie, 2009). Essentially, the employee constantly seeks to balance the exchange relationship.

A concept that is related to supervisory support is the psychological contract, as introduced by Argyris in 1960 and developed by Rousseau in 1989. This concept, also based on the principles of the social exchange theory, refers to the mutual beliefs, perceptions, and obligations between employer and employee. Employees' expectations regarding the supervisory relationship form part of the psychological contract (Mor Barak et al., 2009). Failing to provide the amount of support expected by the employee puts pressure on the psychological contract and may eventually lead to contract breach.

Search Strategy

Relevant databases were searched using the well-defined and broadly used construct *supervisory support* as the key word. *Organizational change* was also added as a key word to narrow down the results to match the context of change management.

Assessing Quality and Relevance

The search that focused on supervisory support in general resulted in more than 1,000 articles. Filtering for meta-analyses and systematic reviews yielded nine results. After screening the titles and abstracts for relevance, three meta-analyses were excluded. Full-text screening and critical appraisal of the remaining articles did not result in further exclusions. The six meta-analyses included represented the results of more than 150 studies. The overall methodological quality was moderate to limited as none of them explicitly included studies that used a control group and/or a before-and-after measurement. The second search, in which the key words *change* and *organizational change* were added, resulted in 105 single studies. After screening the abstracts for relevance, full-text screening, and critical appraisal, 91 studies were excluded. One of the 14 studies was a randomized controlled before-after study, which is almost unique in this field of research. Three studies had a noncontrolled before-after design. The remaining studies used a cross-sectional design.

Main Findings

The first part of this section describes the main findings related to the construct of perceived supervisory support. The second part contains the main findings on supervisory support in the context of organizational change.

1 *Perceived supervisory support has a moderate positive effect on performance and a strong positive effect on job satisfaction and organizational commitment (Level A).*

All meta-analyses that studied the relationship between perceived supervisory support and job satisfaction found positive effects (Edmondson & Boyer, 2013; Luchman & González-Morales, 2013; Mor Barak et al., 2009; Ng & Sorensen, 2008). Several cross-sectional studies, albeit with lower levels of evidence, confirmed this finding (Elias & Mittal, 2011; Mansell, Brough, & Cole, 2006). In addition, perceived supervisory support was found to have a moderate positive effect on performance and a strong positive effect on organizational commitment (Edmondson & Boyer, 2013) and affective commitment (Ng & Sorensen, 2008), a more specific element of organizational commitment. Because the results were consistent throughout all the meta-analyses, evidence Level A was assigned.

2 *Perceived supervisory support has a moderate negative effect on turnover intentions (Level A).*

Two of the meta-analyses included (Edmondson & Boyer, 2013; Ng & Sorensen, 2008) found a moderate negative relationship between perceived supervisory support and turnover intentions. Thus, supervisory support decreases employees' intention to leave the organization. Because the results were consistent throughout all the meta-analyses, evidence Level A was assigned.

The following main findings examined more specifically the role of perceived supervisory support in the context of organizational change.

1 *Perceived supervisory support has a strong positive effect on change outcomes (Level A).*

There is strong evidence that the outcome of a change process is affected by how employees feel their supervisor supports them. A randomized controlled before-after study in which the effects of a change intervention were tested (empowerment among unit managers) showed that the intervention had positive effects only when the perceived supervisory support was strong (Logan & Ganster, 2007). This finding shows the key role of perceived supervisory support during the implementation of organizational change interventions.

2 *Perceived supervisory support has a positive small to medium effect on commitment to change (Level D).*

One cross-sectional study found that when supervisors were perceived as more competent in their work, employees perceived higher levels of supervisory support. Additionally, the evaluation of supervisor competence increased both affective and normative commitment to change through its relationship with perceived supervisory support (Neves, 2011). This result suggests that supervisory support may be an important factor in the development of commitment to change (see Chapter 7).

3   Perceived supervisory support has a positive small to medium effect on a positive change evaluation (Level D).

It was found that perceived supervisory support increases positive change evaluations (Fuchs & Prouska, 2014).

4   Perceived supervisory support has a small to medium negative effect on psychological stress in a context of change (Level D).

It was found that supervisory support lowers psychological stress in the context of organizational change (Chauvin et al., 2014).

Synthesis of Evidence

Over the past 25 years, various scholars have studied the effects of supervisory support and provided a substantial base of evidence with moderate to high quality (hundreds of studies and several meta-analyses). The greater part of this research is related to general organizational constructs, such as organizational commitment, job satisfaction, performance, and turnover intentions, where the effects of supervisory support are moderate to strong. The research published in the specific context of organizational change is less extensive. Nonetheless, the best available evidence in the context of organizational change suggests that supervisory support plays a key role in change interventions. The assumed positive effect of perceived supervisory support on change outcomes was confirmed by a randomized controlled before-after study. Several cross-sectional studies further suggest that supervisory support has a positive influence on commitment to change, increases positive change evaluation, and helps employees to cope with change.

Conclusion

The scientific research literature supports the claim that supervisory support is critical to the success of change. We therefore conclude that, based on the evidence we found, this claim is very likely to be true.

Practical Reflections

Providing supervisory support to employees is recommended when managers aim to meet organizational objectives by managing performance, organizational commitment, job satisfaction, and turnover (Edmondson & Boyer, 2013). Especially in times of organizational change, when employees are often affected by uncertainty, senior management would do well to ensure that supervisors are suitably trained and attuned to be able to provide support to their subordinates (Elias & Mittal, 2011). This emphasizes the essential role of middle management in organizational change. Because they play a key role in driving change at a lower level by both providing and creating support, the involvement of middle management seems essential. Considering this, the relationship between the employee and the supervisor—as the representative of the organization—during change interventions should not be taken lightly, given that empirical evidence indicates that supervisory support is critical to successful change management. Top managers should provide lower management with more support and identify methods to manage employee perceptions of supervisor support. After all, middle management is both subject to change and plays an important role in achieving change by providing supervisory support. Actions that may help improve supervisory support are discussed in Edmondson and Boyer (2013): having an open door policy, offering a flexible work schedule, scheduling time to listen, communicating appreciation, implementing suggestions made by employees, and empathizing with employees' needs.*

'To Realize Change in Organizations, a Powerful Guiding Coalition Is Needed'

Introduction

Nowadays, almost no change process evolves without a coalition of managers and employees initiating and guiding the required actions and interventions. Kotter (1996) introduced the concept of such a guiding coalition in his book *Leading Change*. His book, despite a lack of scientific citations or empirical research, became an international best seller at the time and is still one of the most influential publications in the field of change management.

Kotter (1996) criticized the belief that change can come from a single larger-than-life person. In his book he argues that major change is difficult to accomplish, so a powerful leading coalition is required to sustain the process.

> No one individual, even a monarch-like CEO, is ever able to develop the right vision, communicate it to large numbers of people, eliminate all the key obstacles, generate short-term wins, lead and manage dozens of change projects, and anchor new approaches deep in the organization's culture.
>
> (Kotter, 1996, pp. 53–54)

Nowadays, many change processes are guided by these coalitions of leaders, managers, and employees. However, is the broad application of these coalitions legitimate? And if so, what are key elements that build up to an effective guiding coalition?

What Is Meant by a Guiding Coalition?

The term *guiding coalition* was first introduced and advocated by Kotter (1995). It refers to a team that is able to direct a change effort within an organization. This rather concise definition does not provide a clear perspective on what signifies a guiding coalition. Hence, it is more relevant to look into the essential characteristics of an effective guiding coalition, as Kotter (1996) describes it.

How Does It Work?

In his book, Kotter (1996) describes why guiding coalitions are successful in leading organizational change. He mentions four key characteristics that are considered to be essential characteristics of effective guiding coalitions:

1. **Position power:** are enough key players on board, especially the main line managers so that those left out cannot easily block the progress?
2. **Expertise:** are the various points of view—in terms of discipline, work experience, nationality, etc.—relevant to the tasks at hand adequately represented so that informed, intelligent, decisions will be made?
3. **Credibility:** does the group have enough people with good reputations in the firm so that its pronouncements will be taken seriously by other employees?
4. **Leadership:** does the group include enough proved leaders to be able to drive the change process? . . . You need both management and leadership skills on the guiding coalition, and they must work in tandem, teamwork style. (Kotter, 1996, p. 59)

Gathering a team with enough position power, broad expertise, great credibility, and both leadership and management skills is the first step in establishing a guiding coalition. Then, this team must build on an important element: trust. According to Kotter (1996), all team members must trust each other to create teamwork that is able to drive the changes that are needed (Kotter, 1996).

Finally, this team must create a common goal: "that speaks to the head and touches the heart" (Kotter, 1996, p. 64). This typical goal must bind the members of the team together and make them feel dedicated in achieving the same objective. When mutual trust is present within the team, creating this shared objective becomes much easier, according to Kotter (1996). It allows the members to transcend their individual interests (e.g., regarding their team, department, careers, etc.) and focus on a shared desire (Kotter, 1996).

Search Strategy

Relevant databases were searched using the key words *guiding coalition* or *leading coalition*. Because the concept is widely applied in organizational practice, no synonyms were used to find evidence regarding this claim.

Assessing Quality and Relevance

Our initial search yielded a total of 209 studies. After screening the abstracts for relevance, 189 studies were excluded. Full-text screening of the articles resulted in the exclusion of another 11 studies. The remaining nine articles were critically appraised. Only one of the nine articles was a quantitative study that included a correlation measure; all other studies were qualitative case studies.

Main Findings

1 *The use of a guiding coalition is widely advocated in the scientific literature, but the assumed effect on successful change is not supported with strong scientific evidence.*

Although the use of a guiding coalition in organizational change is widely advocated, we found only one study—a cross-sectional survey—that showed a moderate correlation between the success of the organizational change and the existence of a powerful guiding coalition that directed the change (Abraham, Griffin, & Crawford, 1999). The qualitative case studies stressed the importance of the formation of a guiding coalition as a starting principle for successfully achieving change (Appelbaum, Habashy, Malo, & Shafiq, 2012; Loeser, O'Sullivan, & Irby, 2007; McCracken & McIvor, 2013). However, the effect on the outcome was not measured.

Preliminary Conclusion

Based on the outcome of our search we must conclude that the scientific evidence supporting the effectiveness of a guiding coalition on change outcomes is negligible. The reason for this might lie in the multiformity of the concept. Kotter (1996) distinguishes the following steps in establishing a successful guiding coalition:

1 Gather people with position power, broad expertise, great credibility, and both leadership and management skills.
2 Establish trust.
3 Create a common goal.

To bring some substance to the apparent significance of guiding coalitions in management practice, a second—quick and unsystematic—search was conducted on the characteristics mentioned above. The main findings are summarized below:

1. *Position power, expertise, credibility, and leadership skills have a moderate positive effect on the successful implementation of change (Level D).*

Although little research has focused on how the power of change agents affects successful implementation, some cross-sectional studies suggests that both position power and expert power (expertise) have a moderate positive effect on the achievement of change goals (e.g., Lines, 2007). In addition, it was found that credibility has a positive effect on employees' attitudes and behaviors as well as organizational outcomes (e.g., Gabris, Golembiewski, & Ihrke, 2001; Posner & Kouzes, 1988). This is not surprising as an important component of leadership credibility is trust, a construct that has shown to be an important predictor for change outcomes (see Chapter 5). Finally, several studies indicate that change agents with good leadership skills—such as an ability to coach, communicate, motivate, and support—have a positive effect on successful change (e.g., Gilley, Dixon, & Gilley, 2008). These results indicate that people with position power, broad expertise, great credibility, and both leadership and management skills may have a positive impact on the outcome of change processes.

2. *Trust in leadership has a positive effect on organizational outcomes (Level A).*

In Chapter 5 the available scientific evidence regarding trust as a presumed vital component for effective leadership was analyzed. The outcomes from several meta-analyses show that fostering trust has many benefits. Trust in the leader has a positive effect on attitudinal, behavioral, and performance outcomes. This suggests that, when a guiding coalition enhances trust, this will positively affect change.

3. *Setting common goals increases performance (Level A).*

The results following from Chapter 7 suggest that setting a specific, hard goal positively affects performance. Additionally, it has been shown that commitment to change objectives has a large effect on employees' behavioral support for change initiatives (Chapter 7). These results strongly indicate that a guiding coalition that sets a common goal will most likely have a positive effect on change outcomes.

Synthesis of Evidence

As mentioned earlier, based on the outcome of our search, we must conclude that the scientific evidence supporting the effectiveness of a guiding coalition on change outcomes is negligible: Only one cross-sectional study and a handful of qualitative case studies have directly examined this relationship. From an evidence-based perspective, the scientific evidence offers little foundation for the widespread support of guiding coalitions in practice. However, as pointed out by Carl Sagan, "[A]bsence of evidence is not evidence of absence" (1996, p 213). Put differently, the fact that no high-quality studies were found does not mean that a guiding coalition has no effect. After all, based on experiences and professional judgment, many practitioners call for the formation of a guiding coalition at the start of a change process. In fact, it seems that the establishment of such a coalition—in any form—feels self-evident to practitioners. In addition, each of the characteristics of an effective guiding coalition named by Kotter (1996)—position power, expertise, credibility, trust, and common goals—seems to positively influence the effectiveness of a leader or a group of leaders.

Conclusion

The scientific literature provides little evidence for the assumed effectiveness of a guiding coalition. However, the characteristics of a guiding coalition separately may have a positive effect on change outcomes. We therefore conclude that the claim is likely to be true.

Practical Reflections

As a manager, you would probably not question whether it is wise to establish a guiding coalition. Following the results of our analysis of available evidence, it seems likely that a team of managers with sufficient power, credibility, expertise, and strong leadership skills will be more capable of managing change than a single individual because this team has *more* power, expertise, skills, and so on. One might therefore conclude that it would be wise to see if there is any formal or informal coalition with these characteristics at the start of the change process. And, if this is not the case, establishing a set new coalition (at least to the extent to which this is possible) seems prudent too. A small group consisting of the right people might be capable of initiating a desired movement, clearing the way for others to get involved as the process develops.

However, the literature seems to offer no solid foundation for practical operationalization of this concept. Although we know that all of the characteristics listed are highly relevant for a leader (or group of leaders) when managing change, Kotter (1996) ignores some relevant questions regarding the operationalization and implementation of the concept; for example, which characteristics are especially required in what phase of the change's process? And how do specific contextual and organizational factors influence the effectiveness of a guiding coalition?

'Employees' Capabilities to Change Determine the Organization's Capacity to Change'

Introduction

An organization's change capacity (OCC) is an important concept, especially in an era in which major organizational changes seem to occur with increasing frequency. Change capacity is therefore in the spotlight, and assessing it is felt to be critical in deciding about the quality of an organization and whether it is fit for purpose. Here is an example of how an OCC is defined in practice:

> ... the extent to which groups of people within that organization are willing and able to effectively implement ambitions and objectives and ensure they succeed. It also includes the ability to adjust the process of change if the approach does not seem to be working or if there is a drastic change in circumstances.
>
> (AFM & DNB, n.d.)

This quote shows that the emphasis in change capacity is on employees' capabilities—for example, willingness, readiness, and ability—to change. It thus seems to mainly relate to the human and behavioral dimensions, the soft side of change. Similarly, this assumption is evident in the following quote by a consultancy firm, which states: "Change management begins and ends with your people. Whereas in the past we talked about managing people through change, today we manage change through our people—putting the capacity to change in their hands." Google will give you thousands of hits on change capacity that take you to numerous Web sites and blogs by experts, gurus, and highly esteemed consulting firms that are dedicated to developing an OCC. In academic databases such as Business Source Elite and PsycINFO, a mostly conceptual but rich collection of academic articles is available. Nevertheless, the concept of change capacity in the literature seems quite difficult or even problematic, given the variety of definitions. So the question arises: How is an OCC determined and linked to employees' capabilities, according to the scientific evidence? And how important is change capacity in managing change successfully?

What Is Meant by Change Capacity?

In the literature there is a wide variety of definitions regarding the capacity to change, and there is no single definition that is widely supported (Meyer & Stensaker, 2006). The literature is fragmented (Judge & Elenkov, 2005) without agreement on the constituent parts of change capacity. Moreover, the construct of change capacity resembles that of many other concepts. Examples are 'readiness for organizational change' (Armenakis, Harris, &

Moss Holder, 1993), 'organizational change readiness' (Holt, Armenakis, Feild, & Harris, 2007), 'organizational flexibility' (Gupta & Somers, 1992), 'receptivity to organizational change' (Butler, 2003), 'organizational change capability' (Oxtoby, McGuiness, & Morgan, 2002), 'organizational adaptive capacity' (Staber & Sydow, 2002), and 'organizational becoming' (Tsoukas & Chia, 2002).

In contrast to the definitions used in management practice that primarily focus on employees, the academic definitions of an OCC seem to focus on organizational level, being very abstract and conceptual. Oxtoby et al. (2002), for example, define *organizational change capability* as ". . . generic to all other dynamic capabilities" (p. 311). Bennebroek Gravenhorst, Werkman, and Boonstra (2003) define *change capacity* as ". . . the degree to which aspects of an organization and aspects of a change process contribute to or hinder change" (p. 86). And Judge and Elenkov's (2005) definition is ". . . a broad and dynamic organizational capability that allows the enterprise to adapt old capabilities to new threats and opportunities as well as create new capabilities" (p. 894). In addition, McGuiness and Morgan (2005) define it as ". . . organizational capability of implementing incessant change" (p. 1308) and ". . . a capability for leading and managing a cascading series of inter-related change initiatives that are consistent with an intended type of strategy dynamics" (p. 1312), and Klarner, Probst, and Sopranot (2007) choose to conceptualize it as

> . . . the organization's ability to develop and implement (change process perspective) appropriate organizational changes (change content perspective) to constantly adapt to environmental evolutions (external context) and/or organizational evolutions (internal context) in either a reactive way (adaptation) or by initiating it (pro-action)." (p. 14)

Meyer and Stensaker (2006) define it as ". . . the allocation and development of change and operational capabilities that sustain long-term performance" (p. 217). In their view it consists of the ability (resources and capabilities) to change the organization successfully and the capability to maintain daily operations and implement subsequent change processes. The resource perspective is also present in the definition by Hope-Hailey and Balogun (2002), who talk about "the amount of money available to invest in the change process, and the availability of human resources and managerial time to divert toward the change" (p. 160). Judge and Douglas (2009) talk about it as ". . . a combination of managerial and organizational capabilities that allows an enterprise to adapt more quickly and effectively than its competition to changing situations" (p. 635). Buono and Kerber (2009) contribute with the following description of change capacity: "[a]n organization's ability to successfully navigate an array of changes in response to and in anticipation of ever shifting market conditions, customer demands, competitive pressures, and societal condition" (para. 2).

This variety of definitions shows that the concept of change capacity is not clear-cut. In this research, we use the term OCC as a general concept covering the many different definitions.

How Does It Work?

Although the conceptualization of the construct and its subsequent definition seem ambiguous, the assumed purpose and mechanism of change capacity are very straightforward. When organizations are confronted with a change or choose to change, they need to define *and* deliver. The change has to be translated or conceptualized in a change vision, a change case, or change goals (define change). But to deliver actual change results, one has to have or develop the *change capacity* to carry it out. As Bower (2000) states, purposive change rests in the answers to two questions: What it should be (change vision) *and* how it should be delivered (change capacity). It is therefore assumed that a lack of or underdeveloped change capacity may lead to unsuccessful change.

Search Strategy

Relevant databases were searched to find meta-analyses and studies, using key words such as *change capacity, capacity for change, change readiness, organizational flexibility, receptivity to organizational change, organizational adaptive capacity,* and *organizational becoming*.

Assessing Quality and Relevance

Our initial search yielded a total of 721 studies. After screening the abstracts for relevance, 661 studies were excluded. Full-text screening of the articles resulted in the exclusion of another 22 studies. Finally, after critical appraisal of the remaining 38 articles, a total of 18 studies were included. Of these, not a single article was a meta-analysis or systematic review. The overall quality of the included studies was low (Level D) as they were mainly of a cross-sectional nature. All studies included were published between 2002 and 2015.

Main Findings

No relevant meta-analyses were found to investigate the current assumption. However, the assumption does not imply a causal effect as we mainly looked for an academic conceptualization of the construct of an OCC. The first two findings are thus formulated based on single studies that operationalized the concept of change capacity in an evidence-based way (as much as possible). Moreover, as stated in the introduction paragraph, it is also valuable assessing the importance of an organization's capacity to successful change, which is answered in the third main finding based on our search.

1 *Employees' capabilities, their level, and development are an essential element or dimension in delivering change, thus being part of an OCC (Level D).*

Soparnot (2011) designates elements such as knowledge, experience, practices, and capabilities of individual learning as part of an OCC. Moreover, Buick, Blackman, O'Donell, O'Flynn, and West (2015) assign performance management as a driver for change capacity:

> Performance management can enable employees to cope better with the change through clearly defining what will constitute high performance in the change context; ensuring employees have a clear role purpose and are provided with sufficient mechanisms to adjust this as change occurs; and ensuring employees are aligned with the organizational direction. (p. 284)

Fitzgerald et al. (2007) conclude that in change situations, a leadership constellation at the top of the organization is necessary but not sufficient. There have to be knowledgeable change leaders at several levels throughout the organization. Detert and Pollock (2008) conclude that change may be frustrated by personal interests and capacity constraints and point to the importance of appropriate training, structural support, incentives, and other resources for the real learning that underpins change. They consider the skills of the people involved in achieving new behavior as a precondition in delivering change.

2 *Change capacity consists of more than just employees' capabilities (Level D).*

As shown in the first main finding, employees' capabilities appear to be part of an OCC. However, systems (Buick et al., 2015) and structures (Soparnot, 2011) are also found to contribute to the change capacity of an organization. In this light, Judge, Naoumova, and Douglas (2009) conceptualize an OCC as 'a comprehensive meta-capability' that enables an enterprise to regain competitiveness or remain competitive with other enterprises through effective leadership, adaptive cultures, resilient employees, and an organizational infrastructure conducive to change. "As such, OCC is a 'bigger' and more encompassing concept than absorptive capacity or organizational readiness for change" (p. 1740). Moreover, Soparnot (2011) considers the organization's 'structural flexibility' (besides soft elements such as transformational leadership and trust) also as a crucial part of the change capacity.

3   Change capacity positively relates to the performance of an organization (Level D).

It was found that an OCC relates to performance. Hence, Heckman, Steger, and Dowling (2016) show that an OCC is positively associated with the performance of its change projects. Looking at economic performance, Judge et al. (2009) concluded that the capacity of an organization to change is positively associated with a companies' performance within Russia's transition economy.

With regard to *change readiness* (defined as the change participant's motivation to engage in the change) and performance, Caldwell, Chatman, O'Reilly, Ormitson, and Lapiz (2008) found that change readiness and the quality of leadership are positively related to improving patient satisfaction during large health care change implementations. Caldwell et al. (2008) conclude with the notion that leaders can enhance the results of the change by developing general norms such as teamwork and tolerance for mistakes that increase general readiness for change within the group.

Synthesis of Evidence

A rich collection of academic articles is available regarding an OCC. The results of the current REA, however, leave us with a sense of disappointment. There are hardly any well-conducted, high-quality studies regarding change capacity; most of the studies included in this REA suffer from methodological shortcomings (i.e., the level of evidence and the articles lacking rigor). Based on the meager evidence that we have found, there are indications that employees' capabilities are an important element of an OCC mainly referring to the skills of people. However, there are also indications that change capacity is not limited to these capabilities. Hence, the more hard aspects such as organization's systems and structures are also presented as defining elements of change capacity. Finally, the available evidence suggests that change capacity is related to an organization's (change) performance.

Conclusion

The scientific evidence with regard to change capacity in general and the assumption that employees' capabilities to change determine the organization's capacity to change is very limited and lacks methodological rigor. The research literature provides some corroborating indications but also shows that change capacity is a broad concept and not one that is solely determined by employees' capabilities. Moreover, it has shown that the construct has not yet been conceptualized and investigated in a solid, evidence-based way. However, based on the very limited evidence found, we conclude that employees' capabilities are *one of* the determining elements of change capacity. We therefore conclude that the claim is somewhat likely to be true, although with the important notion that further (high-quality) research is needed to further conceptualize the concept.

Practical Reflections

As a manager, do you need to consider employees' capabilities as a determining element of change capacity when preparing, designing, and implementing change? Clearly, if the capacity to change is underdeveloped or inadequate compared to the challenge, success is unlikely. Employees who are unwilling, unable, or not ready will probably not contribute to successful change. Therefore, and for other psychological and ethical reasons, paying attention to employees' capabilities in a change process seems to make sense. However, developing change capacity should not be limited to developing the capabilities of the people involved. For example, resources such as budgets, time, external expertise, and elements such as organizational leadership, structures, and systems may also determine and contribute to an OCC. Together these elements invigorate every step in a change process, emphasizing the importance of change leaders constantly gauging how the organization stands in relation to these aspects. The question of whether we are capable of achieving this should therefore be asked systematically and reviewed regularly within management circles during the change process.

'Participation Is Key to Successful Change'

Introduction

In management circles one often hears the claim that participation is *the* key to successful change. A quick search on Google with the terms *participation* and *change management* takes you to thousands of Web sites and blogs of experts, gurus, and business leaders, all suggesting that actively encouraging employees to provide input and, where possible, giving them (some) control of the change process is critical for successful change. Even the Web pages of reputed international consulting firms state that employee participation is key to success. What's more, this claim is endorsed by numerous articles and books on change management. For instance, in their book *Choosing Strategies for Change* Harvard professors John Kotter and Leonard Schlessinger state that ". . . participation leads to commitment, not merely compliance. In some instances, commitment is needed for the change to be a success" (1979, p. 401). However, the authors also point out that participation can lead to a poor solution if the process is not carefully managed. The roots of participation within the context of change management go back to at least 1948, when Coch and French (1948)—based on an experiment they conducted in a clothing factory—suggested that resistance to change could be overcome by involving workers in decision making. In the 1980s, it was widely assumed that a top-down, autocratic style of leadership no longer created competitive advantage and that organizations should, instead, rely on workers who are "empowered through extensive involvement in problem-solving, decision making and continuous improvement" (Vidal, 2007, p. 198). Even then, however, not everyone agreed, as shown by this statement by former US President Richard Nixon:

> I would not think of making a decision by going around the table and then deciding on the basis of how everyone felt. Of course, I like to hear everyone, but then I go off alone and decide. The decisions that are important must be made alone.
>
> (Miller & Monge, 1986, p. 727)

What Is Meant by Participation?

Participation is commonly defined as "taking part in an activity or an event" (Cotton, Vollrath, Froggatt, Lengnick-Hall, & Jennings, 1988, p. 12). In the context of change management, it's often related to decision making. A definition that is commonly used in management therefore defines participation as influence sharing among supervisors and subordinates. It should be noted, however, that participation is a heterogeneous concept that ranges from consultation to shared decision making. In addition, it is assumed that the impact of participation will vary with the form of participation and the criteria used to measure effectiveness.

Participation is both subjective and objective. The perceptions and feelings of employees can be measured using self-report questionnaires that include statements such as "Employees are encouraged to participate when important decisions are made in this organization" (Sverke, Hellgren, Näswall, Göransson, & Öhrming, 2008, p. 119). A more objective measure is provided by Heller's typology of participation in decision making, which distinguishes among five levels: (1) leader decides without rationale (tell); (2) leader decides with rationale (tell and sell); (3) leader consults employees and then decides (consultation); (4) joint decision of employees and leader (participation); (5) employees decide themselves (delegation) (Kleingeld, Van Mierlo, & Arenas, 2011).

How Does It Work?

To understand how participation may be effective, three types of theoretical models are proposed: cognitive, affective, and contingency ones. Each assumes a different working mechanism for participation. First, cognitive models assume that participation leads to increased quality of decisions because of decision-making benefits from high-quality information and specific knowledge from employees. Basically, this model builds on the assumed positive effects of information sharing and processing among supervisors and subordinates, leading to "better decisions" (Wagner, 1994). Affective models (also referred to as *motivational models*), however, propose that participation reduces resistance to change and increases motivation because specific needs of employees are satisfied when they are involved in decision making. Finally, proponents of contingency models advocate that no single model is appropriate for all employees in all organizations: Whether someone positively values involvement through participation depends on both the individual's personality and the complexity of decision making (Miller & Monge, 1986).

Search Strategy

Relevant databases were searched using key words such as *participation*, *voice*, and *employee involvement*. Studies were included in the search if participation was related to performance outcomes, behavioral outcomes, or decision-making quality.

Assessing Quality and Relevance

Our initial search yielded a total of 329 studies. After screening the abstracts for relevance, 290 studies were excluded. Full-text screening of the articles resulted in the exclusion of another six studies. Finally, after critical appraisal of the remaining 33 articles, a total of 23 studies were included. Thirteen of the 23 studies included were meta-analyses. The overall quality of the included meta-analyses was moderate: Most of them were based on cross-sectional studies, and only one meta-analysis included studies that used both a control group and a before-and-after measurement. It is notable that almost all meta-analytical reviews (11 out of 13) were written between 1980 and 2000.

Main Findings

1   *Participation has a small to medium effect on organizational and attitudinal outcomes (Level C).*

Participation in decision making was found to be positively associated with productivity (Doucouliagos, 1995; Miller & Monge, 1986). In addition it was found that participation has a positive impact on employee satisfaction. In both cases, however, the effect sizes were small to moderate, and the effect on satisfaction was somewhat stronger than on productivity.

2   *The practical significance of participation as a means of influencing organizational and attitudinal outcomes is very limited (Level C).*

The correlations between participation and both organizational and attitudinal outcomes were small. As a result, the practical significance of participation as a means of influencing performance or employee satisfaction is very limited. This is also reflected in the meta-analysis by Wagner and Lepine (1999), who state that "existing research has not shown that participation has substantial effects on performance or satisfaction." Further support is thus provided ". . . that participation has only limited influence and efficacy in the workplace" (Wagner & Lepine, 1999, p. 725). In addition, a recent meta-analysis on the effect of goal setting on group performance did not confirm the assumed inferiority of a *tell-and-sell strategy* (top-down and authoritarian) as opposed to more participative strategies (Kleingeld et al., 2011) (Level A).

Synthesis of Evidence

Over the past 50 years, various scholars have studied the effects of participation. This has resulted in a number of meta-analytical reviews that were mostly published between 1980 and 2000. Although this large amount of research underlines the continuous advocacy of participation in practice, the outcomes seem to be less favorable: The scientific evidence does not demonstrate that participation is an effective intervention for improving organizational outcomes. This is reflected in the findings of a large number of studies (Wagner, 1994) that indicate that the correlation between participation and relevant organizational outcomes is low.

Conclusion

The scientific research literature does not provide solid support for the claim that participation is *key* to successful change. We therefore conclude that, based on the evidence found, this claim is unlikely to be true.

Practical Reflections

The practical question is this: Is participation an effective strategy when managing change? Unfortunately, there is no simple answer. There is strong scientific evidence suggesting that participation is not *key* to successful change. However, the small correlations that were found between participation and organizational outcomes do not rule out the possibility that participation may have a stronger effect under certain unspecified conditions and circumstances. What's more, several studies have indicated that the quality of a decision-making process increases if the available information regarding the problem and the preferred solution becomes more accurate. It might therefore be helpful to use participation to facilitate the transfer of knowledge among managers and employees who might not otherwise share information (Wagner, Leana, Locke, & Schweiger, 1997).

Most of the research on the effects of participation, however, is based on affective or motivational models. When employee participation primarily focuses on minimizing resistance to change without being clear about the exact purpose of the involvement, employees might well end up disappointed (fake participation). As pointed out in a meta-analysis by Wagner et al. (1997), research on the effects of participation on decision-making and change processes may benefit from moving away from this type of model and focusing instead on cognitive models with an information-processing approach. This shows that sharing knowledge seems to be valuable (and deserves more attention in academic research), whereas nowadays participation is too often applied from a team-wise perspective based on the idea that for everyone to give support to change, they should be involved. However, the lack of knowledge about this underlying causal mechanism raises questions regarding the practical relevance and, hence, applicability of participation in organizational change. The decision whether or not to let employees participate during the change process seems therefore, from this perspective, more a matter of style and personal preference than of evidence-based practice.

'Resistance to Change Is Detrimental to the Success of Change'

Introduction

> One of the most baffling and recalcitrant problems which business executives face is employee resistance to change. Such resistance may take a number of forms—persistent reduction in output, increase in the number of 'quits' and requests for transfer, chronic quarrels, sullen hostility, wildcat or slowdown strikes, and, of course, the expression of a lot of pseudo-logical reasons why the change will not work. Even the more petty forms of this resistance can be troublesome.
>
> (Lawrence, 1954, p. 49)

This is how the seminal article "How to Deal With Resistance to Change," which was published in the highly respected *Harvard Business Review* begins. Although it was published more than 60 years ago, it is still exemplary for what is assumed by numerous managers and leaders to be a general law of organizational change: Resistance to change is a problem that should be overcome or eliminated (e.g., Erwin & Garman, 2010; Mabin, Forgeson, & Green, 2001). In fact, change itself is not the problem but rather employees' resistance to change. Hence popular management books and Web sites on organizational change offer a wide range of tips and advice on how to successfully manage employees' resistance to change, including fostering a culture of trust, establishing a sense of urgency, and participative decision making. Type *resistance to change* in Google, and you will get millions of hits that take you to numerous Web sites and blogs of experts, gurus, and highly esteemed consulting firms that are dedicated to countering resistance to change. In addition, scientific research databases contain hundreds of scientific papers on this topic. But how important is resistance to change for a change leader? And how important is its impact to the outcome of a change process?

What Is Meant With Resistance to Change?

In the literature, no universally accepted definition of resistance to change appears. Numerous books and articles on change management point out that resistance to change is a 'divergent,' 'evolving' construct. Oreg (2006), and Piderit (2000), for example, define it as a multidimensional concept, which includes affective, behavioral, and cognitive components. Put differently, resistance to change is about feeling (affective), behaving (behavioral), and thinking (cognitive). It is assumed that employees who resist change operate in all of these dimensions simultaneously. Faced with organizational change, they might feel that change is unnecessary, feel angry about it, and thus act accordingly. This multidimensional approach is also the basis of the widely used "Resistance to Change Scale"—a validated measurement tool that is used to assess individuals' personality-based inclination to resist change (Oreg, 2003). Resistance to change can therefore be considered to be a broad construct that includes almost any unfavorable reaction, opposition, or force that prevents or inhibits change (Erwin & Garman, 2010).

How Does It Work?

The mechanism of resistance to change is relatively simple: When people perceive the change as a threat (e.g., less pay, loss of status, or loss of control), they are naturally inclined to defend the status quo (Folger & Skarlicki, 1999). As a result they will actively or passively resist to the change. When people actively block change, this will clearly negatively affect the change process. Whether it concerns withholding information, not following through on commitments, or outright sabotaging of the change process, in all these cases the change effort may be seriously affected. However, more remarkable is the presumed negative impact of passive resistance to change (e.g., negative thoughts and emotions) on organizational change.

Search Strategy

Relevant databases were searched using key words such as *resistance to change*, *change resistance*, and *employee resistance*. Studies were included in the search if resistance to change was related to performance outcomes, behavioral outcomes, or decision-making quality.

Assessing Quality and Relevance

The search yielded a total of 548 articles. After screening the abstracts for relevance, 504 studies were excluded. Full-text screening of the articles resulted in the exclusion of another 20 studies. Finally, after critical appraisal of the remaining 24 articles, a total of three studies were included. Most studies were excluded because they had serious methodological shortcomings. The overall quality of the three included studies was low because they used a cross-sectional design. As a result the trustworthiness of the scientific evidence supporting the following main findings is very limited, so they should be interpreted with caution.

Main Findings

1   *Resistance to change is negatively correlated with job satisfaction, intention to quit, and commitment—but the effect sizes are small (Level D).*

It was found that employees who have negative emotions (e.g., stress, anxiety, or anger) because of the change also reported being less satisfied with their jobs. In addition, employees who reported having actively resisted change also reported a stronger intention to leave the organization. Similarly, employees who regarded the change as unfavorable were also less likely to believe it was worth their while to remain in the organization due to loss in commitment (Oreg, 2006). It should be noted, however, that the effect sizes found were small, which makes these findings of limited relevance to practice. In addition, due to the cross-sectional design of the study concerned, the direction of the correlation is unknown. This means that it cannot be excluded that employees who are not satisfied with their jobs or have a strong intention to leave the organization are more likely to resist change.

2   *Resistance to change is weakly negatively linked with goal accomplishment (Level D).*

There were indications that employees who resist change also find it more difficult to work effectively and as a result tend to accomplish a lower number of goals (Kunze, Boehm, & Bruch, 2013). Moreover, this negative effect disappeared when employees were older.

3   *Resistance to change is weakly related to creative performance (Level D).*

It was found that when employees resist change, their creative performance may be negatively affected (Hon, Bloom, & Crant, 2014). A possible explanation for this effect is that the more resistant an individual is to change, the less willing he or she will be to think differently and develop new ways of doing things. The variables of 'modern' organizational climate (e.g., where openness to new experiences, novelty, and rejecting traditional authority are encouraged), empowering leadership, and high levels of support from colleagues decrease the negative effect that resistance to change has on employees creative performance.

4 Resistance to change is associated with a lack of trust in management (Level D).

A low level of trust in the organization's leadership is strongly related to the buildup of anger, frustration, and anxiety regarding the change, which makes it more likely that they will actively resist change (Oreg, 2006). Conversely, employees who feel that the leader of the change knows what he or she is doing and strongly believe that the organization has a good reason to change are more likely to embrace and actively support it.

Synthesis of Evidence

Resistance to change is considered to be one of the most important topics of change management, as shown by the wide coverage of this subject in both the popular management literature and academic publications. Many people have made claims about resistance to change, which is seen as a prominent factor contributing to the failure of organizational change initiatives. The results of this REA however, leave us with a sense of disappointment. There are hardly any well-conducted, high-quality studies, and all of the studies included in this REA suffer from serious methodological shortcomings. Nevertheless, there are indications that components of resistance to change have a small negative effect on job satisfaction, creativity, and churn rates. These outcomes might, to a limited extent, affect the success of the change.

Conclusion

The scientific evidence that suggests that resistance to change negatively affects behavioral and organizational outcomes is very limited and lacks methodological rigor. In addition, the effect sizes found are small and are of limited relevance to practice. The scientific research literature therefore does not support the claim that resistance to change is detrimental to the success of change. We therefore conclude that, based on the evidence found, this claim is somewhat unlikely to be true.

Practical Reflections

As a manager, do you need to minimize resistance to change as much as possible when implementing change? Clearly, change cannot succeed when people display extreme behavior and, for instance, literally block the entrance to the company. Besides, there are also indications that even passive resistance to change may negatively affect organizational outcomes, which are highly important for organizational change to succeed. However, it must be noted that reverse causation cannot be excluded because the quality of the studies is rather low. This means that a lack of trust in the abilities or intentions of a change leader, low employee satisfaction, or little organizational commitment may also be important determinants of resistance rather than vice versa. From a practical perspective, therefore, it seems prudent to measure—or at least take into account—these elements and consider to what extent they are present. In other words, it seems that, based on scientific evidence, the underlying factors might be the real issue for change leaders rather than resistance to change in itself. In that sense, resistance to change can be considered an important signal that demands that we look into the underlying factors that create the conditions for resistance to arise.

'A Fair Change Process Is Important in Achieving Successful Change'**

Introduction

The importance of fairness in organizations has been emphasized in the last decade, partly in response to an increasing number of organizational changes that have had detrimental results for employees (e.g., reorganizations), usually arising from macroeconomic conditions. "Increasing globalization and the economic uncertainty inherent in the recent financial crisis have strained the already tenuous commitment of many employees, making followers' perceptions of justice and trust more critical now than ever before in retaining a loyal workforce" (Pillai, Kohles, Bligh, Carsten, & Brodowsky, 2011, p. 242).

Employees and other stakeholders affected by organizational change perceive the outcomes as either positive or negative. They then further ask themselves whether the organizational change (i.e., the process and its outcome) can be perceived as fair. First and foremost, employees and other stakeholders will wonder whether the allocation of the results of the organizational change is fair (distributive justice). Examples of such outcomes are appointments and promotions as well as status and appreciation. Widely used allocation norms are equality, equity, and the need-based principle (Deutsch, 1975). Apart from the results, employees and other stakeholders will implicitly or explicitly evaluate the fairness of the process by which the outcomes are determined (procedural justice). It is suggested that when the change process is conducted fairly, there is greater acceptance of the outcome, even when this may be negative for those involved. By making the process of the organizational change fairer, resistance is less likely to occur, and the chances of success will be greater.

What Is Meant by a Fair Process?

Fairness or justice is a fundamental concept that takes many forms in different disciplines, such as theology, philosophy, law, and psychology. Greenberg (1987) introduced the construct of organizational justice in psychology. This construct does not refer to a universal or absolute form of justice;

rather, it is about the fairness as perceived by employees—a *subjective* experience. Organizational justice can be divided into three elements: distributive justice (outcomes), procedural justice (process), and interactional justice (interaction). Fair process is essentially a synonym for procedural justice and defined as the following: "Procedural justice reflects the perceived fairness of decision-making processes and the degree to which they are consistent, accurate, unbiased, and open to voice and input" (Colquitt et al., 2013, p. 200). Various researchers have applied different standards and varied in their operationalizations of procedural justice as a construct. Leventhal's (1980) six criteria of procedural justice, for example, are well-known and often used to determine the fairness of procedures:

> (a) the consistency rule, stating that allocation procedures should be consistent across persons and over time; (b) the bias-suppression rule, stating that personal self-interests of decision-makers should be prevented from operating during the allocation process; (c) the accuracy rule, referring to the goodness of the information used in the allocation process; (d) the correctability rule, dealing with the existence of opportunities to change an unfair decisions; (e) the representativeness rule, stating that the needs, values, and outlooks of all the parties affected by the allocation process should be represented in the process; and (f) the ethicality rule, according to which the allocation process must be compatible with fundamental moral and ethical values of the perceiver.
> (Leventhal, 1980, in Cohen-Charash & Spector, 2001, p. 280)

How Does It Work?

An important theory often referred to in research on organizational justice is the equity theory that was introduced by behavioral psychologist John Adams (1965). This theory explains how people appraise the remuneration for their work. What is considered as fair is set against the income-outcome ratio of peers. Getting rewarded too little compared to one's peers, either in money, influence, or prestige, may result in frustration or anger. Getting rewarded too much, on the other hand, may result in feelings of guilt. This nagging sense may cause the employee to invest less rather than more to restore the balance. Explaining the appropriate allocation norms beforehand and striking the right balance, with an emphasis on outcomes, is referred to as *distributive justice*.

To understand the underlying mechanism of why the perception of a fair process may help to increase acceptance of the outcome, it is interesting to consider the first empirical research on procedural justice that was conducted in a judicial setting (Thibaut & Walker, 1975). The researchers compared the inquisitorial system of continental Europe with the

Anglo-Saxon adversarial system of justice. It turned out that, irrespective of the final verdict, the Anglo-Saxon adversarial system was perceived to be fairer. In continental Europe, judges control both decision and process. Under the Anglo-Saxon judicial system, however, those affected by the decision can exert more influence on the judicial proceedings. As Thibaut and Walker indicated, this influence over the process makes the outcome more acceptable, *even* when these outcomes may be disadvantageous in terms of self-interest.

Later empirical research replicated this finding that when procedures are perceived as fair, reactions are favorable, largely irrespective of the outcome. However, when procedures are perceived to be unfair, the importance of the fairness of the outcome increases, that is, distributive justice. This interaction effect is called the *fair process effect* and has been shown empirically in several studies in different contexts (for a review, see Brockner & Wiesenfeld, 1996).

Search Strategy

To gain an overview of the relevant literature on fair process in general, relevant databases were searched using the key words *organizational justice*, *procedural justice*, and *fair process*. In a second search, these key words were combined with *organizational change* to identify studies in which fair process was applied in the context of organizational change.

Assessing Quality and Relevance

Initially, the general search that focused on fair process in general resulted in more than 2,000 articles. Filtering for meta-analyses and systematic reviews, our search yielded 37 results. After screening the abstracts for relevance, 27 studies were excluded. Full-text screening and critical appraisal of the remaining 10 articles did not result in additional exclusions. All the meta-analyses included were of moderate quality (Level B).

The second search, in which the key word *organizational change* was added to narrow down the results to the context of change management, resulted in 43 studies. After screening the abstracts for relevance, 29 studies were excluded. Full-text screening of the articles resulted in the exclusion of another five studies. Critical appraisal of the remaining nine articles did not lead to more exclusions. One of the nine studies was a noncontrolled before-after study. The other eight studies had a cross-sectional study design.

Main Findings

The first part of this section describes the main findings for the construct of procedural justice in organizations (i.e., fair process) *in general*. The second part contains the main findings for procedural justice in the *context of organizational change*.

1 *Fair process has a medium to large positive effect on organizational outcomes (Level A).*

The results showed relationships between the dimensions of justice and certain organizational outcomes, such as performance, productivity, organizational citizenship behavior, satisfaction, and commitment (Cohen-Charash & Spector, 2001; Viswesvaran & Ones, 2002).

More specifically, the meta-analyses clearly illustrated the importance of procedural justice (fair process) in relation to organizational outcomes. Compared to the other types of justice (i.e., distributive justice and interactional justice), procedural justice is the best predictor of work performance, counterproductive work behavior, and affective commitment (Cohen-Charash & Spector, 2001). Viswesvaran and Ones (2002) found similar results: Organizational commitment, organizational citizenship behavior, and productivity were more associated with procedural justice than distributive justice.

The effects that have been found were medium to large. Because the results were consistent throughout all the meta-analyses, evidence Level A was assigned.

2 *Fair process has a medium positive effect on the affective commitment of both survivors and victims of a downsizing operation (Level B).*

Van Dierendonck and Jacobs (2002) presented an overview of the impact of fairness on organizational commitment on both survivors and victims after a downsizing operation. This specific type of organizational change often increases the level of insecurity among employees and triggers sensemaking processes. One of their results revealed that procedural justice mattered more to survivors of the downsizing operation than distributive justice. "Employees who felt that they were given a full and fair explanation of why and how people were dismissed are more likely to accept the layoff process and to remain more positive about the organization" (p. 105). Van Dierendonck and Jacobs also found that fairness in general mattered more when mass layoffs were instigated for profit maximization reasons. These results indicate that attention to fairness in a downsizing process is a vital driver of commitment in the critical time period following a downsizing operation.

To examine more closely the essence of procedural justice in relation to organizational change, several single studies were included that measured perceived justice or injustice during different types of change interventions. Although these single studies had lower levels of evidence, they all supported the claim that procedural justice is an important factor to be taken into account during organizational change.

1   Fair process has a low to medium positive effect on the acceptance of organizational changes (Level D).

The findings of one study indicated that if leaders act in a procedurally fair way, employees are more likely to accept organizational changes (Tyler & De Cremer, 2005). In addition, Saruhan (2014) indicated that effective communication and perceptions of justice are crucial factors in reducing employee resistance and increasing favorable behavior toward change, thereby increasing the possibility that the change process will be successfully implemented. Although the effect sizes of both studies were small to medium, these studies provided the best available evidence on this subject, which makes them relevant for both researchers and practitioners.

2   Fair process has a large positive effect on change commitment (Level D).

One study indicated procedural justice as, in fact, a predictor of change commitment (Bernerth, Armenakis, Field, & Walker, 2007). Procedural justice was found to be strongly positively related to affective change commitment and moderately negatively related to organizational cynicism.

3   An unfair process has a small to medium negative effect on employee behavior further to a breach of the psychological contract (Level D).

Kickul, Lester, and Finkl (2002) found that procedural justice was an important determinant of behavior following breaches of external outcomes (e.g., pay) in terms of the psychological contract between the employer and the employee. When procedural justice was perceived to be low, employees showed less organizational change behavior, satisfaction, and in-role job performance. These employees were also more likely to leave the organization. Although this study showed small to medium effect sizes, the findings may be relevant to the field of organizational change, where psychological contracts play an important role.

Synthesis of Evidence

Extensive research has been done over the past 15 years on the topic of organizational justice and, more specifically, procedural justice, also known as fair process. At least 10 meta-analyses have been published on organizational justice, alongside thousands of other relevant studies. The effects of fair processes on organizational outcomes are significant and show fairly consistent medium to large effect sizes, making them practically relevant. The single studies, designed to measure the effect of organizational justice in the specific change context, also clearly showed the importance of a fair process for change commitment, pro-change behavior, and the acceptance of change. The evidence levels of the studies in very specific change contexts, however, were meager (Level D).

Therefore, based purely on this empirical evidence, caution is advised when generalizing findings. Organizational change is context dependent. Universal guidelines for managing organizational change in a way that is fair cannot be provided on the basis of nine single studies. However, given the direction of the evidence related to organizational change (consistent with the strong evidence concerning organizational outcomes), it has been consistently demonstrated that a fair process is very important to achieving results in change processes.

Conclusion

The scientific research literature supports the claim that a fair change process is important to realizing successful change, given the moderate positive effect of procedural justice on organizational outcomes. Moreover, with the effects mostly small to medium, indications are that there is a positive relationship between procedural justice and acceptance, commitment, and behavior in the specific context of organizational change. We therefore conclude that, based on the evidence found, this claim is likely to be true.

Practical Reflections

The fair process effect in organizations is observed when change leaders increase the degree to which the decision-making process is consistent, accurate, unbiased, and open to employee input. When procedural justice is not taken into account, employees may feel treated unfairly, and dissatisfaction may increase. To actively design a fair change process, the six classic criteria for procedural justice named by Leventhal (1980)—which are still used by many researchers—may serve as a useful checklist. These criteria can be turned into practical guidelines for the purpose of organizational change as follows: (1) the change approach needs to be consistently applied to all employees at all times; (2) it needs to be impartial, meaning that prejudice or stereotyping are eliminated; (3) the information on which decisions are based needs to be accurate; (4) if the situation demands it, opportunities should be provided to correct or change plans or processes; (5) those responsible for the organizational change (the change managers or executives responsible) need to represent the interests of all those affected by the change; and (6) the ethical standards and values of those involved should never be disregarded. Although this all sounds logical and righteous, in practice it is not always possible to fully apply all guidelines. Sometimes change leaders simply do not have enough time or resources to apply to all of these criteria. Sometimes—for example, in times of conflict within a multiparty organization—it is impossible to represent all of the interests of all stakeholders, given the complexity of those involved and their stakes in possible outcomes. In such cases, it seems prudent only to deviate from the criteria for a fair process intentionally and transparently, which for example, means explaining the choices that have been made as these can reduce the overall fairness of the change process.

Notes

* The two other elements of perceived social support are perceived coworker support and perceived organizational support.

** This paragraph is based on research by Leonard Millenaar, and parts of this paragraph have been published before in: Millenaar, J. L., Graamans, E., & Ten Have, W. D. (2015). Rechtvaardigheid als bepalende factor bij organisatieverandering. *De Psycholoog, 3*, 10–18.

References

Abraham, M., Griffin, D., & Crawford, J. (1999). Organisation change and management decision in museums. *Management Decision, 37*(10), 736–751.

Adams, J. S. (1965). Inequity in social exchange. In L. Berkowitz (Ed.), *Advances in experimental social psychology* (pp. 267–299). New York, NY: Academic Press.

AFM, & DNB. (n.d.). *Capacity for change in the financial sector*. Retrieved February 3, 2016, from https://www.afm.nl/~/profmedia/files/brochures/2014/verandervermogen-banken-verzekeraars-2.ashx

Appelbaum, S. H., Habashy, S., Malo, J. L., & Shafiq, H. (2012). Back to the future: Revisiting Kotter's 1996 change model. *Journal of Management Development, 31*(8), 764–782.

Argyris, C. (1960). *Understanding organizational behavior*. Homewood, IL: Dorsey Press.

Armenakis, A. A., Harris, S. G., & Mossholder, K. W. (1993). Creating readiness for organizational change. *Human Relations, 46*(6), 681–703.

Bennebroek Gravenhorst, K. M., Werkman, R. A., & Boonstra, J. J. (2003). The change capacity of organisations: General assessment and five configurations. *Applied Psychology, 52*(1), 3–105.

Bernerth, J. B., Armenakis, A. A., Field, H. S., & Walker, H. J. (2007). Justice, cynicism, and commitment: A study of important organizational change variables. *The Journal of Applied Behavioral Science, 43*(3), 303–326.

Bower, J. L. (2000). The purpose of change: A commentary on Jensen and Senge. In M. Beer, & N. Nohria (Eds.), *Breaking the code of change* (pp. 83–95). Boston, MA: Harvard Business School Press.

Brockner, J., & Wiesenfeld, B. M. (1996). An integrative framework for explaining reactions to decisions: The interactive effects of outcomes and procedures. *Psychological Bulletin, 120*(2), 189–208.

Buick, F., Blackman, D. A., O'Donell, M. E., O'Flynn, J. L., & West, D. (2015). Can enhanced performance management support sector change? *Journal of Organizational Change Management, 28*(2), 271–289.

Buono, A. F., & Kerber, K. W. (2009, June). *Building organizational change capacity*. Unpublished paper presented at the Management Consulting Division International Conference. Vienna, Austria.

Butler, M. J. R. (2003). Managing from the inside out: Drawing on 'receptivity' to explain variation in strategy implementation. *British Journal of Management*, 14(1), 47–60.

Caldwell, D. F., Chatman, J., O'Reilly, A. C., Ormitson, M., & Lapiz, M. (2008). Implementing strategic change in a health care system: The importance of leadership and change readiness. *Health Care Manage Review*, 33(2), 124–133.

Chauvin, B., Rohmer, O., Spitzenstetter, F., Raffin, D., Schimchowitsch, S., & Louvet, E. (2014). Assessment of job stress factors in a context of organizational change. *European Review of Applied Psychology*, 64(6), 299–306.

Coch, L., & French, J. R. P. (1948). Overcoming resistance to change. *Human Relations*, 1(4), 512–532.

Cohen-Charash, Y., & Spector, P. E. (2001). The role of justice in organizations: A meta-analysis. *Organizational Behavior and Human Decision Processes*, 86(2), 278–321.

Colquitt, J. A., Scott, B. A., Rodell, J. B., Long, D. M., Zapata, C. P., Conlon, D. E., & Wesson, M. J. (2013). Justice at the millennium, a decade later: A meta-analytic test of social exchange and affect-based perspectives. *Journal of Applied Psychology*, 98(2), 199–236.

Cotton, J. L., Vollrath, D. A., Froggatt, K. L., Lengnick-Hall, M. L., & Jennings, K. R. (1988). Employee participation: Diverse forms and different outcomes. *Academy of Management Review*, 13(1), 8–22.

Detert, J. R., & Pollock, T. G. (2008). Values, interests, and the capacity to act understanding professionals' responses to market-based improvement initiatives in highly institutionalized organizations. *The Journal of Applied Behavioral Science*, 44(2), 186–214.

Deutsch, M. (1975). Equity, equality, and need: What determines which value will be used as the basis for distributive justice? *Journal of Social Issues*, 31(3), 137–149.

Doucouliagos, C. (1995). Worker participation and productivity in labor-managed and participatory capitalist firms: A meta-analysis. *Industrial and Labor Relations Review*, 49(1), 58–77.

Edmondson, D. R., & Boyer, S. L. (2013). The moderating effect of the boundary spanning role on perceived supervisory support: A meta-analytic review. *Journal of Business Research*, 66(11), 2186–2192.

Elias, S. M., & Mittal, R. (2011). The importance of supervisor support for a change initiative: An analysis of job satisfaction and involvement. *International Journal of Organizational Analysis*, 19(4), 305–316.

Erwin, D. G., & Garman, A. N. (2010). Resistance to organizational change: Linking research and practice. *Leadership & Organization Development Journal*, 31(1), 39–56.

Fitzgerald, L., Ferlie, E., Addicott, R., Baeza, J., Buchanan, D., & McGivern, G. (2007). Service improvement in healthcare: Understanding change capacity and change context. *Clinician Management*, 15(2), 61–74.

Folger, R., & Skarlicki, D. (1999). Unfairness and resistance to change: Hardship as Mistreatment. *Journal of Organizational Change Management*, 12(1), 35–50.

Fuchs, S., & Prouska, R. (2014). Creating positive employee change evaluation: The role of different levels of organizational support and change participation. *Journal of Change Management*, 14(3), 361–383.

Gabris, G. T., Golembiewski, R. T., & Ihrke, D. M. (2001). Leadership credibility, board relations, and administrative innovation at the local government level. *Journal of Public Administration Research & Theory*, 11(1), 89–108.

Gilley, A., Dixon, P., & Gilley, J. W. (2008). Characteristics of leadership effectiveness: Implementing change and driving innovation in organizations. *Human Resource Development Quarterly, 19*(2), 153–169.

Greenberg. (1987). A Taxonomy of organizational justice theories. *Academy of Management Review, 12*(1), 9–22.

Gupta, Y. P., & Somers, T. M. (1992). The measurement of manufacturing flexibility. *European Journal of Operational Research, 60*(2), 166–182.

Heckmann, N., Steger, T., & Dowling, M. (2016). Organizational capacity for change, change experience, and change project performance. *Journal of Business Research, 69*(2), 777–784.

Holt, D. T., Armenakis, A. A., Feild, H. S., & Harris, S. G. (2007). Readiness for organizational change: The systematic development of a scale. *The Journal of Applied Behavioral Science, 43*(2), 232–255.

Hon, A. H. Y., Bloom, M., & Crant, J. M. (2014). Overcoming resistance to change and enhancing creative performance. *Journal of Management, 40*(3), 919–941.

Hope-Hailey, V., & Balogun, J. (2002). Devising context sensitive approaches to change: The example of Glaxo Wellcome. *Long Range Planning, 35*, 153–178.

Judge, W., & Douglas, T. (2009). Organizational change capacity: A systematic development of a scale. *Journal of Organizational Change Management, 22*(6), 635–649.

Judge, W. Q., & Elenkov, D. (2005). Organizational capacity for change and environmental performance: An empirical assessment of Bulgarian firms. *Journal of Business Research, 58*(7), 893–901.

Judge, W. Q., Naoumova, I., & Douglas, T. (2009). Organizational capacity for change and firm performance in a transition economy. *The International Journal of Human Resource Management, 20*(8), 1737–1752.

Kickul, J., Lester, S. W., & Finkl, J. (2002). Promise breaking during radical organizational change: Do justice interventions make a difference? *Journal of Organizational Behavior, 23*(4), 469–488.

Klarner, P., Probst, G., & Soparnot, R. (2007). *From change to the management organizational change capacity: A conceptual approach*. Retrieved February 3, 2015, from http://archive-ouverte.unige.ch/unige:5739

Kleingeld, A., Van Mierlo, H., & Arenas, L. (2011). The effect of goal setting on group performance: A meta-analysis. *Journal of Applied Psychology, 96*(6), 1289–1304.

Klonsky, E. J. (2010, September 10). *How to support your staff*. Retrieved November 16, 2015, from http://www.inc.com/guides/2010/09/how-to-support-your-staff.html

Kotter, J. P. (1996). *Leading change*. Boston, MA: Harvard Business Review Press.

Kotter, J. P., & Schlesinger, L. A. (1979). Choosing strategies for change. *Harvard Business Review, 86*(7/8), 130–139.

Kunze, F., Boehm, S., & Bruch, H. (2013). Age, resistance to change, and job performance. *Journal of Managerial Psychology, 28*(7/8), 741–760.

Lawrence, P. R. (1954). How to deal with resistance to change. *Harvard Business Review, 32*(3), 49–57.

Leventhal, G. S. (1980). What should be done with equity theory? New approaches to the study of fairness in social relationships. In K. Gergen, M. Greenberg, & R. Willis (Eds.), *Social exchange: Advances in theory and research* (pp. 27–55). New York, NY: Plenum Press.

Lines, R. (2007). Using power to install strategy: The relationships between expert power, position power, influence tactics and implementation success. *Journal of Change Management, 7*(2), 143–170.

Llopis, G. (2012, July 16). *6 things that will make you (and your manager) a better leader*. Retrieved November 16, 2015, from http://www.forbes.com/sites/glennllopis/2012/07/16/6-things-that-will-make-you-and-your-manager-a-better-leader/

Loeser, H., O'Sullivan, P., & Irby, D. M. (2007). Leadership lessons from curricular change at the University of California, San Francisco, School of Medicine. *Academic Medicine, 82*(4), 324–330.

Logan, M. S., & Ganster, D. C. (2007). The effects of empowerment on attitudes and performance: The role of social support and empowerment beliefs. *Journal of Management Studies, 44*(8), 1523–1550.

Luchman, J. N., & González-Morales, M. G. (2013). Demands, control and support: A meta-analytic review of work characteristics interrelationships. *Journal of Occupational Health Psychology, 18*(1), 37–52.

Mabin, V. J., Forgeson, S., & Green, L. (2001). Harnessing resistance: Using the theory of constraints to assist change management. *Journal of European Industrial Training, 25*(2/3/4), 168–191.

Mansell, A., Brough, P., & Cole, K. (2006). Stable predictors of job satisfaction, psychological strain, and employee retention: An evaluation of organizational change within the New Zealand customs service. *International Journal of Stress Management, 13*(1), 84–107.

McCracken, M., & McIvor, R. (2013). Transforming the HR function through outsourced shared services: Insights from the public sector. *The International Journal of Human Resource Management, 24*(8), 1685–1707.

McGuiness, T., & Morgan, R. E. (2005). The effect of market and learning orientation on strategy dynamics: The contributing effect of organizational change capability. *European Journal of Marketing, 39*(11/12), 1306–1326.

Meyer, C., & Stensaker, I. (2006). Developing capacity for change. *Journal of Change Management, 6*(2), 217–230.

Miller, K. I., & Monge, P. R. (1986). Participation, satisfaction, and productivity: A meta-analytic review. *Academy of Management Journal, 29*(4), 727–753.

Mor Barak, M. E., Travis, D. J., Pyun, H., & Xie, B. (2009). The impact of supervision on worker outcomes: A meta-analysis. *Social Service Review, 83*(1), 3–32.

Neves, P. (2011). Building commitment to change: The role of perceived supervisor support and competence. *European Journal of Work and Organizational Psychology, 20*(4), 437–450.

Ng, T. W. H., & Sorensen, K. L. (2008). Toward a further understanding of the relationships between perceptions of support and work attitudes. *Group & Organization Management, 33*(3), 243–268.

Oreg, A. (2006). Personality, context, and resistance to organizational change. *European Journal of Work and Organizational Psychology, 15*(1), 73–101.

Oreg, S. (2003). Resistance to change: Developing an individual differences measure. *Journal of Applied Psychology, 88*(4), 680–693.

Oxtoby, B., McGuiness, T., & Morgan, R. (2002). Developing organizational change capability. *European Management Journal, 20*(3), 310–320.

Piderit, S. K. (2000). Rethinking resistance and recognizing ambivalence: A multidimensional view of attitudes toward an organizational change. *Academy of Management Review, 25*(4), 783–794.

Pillai, R., Kohles, J. C., Bligh, M. C., Carsten, M. K., & Brodowsky, G. (2011). Leadership in "Confucian Asia": A three-country study of justice, trust, and transformational leadership. *Organization Management Journal*, 8(4), 242–259.

Posner, A. Z., & Kouzes, J. M. (1988). Relating leadership and credibility. *Psychological Reports*, 63, 527–530.

Rousseau, D. M. (1989). Psychological and implied contracts in organizations. *Employee Responsibilities and Rights Journal*, 2(2), 121–139.

Sagan, C. (1996). *The demon-haunted world: Science as a candle in the dark*. New York, NY: Random House.

Saruhan, N. (2014). The role of corporate communication and perception of justice during organizational change process. *Business and Economics Research Journal*, 5(4), 143–166.

Soparnot, R. (2011). The concept of organizational change capacity. *Journal of Organizational Change Management*, 24(5), 640–661.

Staber, U., & Sydow, J. (2002). Organizational adaptive capacity: A structuration perspective. *Journal of Management Inquiry*, 11(4), 408–424.

Stinglhamber, F., & Vandenberghe, C. (2003). Organizations and supervisors as sources of support and targets of commitment: A longitudinal study. *Journal of Organizational Behavior*, 24(3), 251–270.

Sverke, M., Hellgren, J., Näswall, K., Göransson, S., & Öhrming, J. (2008). Employee participation in organizational change: Investigating the effects of proactive vs. reactive implementation of downsizing in Swedish hospitals. *Zeitschrift für Personalforschung*, 22(2), 111–129.

Thibaut, J. W., & Walker, L. (1975). *Procedural justice: A psychological analysis*. Hillsdale, NJ: Erlbaum.

Tsoukas, H., & Chia, R. (2002). On organizational becoming: Rethinking organizational change. *Organization Science*, 13(5), 567–582.

Tyler, T. R., & De Cremer, D. (2005). Process-based leadership: Fair procedures and reactions to organizational change. *The Leadership Quarterly*, 16(4), 529–545.

Van Dierendonck, D., & Jacobs, G. (2002). Survivors and victims, a meta-analytical review of fairness and organizational commitment after downsizing. *British Journal of Management*, 23(1), 96–109.

Vidal, M. (2007). Manufacturing empowerment? 'Employee involvement' in the labour process after Fordism. *Socio-Economic Review*, 5, 197–232.

Viswesvaran, C., & Ones, D. S. (2002). Examining the construct of organizational justice: A meta-analytic evaluation of relations with work attitudes and behaviors. *Journal of Business Ethics*, 38(3), 193–203.

Wagner, J. A. (1994). Participation's effects on performance and satisfaction: A reconsideration of research evidence. *Academy of Management Review*, 19(2), 312–330.

Wagner, J. A., & Lepine, J. A. (1999). Effects of participation on performance and satisfaction: Additional meta-analytic evidence. *Psychological Reports*, 84(3), 719–725.

Wagner, J. A., Leana, C. R., Locke, E. A., & Schweiger, D. M. (1997). Cognitive and motivational frameworks in U.S. research on participation: A meta-analysis of primary effects. *Journal of Organizational Behavior*, 18(1), 49–65.

7 Examining the Story of Change
Part III

Introduction

This chapter handles the last part of the 'Story of Change,' presenting the scientific evidence base of the final six assumptions:

> *"It's all about behavior. Organizational culture can be an effective tool for stimulating performance, but it's difficult—and time-consuming—to change the organizational culture. However, goal setting combined with feedback is a powerful tool for change leaders. Employee commitment to change is an essential component of a successful change initiative, and commitment is positively correlated with performance. Financial incentives are an effective way to encourage and improve performance. Self-managing teams perform better in realizing change than traditionally managed teams."*

In contrast to the previous two chapters and in addition to Chapter 4, we start with a clarification on some methodological issues regarding the assumptions about organizational culture.

Problematic Case: Qualitative Approaches, Theoretical Foundations, and Culture

While carefully following the steps described in Chapter 4 (Methodology), the team of researchers assigned to finding evidence for the two claims related to organizational culture was faced with two interesting dilemmas. The first dilemma relates to the fact that *culture* is used as an all-purpose term. Second, there is disagreement in the academic world about whether the phenomena implied by the wide scope of the term *culture* can be captured in questionnaires and quantitatively analyzed in a way that is meaningful.

First, we will expound on the dilemma of *culture* as an all-purpose word. Generally, it is used to imply a wide range of forces, both tangible and intangible, that steer or influence the behavior of individuals in groups or groups as a whole. Culture is often reified and given agency, meaning it is attributed with an external causal influence on behavior. It may also be used to directly imply collective behavior, thoughts, and feelings. Often organizational culture typologies are made or cross-cultural differences between organizations are analyzed based on a limited set of parameters—all under the banner of studying culture.

The claims or assumptions related to culture in this book have been formulated in the broadest possible sense with no preconceived notion, approach, or framework in mind, with the intention of arriving at an overall conclusion about how the concept of culture is applied. The team of assessors was faced with the dilemma that there is little consensus in the academic literature about what organizational culture really is. Formulating inclusion criteria and building a suitable search string for the databases proved to be a complex endeavor, more so than with some of the other assumptions formulated in this book, not because there was too little research in which words such as *culture* or *cultural* were used but rather because there was too much. When closely scrutinized, such studies often assumed or implied very different things and therefore were difficult to compare. So although the initial searches with key words related to organizational culture yielded many results, many proved to be of little or no use to us. One of the main reasons for this was the lack of consensus on what culture is and how it relates to actual behavior. Similar to what is seen in everyday practice, even in the literature, the word *culture* is widely used without proper definition.

This led to the second dilemma. It is generally accepted that to study effects, phenomena have to be narrowed down to quantifiable elements, counted, and compared. Social science researchers are careful to select relevant parameters and operationalize and analyze according to clear psychometric standards. That is the recognized approach. But this can become a problem if the notion under investigation implies a wide range of contextual factors, both visible and invisible. Organizational culture may imply processes, group dynamics, the clothes people wear to work, mannerisms, norms and values, underlying assumptions, unwritten rules and explicit agreements, as well as behavioral drivers, and so on. Different measures focus on different parameters as deemed relevant by the researcher but also narrows them down in such a way that they can hardly be described by the broader term *culture*. In similar fashion culture change interventions may imply many different things. Does the intervention focus on emphasizing new values (e.g., a switch to a more suitable type of culture (from a family culture to a market culture or on aligning unwritten rules with explicit agreements)? Or is the focus on very specific levers of change (incentives, structure, processes, etc.) with the intent that this will eventually change the culture? In practice, it can and does mean all those things. But it is clear that each case must be considered individually together with a critical appraisal of the theoretical foundations that the researchers are building on or on which an intervention is based before all the studies that include the term *culture* or *cultural* as an adjective can be lumped together. And in view of this, it is prudent to place more emphasis and importance on thorough qualitative case studies in organizations including (rather than eliminating) as much context as possible because these studies will provide us with the most information on what is actually happening. As indicated in Chapter 4 (Methodology), all research adheres to a set of generic inclusion criteria that place a strong emphasis on quantitative research. Even if a qualitative study were to be included for purposes described earlier, and that study scored sufficiently on all criteria as defined in this methodology, based on the appraisal, it would never reach a level higher than D.

The REA methodology is not an end in itself but á method designed to filter academic articles in a way that is both objective and reproducible to be able to draw conclusions about effects based on a thorough assessment of the content. In view of the problematic nature of the culture construct (i.e., the murky relationship between culture and actual behavior, persistent circular reasoning, measurability, etc.), the team assigned to assessing academic articles related to organizational culture slightly deviated from this method, with the risk that some researchers' individual preferences and theoretical backgrounds could come into play. Search strings were built, more than 1,000 articles were scanned, appraisals were made, but equal weight was given to describing and identifying the many different theoretical approaches that can be taken toward organizational culture and its assumed relationship with organizational change, organizational performance, and human behavior in general.

Because the term *culture* is so commonplace and important in actual change management practice, two claims were formulated to serve as a basis for further research and exploration:

- Organizational culture change is time-consuming and difficult.
- Organizational culture is related to performance.

'Changing Organizational Culture Is Time-Consuming and Difficult'*

Introduction

When there is a need to change the more persistent behavioral patterns of groups of employees, organizational culture change may be attempted. But what do managers and consultants mean when they talk about organizational culture? A quick search on Google with the terms *organizational culture* and *change management* takes you to thousands of Web sites and blogs by experts, gurus, and business leaders, all giving different descriptions of how to change organizational culture. They do seem to agree on one thing: that it is a difficult endeavor. And tangible results will take a long time to manifest. In general, when the adjective *cultural* is added to *behavioral change*, it almost directly implies that this kind of group behavior is more resistant to change. We want to examine if this is really the case, and if so, why.

What Is Meant by Organizational Culture?

In 1984, Allaire and Firsirotu noted 164 definitions of organizational culture. It is used as an explanation for almost anything that is poorly understood in an organization. Often culture is treated as an independent variable (Smircich, 1983) that influences the behavior of the workforce in unseen ways, almost like a superindividual who affects the behavior of each individual employee from above (Greenwood, 1994). This assumption poses the clear and present danger of false explanations and/or circular reasoning (culture as a synonym for behavior to explain behavior). The epistemological problem of how culture relates to actual (group or individual) behavior has so far not been solved (Verheggen, 2005). What we are dealing with here is a clear-cut reification fallacy; that is, culture, which is an abstraction, is treated as a real thing. Not only that, but this abstraction is then given agency, an independent causal influence over individual and group behavior.

Smircich (1983) noted that organizational culture is also treated as an internal variable; that is, organizations themselves are seen as cultures or 'culture-producing phenomena' (e.g., Tichy, 1982, in Smircich, 1983, p. 344). Culture serves as the context of different organizational elements put together or as "social or normative glue that holds an organization together" (e.g., Tichy, 1982, in Smircich, 1983, p. 344). Again the way researchers tackle the problem of how culture relates to actual behavior within this perspective varies widely.

When it comes to organizational culture *change*, more problems arise. However, we try to tackle the issue. How can you change something that does not really exist, yet is a reified super-identity? Or how can you change something that consists of so many factors, known and unknown, and that in itself is part of a multitude of larger systems? And what is the rationale behind trying to change something that is not related to actual behavior or is very complex and poorly understood? We are left with only one conclusion: that organizational culture change is difficult and time-consuming, if feasible at all.

Search Strategy

Relevant databases were searched using key words such as *organizational culture* and *change*. We chose a broad search strategy. Earlier attempts with search strings more closely related to the question were unsuccessful as no relevant articles were found. After sifting through the abstracts, we finally included four articles. We followed an extra search string using key words such as *innovation culture*, *safety culture*, and *market culture* to look for common themes and interventions that might falsify our assumption that organizational culture change is always difficult. We therefore included another four articles. Furthermore we snowballed, based on leads in the articles we scanned, leading to the inclusion of another five articles, totaling 13, consisting of several meta-analyses, systematic reviews, and a few qualitative case studies to gain insight into the assumed mechanisms of organizational culture change.

Assessing Quality and Relevance

To test this assumption we sought studies that specifically address the difficulty of organizational culture change or, to falsify this assumption, studies that exemplify how organizational culture change can be realized quickly and easily. We found none. In all of the studies about organizational culture change under review, difficulty is implicitly or explicitly assumed. Whether one defines *culture* as "a pattern of basic assumptions . . ." (Schein, 1996, p. 111), "the collective programming of the mind . . ." (Hofstede, 1980, p. 25), or in any other way, if it was easy to change, it was probably *not* the organizational culture that was changed. In the words of Shier, Khodyakov, Cohen, Zimmerman, and Saliba (2014), "Culture change interventions are, by their nature, complex. Most culture change interventions target more than one domain of culture change, and full, consistent implementation of care processes may require long time periods" (p. 14).

To take a closer look at the practice of organizational culture change, how it is researched and what makes it so difficult, we focused on studies on, for example, *changing* or *developing* hospital safety culture (e.g., Clay-Williams, Nosrati, Cunningham, Hillman, & Braithwaite, 2014; Groves, 2014) or innovativeness culture (e.g., Leong & Anderson, 2012; Rubera & Kirca, 2012). Cross-cultural organizational culture research, mainly but not exclusively based on Hofstede's (1980) cultural parameters, was excluded. The emphasis in these kinds of studies is on mapping differences and not necessarily on change.

The best way to investigate the *actual practice* of organizational culture change would be the extensive case study because those types of studies do not just focus on preconceived parameters as captured in a questionnaire but often take a broader perspective, allowing more contextual factors to be included. From the perspective of an REA, these kinds of studies have a lower level of evidence (both D). But, even if we do include them, the qualitative studies based on the paradigm set forth by Schein (1996), for example, inherently suggest that sustainable culture change is always difficult because durable change requires changing underlying assumptions that are taken for granted and thus hard to decipher. So research, interventions, or approaches genuinely based on Schein's framework will always be thorough and long-term endeavors.

We also included quantitative studies and meta-analyses. These do not reveal the mechanisms of organizational culture change as extensively as a qualitative case study does. But they may provide insight into specific cause-and-effect relations, what works and what does not, and generalizability. The problem with the quantitative approach to culture is that it tends to oversimplify what is generally understood as culture, a complex phenomenon that includes many contextual factors that are unique to a specific organization. What happens is that culture is either reduced to certain parameters, as Hofstede (1980) does with his national culture dimensions, or to a small set of types, such as those based on Cameron and Quinn (2011). Schein has the following to say about parameters of culture: "Not only does this create fuzzy theory and research that is made significant only by massaging the data statistically, but the results are often useless to the practitioner" (1996, p. 232). Then there are the often-used typologies such as adhocracy, hierarchy, clan, or market culture (Cameron & Quinn, 2011). But here we run the risk of oversimplification and stereotyping organizations into neatly fitting categories with little relevance. However, most of the meta-analyses we found used Cameron and Quinn's (2011) or Quinn and Rohrbaugh's (1983) typology derived from the Competing Values Framework (e.g., Büschgens, Bausch, & Balkin, 2013; Hartnell, Ou, & Kinicki, 2011). Probably because it is accompanied by an easy-to-use, validated questionnaire (OCAI), which makes researching a complex phenomenon such as organizational culture all the more manageable, and makes the studies comparable through meta-analyses, but does not do justice to the often well-written introductions about the complexity of the phenomenon that is organizational culture.

We have included a few qualitative studies that are very insightful in understanding how an organizational culture develops and how it can be understood to affect behavior in the context of organizational change. Like many others authors, Heracleous (2001) starts with this: "Understanding culture in any particular context, however, is not an easy task" (p. 426). If understanding is not easy, it seems fair to conclude that influencing it might be an even more difficult task. Heracleous's study "illustrates how an organization's cultural assumptions develop historically, underpin values and beliefs, and have subtle but nevertheless pervasive effects on organizational actors' interpretations and actions, as well as on organizational arrangements" (p. 439). What is very clear from this quotation is that Heracleous uses Schein's paradigm to understand organizational cultural phenomena, whereby assumptions underpin values that in turn have a pervasive effect on observable behavior. By using this framework, culture bottlenecks of organizational change become understandable and predictable. In Heracleous's own words his study ". . . illustrates empirically why organizational cultures are so inertial and resistant to change" (p. 440). Insights derived from these kinds of studies might help to tackle resistance to change more proactively and smartly by aligning change with how people think and what drives them (assumptions and values). Heracleous noted that ". . . suggestions generally helpful to change programs but which in this case challenged cultural 'sacred cows' of the organization were ignored" (p. 442). This explains the often-heard complaint that although a plan may seem rational, somehow some plans just don't seem to land in the organization because they don't relate to how employees experience reality and what they deem as important (so-called sacred cows).

So these kinds of empirical studies are relevant if they are conducted thoroughly and through the lens of a developed paradigm. But, being qualitative in approach, they score a lower level of evidence. Heracleous (2001) scored a D. Leong and Anderson (2012) in contrast use the same paradigm but score an F. We cannot draw broadly generalizable conclusions based on these studies. When we searched for quantitative studies on (the difficulty of) organizational culture change, we were confronted with the problem of how to quantify a polythetic (or even *reified*, as some critics proclaim) construct such as organizational culture in a meaningful way. Schein (1996) already expressed his doubts in the following manner:

> . . . [W]hen I see my colleagues inventing questionnaires to 'measure' culture, I feel that they are simply not seeing what is there, and this is particularly dangerous when one is dealing with a social force that is invisible yet very powerful. We are in grave danger of not seeing our own culture, our assumptions about methods, about theory, about what is important to study or not study, and, in that process, pay too much attention to only what suits our needs. (p. 239)

This does not stop researchers from trying to quantify that which by its very nature is hard to quantify. We are left with a plethora of scales and questionnaires, but many put together pragmatically, opportunistically, or for convenience sake. Very often researchers make use of Quinn and Rohrbaugh's (1983) Competing Values Framework and corresponding questionnaire. This enables them to classify an organizational culture as either an adhocracy, hierarchy, clan, or market culture. However limited these types may be, from the point of relevance and providing concrete levers for change, they are tested and proved somewhat or moderately valid (for a critical review of the framework, read Hartnell et al.'s 2011 meta-analysis). They also make it possible to compare studies and hopefully draw more generalizable conclusions. The quantitative studies we found, although scoring higher on level of evidence, were markedly less relevant for accepting or refuting our assumption. In the introductions of many articles, it is either casually assumed that organizational culture change is difficult (with or without reference to other authors) or disregarded. What we do sometimes find within studies using a quantitative paradigm to organizational culture is the idea that culture can be established or implemented instrumentally . . . as a tool. For example Büschgens et al. (2013) recommend:

> Therefore, managers that follow a (radical) innovation strategy should establish a developmental culture in their organization. If innovation

rather represents a minor aspect of the firm's long-term objectives, the efficiency-orientated rational culture or group culture may also be the right choice. (p. 763)

Here researchers and managers run the risk of falling prey to the reification fallacy when the kind of concrete behavioral patterns implied with the label, abstraction, or type used are not or only partially clear. Between the lines we might read in the previous quote that you can relatively easily choose a culture that best fits a manager's purpose! This is clearly a mistake, though. Nowhere is evidence presented to show that organizational culture change is easy. What these studies (e.g., Büschgens et al., 2013) do is establish relationships or correlations between culture types or culture as measured and certain organizational outcomes, that is, performance. Organizational culture can change rapidly, for example, by relocation (Christersson & Rothe, 2012) but not in a choose-and-pick way and not necessarily leading to the desired behavior. Groves's (2014) systematic review is illustrative of the many problems still to be solved in establishing a relationship to (hospital safety) culture and (patient safety) outcomes. She found no relation. And one of the reasons she gives is the scarcity of valid and reliable measures that operationalize culture in a relevant manner. Another reason is the lack of coherent theories linking culture as measured to actual behavior on the work floor and desired organizational outcomes (see next assumption on the assumed relationship between culture and performance in this chapter).

It's important to note here that the kind of quantitative and meta-analytical studies included (although they score higher levels of evidence) do not directly tackle the assumption under investigation. They deal with establishing or refuting static relationships between cultural parameters or types and do not directly deal with how difficult organizational culture change might be. At best they give us an indication of the intricacies of working on the organizational culture change project.

Main Findings

1 *Organizational culture change is difficult and time-consuming (Levels D, B, B, and F, not extensive or illustrative).*

"The results indicated that the underlying beliefs, values, and worldviews of the organization seem to have been resistant to change . . ." (Faull, Kalliath, & Smith, 2004, p. 40—a qualitative case study Level D).

> Studies varied widely in scope and outcomes. Most addressed more than one culture change domain; resident direction, home environment, and close relationships were most common. Few studies measured culture change implementation, but most used validated tools to measure

outcomes. Although few studies reported negative outcomes, there was little consistent evidence of positive effects.

> (Shier et al., 2014, p. 6—a systematic review level B, relevant to nursing homes).

"Common findings show the difficulty of introducing large-scale interventions, and that effective leadership and clinical champions, adequate financial and educational resources, and dedicated promotional activities appear to be common factors in successful system-wide change" (Clay-Williams et al., 2014, abstract—a meta-analysis Level B, relevant to health care). "Building an innovative culture is challenging in a large organization, but progress has been achieved. Sustaining effort over time, utilizing a variety of approaches and developing positive sub-cultures among motivated staff have been found to be beneficial" (Leong & Anderson, 2012, abstract—a qualitative case study Level F).

Synthesis of Evidence

The volume of scientific literature on organizational culture is vast. The bulk theorizes about what organizational culture actually is, how it can be measured, and so on. And a great deal has been written on how organizational culture might be changed. Much less research is published on thorough and rigorous empirical tests on the effects of organizational culture change interventions. Some studies cast doubt about whether there is a clear-cut relationship between culture and performance in the first place, thereby placing a bomb under the rationale for organizational culture change (see the assumption on culture and performance). There is widespread agreement that organizational culture change is a complex and difficult (if possible at all) from whatever perspective or paradigm. Our findings do seem to support that, above and beyond what common sense and intuitive appeal tell us.

Conclusion

Based on the empirical studies included in our research, we conclude that there is some support for the claim that changing organizational culture is difficult and time-consuming. From the perspective of theory, common sense, or intuitive appeal, it might seem undisputed, although it is much harder to be empirically sure because culture is an elusive and polythetic construct.

Practical Reflections

The practical implication of our findings on culture is that careful analysis of the problem is warranted before deciding to go ahead with an organizational culture intervention. When managers or employees 'hide' behind the hazy construct of culture, it is essential to refine this and comprehend the real, specific problem. First, some problems might be relatively easy to solve. Employees can change their behavior individually or collectively if the rationale is clear and the process is seen to be fair or if there are no other options. Purposive interventions then might shape new collective behavior, although it remains unclear whether this actually changes organizational culture. Labeling the problem as a cultural problem might be setting yourself up for failure. What's more, notwithstanding the large volume of literature written and still being written on the topic, we do not know exactly how culture is related to actual behavior (see the next assumption concerning organizational culture and performance).

'Organizational Culture Is Related to Performance'*

Introduction

Since Pettigrew in his 1979 article "On Studying Organization Cultures" first proposed the idea that so-called soft aspects of management can either contribute or hinder an organization's competitiveness and performance, the popularity of the organizational culture concept has grown without interruption. Pettigrew saw culture as a root concept with offshoots in the shape, for example, of symbols, language, ideology, rituals, and myths. In developing his ideas, he drew heavily on anthropology, as did most of his scientific contemporaries. Since then, several best sellers, such as *In Search of Excellence* (Peters & Waterman, 1982), *Built to Last* (Collins & Porras, 1997), and *Good to Great* (Collins, 2001) followed in Pettigrew's footsteps in identifying culture as a distinct characteristic of high-performance organizations (HPO). De Waal (2007) describes such organizations as follows:

> A HPO empowers people and gives them freedom to decide and act by devolving decision making authority and giving autonomy to organizational members to operate, within clearly established boundaries and constraints of what is allowed and what not. A HPO establishes clear, strong and meaningful core values and makes sure they are widely shared within the company. A HPO develops and maintains a performance-driven culture by fighting inertia and complacency, challenging the enemies of a winning mindset, focusing strongly on getting high excellence in whatever the organization does, and stimulating people to achieve high performance. A HPO creates a culture of transparency, openness and trust by establishing a shared understanding, openly sharing information and fostering informality. A HPO creates a shared identity and a sense of community by 'uniting the tribe', cultivating a feeling of 'corporateness' and adopting and fostering an 'all for one, one for all' mentality. (p. 184)

The underlying assumption is that culture is not only related to performance in a very direct way but also that culture can be managed or changed for the purpose of contributing to organizational goals. Advocates of the concept, however, typically resort to vague and abstract notions when discussing it; De Waal's (2007) references to a "culture of transparency," "shared understanding," and "a feeling of corporateness" (p. 184) are good examples. As mentioned earlier, our claim is that organization culture change is time-consuming and difficult. So, in spite of the strong appeal of the concept of the culture–performance connection in organizations, a closer examination and critical appraisal of the existing literature seemed to us to be warranted.

What Is Meant by Culture in Its Relationship to Performance?

We found some support in the literature for the claim that changing organizational culture is difficult and time-consuming. However, culture is a highly illusive construct. Indeed, whether it is defined more cognitively as the "collective programming of the mind" (Hofstede, 1980, p. 25), or as a "pattern of basic assumptions" (Schein, 1990, p. 111), or seen as being embodied in practices (e.g., Voestermans & Verheggen, 2013), culture seems to be inherently hard to define.

There are many reasons for changing an organization's culture, but the most common one is a desire to change the culture to one that is better aligned with, or best suited to, the organization's strategy and desired organizational outcomes. The perception is that certain cultures seem to be of a destructive kind and need to be eliminated: Fear, bullying, or arrogance cultures would be examples. Others seem to be more constructive and are often aspired to: innovation, safety, or performance-driven cultures, for instance. While still others, like market or clan cultures, seem to be dependent on, or related, or best suited to specific internal and external environments. Whatever the specifics, the idea underlying all this is that culture is related to performance, either directly or as moderated or mediated by some other variable.

Certain cultures, especially performance-driven ones, are said to characterize HPOs. But we have to be very careful here. If the actual behaviors or behavioral patterns underlying performance-driven cultures as well as the intended outcomes are not clearly specified or remain only vaguely and abstractly described (see characteristics of an HPO), there is a danger of engaging in a form of circular reasoning, or of stating the obvious, namely: Performance culture is related to performance. This kind of statement gives credence to the notion of some social researchers that culture as a construct does not have any added value in explaining and/or predicting behavior (e.g., Verheggen, 2005).

How Does the Culture–Performance Dynamic Work?

Even though organizational culture is defined (Allaire & Firsirotu, 1984), measured, described, or analyzed in a wide variety of ways, often the assumed framework of the relationship between culture and performance, both in the popular and much of the scientific management literature, can be summarized graphically, as shown in Figure 7.1. Culture here is more or less, either explicitly or implicitly, assumed to be an independent variable (Smircich, 1983). The relation between culture and performance can be straightforward or can be mediated or moderated by some other variable.

Inclusion Criteria and Search Strategy

We searched the relevant databases using key words such as *organizational culture*, *performance*, and *(organizational) outcomes* to identify empirical studies that specifically tested the assumed culture–performance correlation. Cross-cultural studies, often based on Hofstede's parameters, were usually excluded—unless they were part of a meta-analysis or systematic review—as was a large group of articles that propose or deal with prescriptive theories unsupported by empirical data.

Assessing Quality and Relevance

Our initial search yielded a total of 455 studies. After screening the abstracts for relevance, 429 studies were excluded. Most (21) of the remaining 26 studies were cross-sectional studies. We also included one systematic review. The majority (15) of the cross-sectional studies were appraised on Level E, whereas the systematic review was appraised at Level B.

Organizational culture in the included studies was mostly measured using scales based on Quinn and Rohrbaugh's (1983) Competing Values Framework, the Organizational Culture Inventory (Cooke & Lafferty,

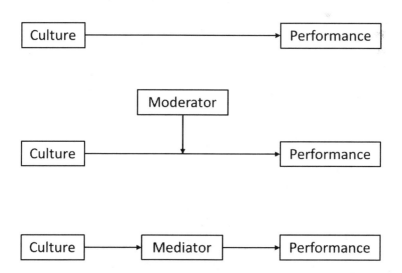

Figure 7.1 Assumed Framework of the Relationship Between Culture and Performance

1989), and the Denison Organizational Culture Survey (Denison & Neale, 1996). Because our goal was to investigate the assumed cause-and-effect relationship between culture and performance, we followed the appropriate practice, as explained in the introduction of this book, of looking for randomized controlled before-after studies on the issue. Considering the complexity—or, we would argue, the impossibility—of successfully conducting such studies on the culture in actual organizations, we usually encountered some kind of cross-sectional approach. In their search for hard quantifiable data on cause-and-effect relations, researchers have tried to capture organizational culture within the framework of off-the-shelf questionnaires, thereby ignoring all kinds of possibly relevant contextual factors that could actually constitute the very thing they are attempting to measure. As said in the previous chapter about the difficulty of organizational culture change, several students of culture and organizational culture, most notably Schein (1996), have criticized this approach for being either too narrow or completely beside the point.

Main Findings

1   *The different studies on organizational culture and performance are difficult to compare.*

When going through scientific articles on organizational culture and its presumed influence on performance outcomes, one is almost immediately confronted with such a plethora of approaches, theories, and measurement techniques that it is hard, if not impossible, to compare the studies on large scale. Take for example Acar and Acar (2014), Level D, who conducted a study in 99 Turkish hospitals and found that hierarchy culture and market culture were related to different performance outcomes. They based these culture types on the aforementioned Competing Values Framework, as did Farley, Hoenig, and Ismail (2008), Level E; Naor, Goldstein, Linderman, and Schroeder (2008), Level E; Prajogo and McDermott (2010), Level E; and Zhang, Li, and Wei (2008), Level E. Biswas (2009), Level D, on the other hand, found a relatively significant correlation between organizational culture and employee performance, but used the Denison Organizational Culture Survey. Others (Boyce, Nieminen, Gillespie, Ryan, and Denison, 2015, Level B; Chan, Schaffer, and Snape, 2004, Level E; Imran, Zahoor, and Zaheer, 2012 Level E; and Kotrba et al., 2012, Level D–) also used the Denison Organizational Culture Survey or similar instruments based on Denison's dimensions: involvement, consistency, adaptability, and mission. Mousavi, Hosseini, and Hassanpour (2015), Level E, actually found some inverse correlations: Involvement and adaptability were negatively related to performance. And these are just two approaches (Competing Values Framework and Denison Organizational Culture Survey) based on different theoretical foundations of the many we came across. Dauber (2012), Level B, in his literature review on culture and performance in the context of mergers and acquisitions (M&A) was confronted with a similar problem:

> This paper has reviewed articles in the field of M&As with a strong focus on culture, integration and performance. It has been shown that findings of existing studies are inconsistent and difficult to interpret when compared on a large scale. Three major reasons for this dissent in the field have been identified: (1) most studies treat 'integration' as an umbrella term for different acculturation strategies, which reflect completely different processes; (2) some studies measure culture at different levels of analysis, i.e. organizational vs. national culture; and (3) the definition of 'M&A success' is very broad, caused by several measurement approaches to M&A performance.
> (Dauber, 2012, p. 393)

We would like to add that in our search, we were not only confronted with a wide variety of measurement approaches to performance outcomes but to the concept of culture itself. The theories and approaches, for example, of Denison (1990), Quinn and Rohrbaugh (1981), Hofstede (1980), or Schein (1996) are all about *culture* or employ *cultural* as an adjective but are not always meant in the same way.

2 *In most studies organizational culture as measured is related to performance.*

Although this finding, with a few exceptions, does seem rather consistent across different studies, the thrust of Finding 1, namely, that these studies are very hard to compare given their different approaches, constitutes a significant disclaimer. Therefore, a generalizable conclusion that organizational culture is related to performance in a meaningful way is not justified, even though most studies point in that direction. It would in any way be either a too general or hollow conclusion to be meaningful. We also would not want to be stating the obvious, as do Uzkurt, Kumar, Kimzan and Eminoğlu:

> An innovative organizational culture is open to the risks and opportunities of innovations and new ideas. An organization which recognizes and nurtures the uniqueness of its employees and empowers the managers to follow their vision will have an innovative culture. The existence of such climates and culture will motivate and support innovation in business.
> (Uzkurt et al., 2013, p. 111)

Cross-sectional studies also do not justify a definitive conclusion that culture *causes* certain performance outcomes.

Synthesis of Evidence

In popular and scientific management literature, there is no lack of publications about organizational culture. The use of the concept in explaining organizational performance has not diminished from the moment it gained popularity after its introduction by Pettigrew in 1979 and the subsequent boost given by best sellers like *In Search of Excellence* (Peters & Waterman, 1982). However, in spite of the large amount of research and publications on the issue, much remains unclear, except for the apparent fact that culture sells. Indeed, it functions as a mystifying X factor that explains everything that organizational structure cannot. But researchers cannot come to grips with what culture actually is or what the notion is supposed to represent. Even when there is agreement on some abstract definition, the way researchers operationalize organizational culture can vary widely. This renders comparisons very difficult. It seems that drawing hard and definite conclusions based on this plethora of studies is not justified.

Conclusion

The studies included in our assessment seem to generally indicate that there is some support for the claim that organizational culture has a causal influence on organizational performance, *as measured* specifically in each study. However taking into account the problematic nature of the organizational culture construct in explaining behavior and the many definitions of the construct itself, emphasis is placed on the words *as measured*.

Practical Reflections

The finding that, in most studies, organizational culture *as measured* is related to performance, together with an appreciation of the difficulty of inter-study comparisons—given the variety of definitions and operationalizations of the construct—has several tentative implications for practice.

We do not deny the value of all the research done with the aim of better understanding the underlying mechanisms of group behavior in organizations. Social researchers from many different disciplines have made valuable contributions and offered many insights. However, we do contend that both in the management literature, and in actual practice, the concept of culture is often abused, either as a sophisticated adjective that provides a quasi-scientific allure to a specific proposition or as an all-purpose tag to describe something that is very poorly understood.

The problem with the concept of organizational culture is not that it lacks meaning but that it has too many meanings. This explains the many different approaches we came across in the management literature. At a deeper level, the concept of culture itself is of course amorphous and intractable, having been the object of study by many specialists, including philosophers and behavioral scientists who grapple interminably in search of a definite conclusion. How culture is related to equally confusing concepts such as agency and free will is the subject of unending debate. And the part played by culture in motivating individuals poses an unresolved psychosociological problem (e.g. Verheggen, 2005).

For these reasons, managers should not be satisfied with broad generalizations and vague abstractions of what is actually a complex set of patterned group behaviors within their organization. The first thing they need to do is to look beyond the abstract notions and justifications that people give for their or others' behavior. Managers have to try to take the perspective of a (cultural) psychologist with a keen eye for group dynamics and context. They might still decide to gather extra data with the help of one of the off-the-shelf culture questionnaires to gain insight into some (limited) parameters of group behavior but should always remain conscious of the fact that these instruments never capture *the* culture of a (whole) organization. At best, they throw light on some specific aspect that might be of some relevance to the question at hand—such as increasing performance, safety, or innovation.

Voestermans and Verheggen (2013) warn us that the notion of culture is often improperly used either as a label, metaphor, or excuse. Each of these carries certain risks. Managers must be mindful that certain people within subgroups of their organizations may simply be stereotyped when they're labeled as representing a certain type of culture, whereas the real people involved and what drives them get lost in metaphorical descriptions or are ignored when culture is used to cover up the true causes of a problem. Moreover, when managers try to replicate the success of some other HPO, they might be better advised to focus on what people actually *do* rather than identify the organization's culture as the cause because everybody knows that performance culture is related to performance. And such circular arguments, including those hidden behind complicated study designs and described in abstruse texts, won't help us.

'Goal Setting Combined With Feedback Is a Powerful Tool for Change Leaders'

Introduction

Goal setting and performance feedback provide change leaders with the information they need to successfully manage change and give their organizations a competitive edge in the market. The origin of this assumption seems to find its way back to the statements 'what gets measured gets done' and 'if you can't measure it, you can't manage it.' In management and business it is common knowledge that when you set clear, ambitious goals that can be expressed—and therefore measured—in numbers, you can provide performance feedback to employees to keep their behavior directed toward the right targets. As the scientist Lord Kelvin said in 1883, ". . . when you cannot measure it, when you cannot express it in numbers, your knowledge is of a meager and unsatisfactory kind . . ." (William Thomson, n.d., para 1). Setting measurable goals is therefore regarded as an important leadership skill. Most lists of 'Top X Skills Every Great Leader Needs to Succeed' in popular management books and on the Internet include goal setting and/or performance feedback. Although goal setting and feedback can be seen as two separate tools, it is widely assumed that one is effective only in combination with the other. As Gary Latham, one of the founding fathers of goal-setting theory, states:

> Both goal-setting theory and empirical research indicate that in the absence of goal setting, feedback has no effect on performance. This is because feedback is only information; its effect on action depends on how it is appraised and what decisions are made with respect to it.
> (Latham, 2009, p. 163)

In the past few decades, goal setting has become a hot topic not only in business but also in the self-help industry. There are a wide range of theories and models marketed as 'the best way' to set goals. Most managers are familiar with the acronym SMART and have learned that goals should be ambitious and challenging. However, opponents argue that for complex tasks, goal setting may impair performance (Csikszentmihalyi, 1998) and that by simply focusing on an outcome without openness to exploration, goal setting may seriously hinder personal and organizational learning. In addition, it is argued that feedback may not always be effective. In fact, several researchers have pointed out that feedback interventions have highly variable effects on performance—in some situations feedback improves performance, but in other situations it has no apparent effect or even harms performance (Kluger & DeNisi, 1996). Clearly opinions vary, but most managers and academics tend to agree that setting goals, measuring results, and providing feedback during organizational change is a powerful tool for change leaders. What does the scientific evidence tells us about this claim?

What Is Meant by Goal Setting and Feedback?

In the personal sphere of life, a goal is simply something you are trying to do or achieve. In the domain of management, a goal can be defined as an observable or measurable organizational outcome to be achieved within a fixed timeframe. Subsequently, goal setting is the process of consciously deciding goal(s) you or the organization want(s) to accomplish and within what timeframe. Goal setting is one of the most researched topics in the field of industrial and organizational psychology. Goal-setting theory was jointly developed by Edwin Locke and Gary Latham (1990). Its basic assumption is that specific and challenging goals along with appropriate feedback contribute to higher and better task performance.

Feedback is the process in which the result or effect of an action is returned (fed back) to modify or improve the next action. It is often defined as "actions taken by (an) external agent(s) to provide information regarding some aspect(s) of one's task performance" (Kluger & DeNisi, 1996, p. 255). The most common form of feedback is *knowledge of results* interventions, in which information about an outcome is provided (e.g., 'your average typing speed is 100 words per minute' [p. 255]), but feedback can also contain information about how a result is achieved (e.g., 'you do not use your thumb for typing' [p. 255]).

How Does It Work?

Basically, goal setting and feedback are presumed to positively affect performance by providing the necessary information and motivation regarding one's work performance. There are two underlying mechanisms that can explain the superiority of combining feedback and goal setting over goal setting alone, namely (1) outcome-related and (2) process-related feedback.

Outcome-related feedback assumes that informing an employee about the discrepancies between the goal and his or her current performance will motivate the employee to put more effort into achieving the goal. It is suggested, however, that the gap between performance and the goal should not be so large that it reduces the employee's self-esteem and commitment to reaching the goal (Neubert, 1998). Process-related feedback, on the other hand, enhances performance by providing information that allows an employee to evaluate to what extent his or her previous strategies or behaviors were successful in attempting to reach the goal. Therefore, goal-setting theory states that employees provided with either process- or outcome-related feedback together with goals are likely to outperform employees who are provided with only goals.

Search Strategy

Relevant databases were searched using the key words *goal setting* and *feedback*. Studies were included for further analysis if they were related to behavioral or organizational outcomes such as motivation or performance.

Assessing Quality and Relevance

Our initial search yielded a total of 280 studies. After screening the abstracts for relevance, 230 studies were excluded. Full-text screening of the articles resulted in the exclusion of another 25 studies. Finally, after critical appraisal of the remaining 25 articles, a total of six studies were included. Five of these studies concerned meta-analyses, representing the results from more than 150 single studies. The overall quality of the meta-analyses included was moderate to high: Most of them were based on cross-sectional studies, and one included study used both a control group and a before-and-after measurement. The single study included was a well-conducted randomized controlled study.

Main Findings

1 Goal setting has a moderate positive effect on employee performance. Specifically, SMART and challenging goals lead to higher performance than easy goals, vague goals, or no goals (Level A).

Several meta-analyses have found a positive relationship between goal setting and employee performance. Specifically, SMART and challenging goals have been consistently demonstrated to have a higher impact on employee performance than easy goals, vague goals (e.g., 'do your best'), or no goals. In addition, this effect was found to be consistent across a variety of tasks, disciplines, and settings (Erez, 1977; Mento, Steel, & Karren, 1987; Tubbs, 1986).

2 Most feedback interventions have a strong positive effect on performance, but more than one-third have a negative effect on performance (Level A).

In the seminal meta-analysis by Kluger and DeNisi (1996), it was found that overall feedback strongly improves employee performance. However, in more than one-third of the cases, feedback reduces performance. This variability may be due to individual differences. For instance, performance improvement was shown to be more likely when recipients had a positive view of feedback, whereas when feedback was perceived as threatening one's self-esteem, it was found to have a lower or even negative effect. In addition, it was found that the positive effect of feedback on performance is greater if the feedback enhances motivation and stimulates learning processes (Kluger & DeNisi, 1996).

3 Employee performance increases strongly by adding feedback to goal setting (Level A).

There is strong and consistent evidence that feedback is a necessary condition for the positive goal setting–performance relationship (Erez, 1977; Kluger & DeNisi, 1996; Locke, 1968; Neubert, 1998). A possible explanation for this combined effect is that the feedback informs the employee about the discrepancy between the goal and his or her current performance, which (1) enables the employee to reflect on his or her past performance and (2) motivates the employee to put in more effort or try out an alternative strategy.

4   *The positive effect of goal setting combined with feedback is moderated by the nature of the task (Level A).*

Although there seems to be no single answer to the question of which specific task properties moderate the positive goal setting–feedback effect, it was nevertheless found that the effect on performance was considerably larger for complex tasks (Kluger & DeNisi, 1996). Presumably this is caused by the fact that simple tasks imply fewer strategic choices and for which both process- and outcome-related feedback are less important.

Synthesis of Evidence

Research on goal setting and feedback, which dates back more than 80 years, continues to be an important topic in organizational research. This has resulted in numerous meta-analytical reviews that underlie the continuous advocacy of the application of goal setting and feedback in management practice. The scientific evidence not only demonstrates that goal setting is an effective way to enhance employee performance but also that adding feedback to it is an even more effective intervention for more consistently improving organizational outcomes. Clearly, feedback may be less effective if not properly given. Although more research is needed to determine what variables moderate these effects, empirical research consistently demonstrates that feedback interventions focusing on task learning or task motivation have a consistent, strong effect on employee performance.

Conclusion

The scientific research literature unequivocally supports the claim that goal setting combined with providing feedback is a powerful tool for change leaders. We therefore conclude that, based on the evidence found, this claim is very likely to be true.

Practical Reflections

The scientific evidence found regarding both goal setting and feedback provides support for our widespread use of goal-setting techniques and the implementation of numerous feedback loops within management processes. SMART goals, feedback loops, and short iterations—they all seem to be vital to an organization's performance. By managing employees around specific, concrete goals and regularly providing process- and outcome-related feedback, we can manage organizations around measurable, objective, morally neutral criteria. Of course, this also applies to change leaders, who can manage those elements that the organization highly values. However, questions regarding measuring more purposive, moral elements (those things we can't measure but need to be managed) are still relevant and do not need to be disregarded by practitioners.

The evidence tells us that feedback regarding these criteria or elements is most effective when it focuses on learning and goal attainment because employees then tend to focus less on protecting their image and more on learning and mastering the task at hand. On the other hand, when feedback merely focuses on a meta-level such as praise or discouragement, or when it tends to affect someone's ego or self-esteem, one may unintentionally change an employee's focus. For example, if a task is complex or unfamiliar, telling employees they are doing it incorrectly may cause them to focus their mental energy on protecting their image (e.g., not looking incompetent), rather than on the task at hand, and subsequently impair performance (Kluger & DeNisi, 1996).

'Commitment to Change Is an Essential Component of a Successful Change Initiative'

Introduction

According to many sources on the Internet, commitment to change is considered to be one of the most important components for change to be successfully implemented. One will find quotes such as these: "If people in an organization are not committed to the change process and are not trusting of management, meaningful and lasting change will almost never occur" (Quantum Health Resources & Associates, n.d.) or "Only when your employees are committed to the change will they engage in the needed activities . . ." (Turner, 2015). These are just some of the many claims that can be found on the numerous Web sites of self-proclaimed change experts and consulting firms. However, the claim can also be found in the scientific literature. Many academics in the field of organizational behavior regard commitment to change as indicative of employees' supportive behavior toward change and therefore consider it an important predictor for successful change (Abrell-Vogel & Rowold, 2014; Herscovitch & Meyer, 2002; Jaros, 2010; Meyer, Srinivas, Lal, & Topolnytsky, 2007; Seo et al., 2012). Jaros (2010) argues that ". . . managers who can get their subordinates to commit to new goals, programs, policies, and procedures may stand a better chance of having these critical business activities successfully implemented" (p. 79). This all suggests that the claim is not only an important professional insight but also firmly grounded in literature.

What Is Meant by Commitment to Change?

Being committed means that you are willing to give your time and energy to something (or someone) that you believe in. *Commitment to change* is often defined as "a force (mind set) that binds an individual to a course of action deemed necessary for the successful implementation of a change initiative" (Herscovitch & Meyer, 2002, p. 475). It is assumed to be a multidimensional construct—rather than a single, undifferentiated psychological state—that can be divided into three distinctive components: affective (attitudinal) commitment, normative commitment, and continuance commitment.

Affective commitment is the degree of emotional attachment with the organization or the change project (Shum, Bove, & Auh, 2008). This component reflects an employee's emotional attachment to the organization and is one of the most studied variables in organizational behavior research.

Normative commitment is driven by moral obligations, suggesting that employees attach themselves to an organization or a change initiative because they feel it is the right way to behave (Herscovitch & Meyer, 2002).

Continuance commitment, the third component, is driven by an employee's belief that leaving the company (or a change project) would have negative consequences in terms of status, pay, responsibility, or career opportunities (Herscovitch & Meyer, 2002).

In short, employees may feel the need to support change because they want to (affective commitment), ought to (normative commitment), or have to (continuance commitment).

How Does It Work?

Commitment to change is assumed to 'bind' people to the change initiative—they support the change because of the benefits and advantages it brings to both the individual and the organization, thereby wanting to go the extra mile to make sure the change goals will be met. Employees who are committed therefore work harder and more passionately, increasing their overall job performance. Commitment is seen as "the glue that provides the vital bond between people and change goals" (Conner, 1992, p. 148).

Search Strategy

To gain an overview of the relevant literature on commitment in general, relevant databases were searched using the key words *organizational commitment* and *performance*. In a second search, the key word *commitment* was combined with *organizational change* to identify studies in which commitment was researched in the context of organizational change.

Assessing Quality and Relevance

Our search that focused on organizational commitment and performance yielded more than 1,000 studies. Filtering for meta-analyses and systematic reviews, our search yielded 46 results. Screening the abstracts for relevance led to the exclusion of 40 studies. Critical appraisal of the remaining six studies did not lead to more exclusions. The overall quality of the studies included was moderate to high. None of the meta-analyses were based on controlled studies, and only one was based on studies that used a before-and-after measure. The meta-analyses represented results from more than 200 single studies.

The second search, in which the key word *organizational change* was added, resulted in 342 single studies and three meta-analyses. After screening the abstracts for relevance, 327 single studies and one meta-analysis were excluded. Full-text screening of the remaining 17 studies resulted in the exclusion of another 11 single studies. Critical appraisal of the remaining studies led to the exclusion of another meta-analysis. The methodological quality of the four single studies included was moderate to low—all used a cross-sectional design. The meta-analysis was based on 17 single studies that were also cross-sectional in nature, and was of moderate quality.

Main Findings: Commitment and Performance

1   There is a positive relationship between affective commitment and performance; the effect, however, is small (Level B).

There is strong evidence that employees who feel attached to and identify with their organization perform better. However, the correlation between affective commitment and job performance is fairly small but nevertheless relevant for practice (Riketta, 2002).

2   Affective commitment is more strongly related to contextual performance than to task performance (Level B).

Job performance can be broken down into two subcategories: task performance and contextual performance. Task performance is directly linked to the organization's core business: teaching a school class as a teacher, for example, or performing surgery as a surgeon. These tasks are formally written down in the contract between employer and employee. Contextual performance, on the other hand, is about the social and psychological environment in which the task must be performed. Examples are investing in good relationships with colleagues, having extra enthusiasm for completing your tasks, or carrying out tasks that are not formally part of your job description (Motowildo, Borman, & Schmit, 1997). The scientific evidence suggests that affective commitment has a stronger effect on a person's contextual performance than on his or her task performance (Harrison, Newman, & Roth, 2006). Put differently, employees who feel attached to and identify with their organization are likely to do more work for the organization that is not in their job description, for example, helping a colleague with a project or volunteering to undertake an extra task during the weekend.

3   *Affective commitment becomes moderately negatively related to task performance when organizational trust and organizational identification are taken into account (Level C).*

A recent meta-analysis based on 118 studies found a moderate negative correlation between affective organizational commitment and task performance (Ng, 2015). The explanation for this might be that the effect of affective commitment on task performance is highly dependent on the level of organizational trust and identification perceived by employees. The evidence in this meta-analysis suggests that organizational trust and identification may be a better predictor for task performance than affective commitment.

4   *Job tenure has a strong effect on the relationship between affective commitment and performance (Level C).*

When starting a new job in a new company, affective commitment to the organization tends to have a strong effect on job performance. However, the longer the employee works in the company, the smaller the effect. After 10 years, affective organizational commitment has almost no effect on job performance (Wright & Bonett, 2002).

Main Findings: Commitment to Change

1   *Commitment to change is a better predictor of behavioral support for a change initiative than organizational commitment (Level D).*

The constructs *employee commitment*, or *organizational commitment* and *commitment to change* show a large degree of overlap. Both are considered to be multidimensional constructs that can be divided into three distinctive components: affective, normative, and continuous commitment. However, it was found that commitment to change is a better predictor of behavioral support for a change initiative than organizational commitment, suggesting that the two are separate constructs (Herscovitch & Meyer, 2002).

2   *Both affective and normative commitment to change have a large, positive effect on behavioral support, but continuance commitment has a small negative effect (Level B).*

It was found that beliefs about the value of the change, in combination with the pressure felt to follow the norm, positively shape people's intentions toward a change initiative and their behavior. As a result, people are more likely to go that extra mile or strongly support the change initiative out of loyalty toward the organization or the expectation of gaining mutual benefits and advantages for both the individual and the organization (Bouckenooghe, Schwarz, & Minbashian, 2015). Continuance commitment, however, tends to have a small negative effect on change outcomes. A possible explanation is that employees with a high continuance commitment may feel they have to make personal sacrifices in situations where it is uncertain whether their investment will pay off.

Synthesis of Evidence

Considerable research has been carried out in recent decades on the topic of commitment—our search yielded hundreds of studies and numerous meta-analyses. The research on commitment to change is less extensive—we found only a handful of cross-sectional studies and one meta-analysis. Overall there is strong evidence demonstrating that commitment is positively correlated to several organizational outcomes, such as job performance. When affective and normative commitment are high, performance is likely to increase, especially contextual job performance. A remarkable finding is that the relationship between affective commitment and performance depends on an employee's tenure and that continuance commitment seems to have a negative effect. However, the effect sizes are small to moderate, and there are some indications that organizational trust might be a better predictor. There are strong indications that this does not apply to commitment to change. Although the research on this topic is limited in terms of volume and rigor, it was consistently found that commitment to change has a large effect on employees' behavioral support for change initiatives, which makes it a relevant factor to take into account.

Conclusion

The scientific evidence suggests that employees' commitment has a small to moderate effect on performance. The evidence demonstrating that commitment to change has a positive impact on change outcomes is considerably smaller, but the effect sizes found are large. We therefore conclude that, based on the evidence found, this claim is somewhat likely to be true.

Practical Reflections

When implementing change, enhancing employees' commitment to it may have a positive effect on support for the change. Support for a change initiative, however, is no guarantee that the change will succeed. In fact, other factors may be even more important—such as trust in the leadership (Chapter 5) or supervisory support (Chapter 6)—making commitment to change a relevant but not necessarily an essential factor. After all, it seems self-evident that if employees commit to the change objectives, they are likely to support the activities that sustain the desired change as well. This is also supported with evidence: No negative relationships were found between commitment to change and change outcomes. Measuring employees' commitment to change and using the outcome to manage the process therefore can be recommended for most change projects.

'Financial Incentives Are an Effective Way to Encourage Change and Improve Performance'

Introduction

Providing financial incentives to reinforce employees' motivation and subsequent performance is common in management practice and a hot topic in organizational research. The assumed positive effect of financial incentives originates from the era in which employee performance was mainly driven by managers using a 'carrot and stick.' This principle has evolved in the past century, highly influenced by Douglas McGregor, who introduced Theory X and Theory Y. Theory X assumes that people are unmotivated, dislike working, have to be driven and supervised, and therefore need carrots and sticks to compel them to do their best. By contrast, Theory Y assumes that people have a psychological need to work, are self-motivated, and seek responsibility, which reduces the need for carrots and sticks (McGregor, 1960). Although current management practice has more or less embedded the fundamentals of Theory Y, financial incentives are still largely regarded as an effective means to improve motivation and therefore performance (Garbers & Konradt, 2014). As such, high bonuses are still very common in, for instance, the financial industry. In addition, several theories of human motivation such as the self-determination theory, support the use of financial incentives as an effective technique (Weibel, Rost, & Osterloh, 2010). Despite compelling theoretical explanations, opponents of incentivizing also have a solid presence. In Dan Pink's well-known speech *The Puzzle of Motivation* (Pink, 2009), he states that incentives dull thinking and block creativity. He argues that, for many tasks, especially those in today's organizations, mechanistic rewards and punishments do not work and often cause harm.

What Is Meant by Financial Incentives?

An *incentive* is commonly defined as "something that encourages a person to do something or to work harder" (Incentive, n.d.). In the domain of management, *incentives* can be defined as ". . . plans that have predetermined criteria and standards, as well as understood policies for determining and allocating rewards" (Greene, 2011, p. 219). Incentives include all forms of rewards (and punishments) that are based on an employee's performance or behavior. Promotions, grades, awards, praise, and recognition are therefore all incentives. However, financial incentives such as money, bonus plans, or stock options are the most commonly used (Cerasoli, Nicklin, & Ford, 2014). Formally, incentives differ from rewards. Incentives refer to all stimuli that are provided in advance, whereas rewards are offered after a given performance (Garbers & Konradt, 2014). In the scientific literature and management practice, however, these terms are used interchangeably.

How Does It Work?

Although financial incentives are opposed by some, it is still widely believed that they are an effective way to change employee behavior—it increases employees' motivation to work harder and subsequently perform better. Researchers, however, distinguish within and between the main concepts of incentives, motivation, and performance, resulting in different expectations regarding the assumed effects. As self-determination theory argues, motivation is not a uniform phenomenon because people experience different kinds of motivation, for example, intrinsic and extrinsic motivation. The latter refers to motivation from external sources such as financial incentives, whereas intrinsic motivation refers to doing something because it is inherently interesting or enjoyable (Ryan & Deci, 2000). It is suggested that an employee's intrinsic motivation is effected by financial incentives. More directly performance-salient incentives (characterized by a clear link between incentive and performance, such as sales commissions), rather than indirectly performance-salient incentives (e.g., base salary or training courses) may even damage the positive relationship between intrinsic motivation and performance. In addition, in the case of rewarding teams, incentives can be distributed either equitably (fairly differentiated based on individual performance) or equally (uniformly based on group performance) among team members, and each of these may have a different effect. Finally, the effect of financial incentives may also differ depending on the type of task (e.g., complexity of task, interesting vs. non-interesting tasks) and team size.

Search Strategy

Relevant databases were searched using the following key words: *financial rewards, financial incentives, incentive fee, incentive pay, pay for performance, performance-related pay, productivity reward, productivity incentive, monetary reward, outcome-based incentive,* and *incentive plan*. Studies were included for further analysis if they were related to behavioral or organizational outcomes such as *motivation* and *performance*.

Assessing Quality and Relevance

Our initial search yielded a total of 213 studies. After screening the abstracts for relevance, 186 studies were excluded. Full-text screening of the articles resulted in the exclusion of another 14 studies. Finally, after critical appraisal of the remaining 13 articles, a total of four meta-analyses—representing results from more than 200 single studies—were included. The overall quality of the meta-analyses was moderate to high: Two of them included studies that used a control group and before-and-after measurement. All four meta-analyses were published between 2010 and 2014.

Main Findings

1. *Overall, financial incentives have a moderate positive effect on performance (Level A).*

There is strong evidence that financial incentives tend to have a moderate positive effect on performance (Cerasoli et al., 2014; Garbers & Konradt, 2014; Wegge et al., 2010; Weibel et al., 2010). This positive effect is often referred to as the *price effect*: The financial incentive increases the intention to perform well because of the monetary benefit. However, this effect differs among forms of incentives, types of motivation, and performance outcomes, as described in the following findings.

2. *Indirectly performance-salient incentives positively affect the relationship between intrinsic motivation and performance, whereas this relationship is weakened by directly performance-salient incentives (Level B).*

Several studies indicate that the effect of indirectly (e.g., base salary and education) and directly (e.g., sales commissions) performance-salient incentives differs between intrinsic and extrinsic motivation (Cerasoli et al., 2014). It was found that indirect incentives moderately strengthen the relationship between intrinsic motivation and performance. In contrast, this relationship is weakened by the presence of direct incentives. This negative effect on employees' intrinsic motivation is often referred to as the *crowding-out effect*. It occurs when direct incentives rather than intrinsic motivation become the primary motivation for performance. Indirect incentives do not seem to cause this crowding-out effect and therefore tend to stimulate performance.

3. *Intrinsic motivation is a better predictor for quality of performance, whereas financial incentives are a better predictor for quantity of performance (Level B).*

Extrinsic incentives are found to be a better predictor of performance quantity outcomes, for instance when commissions are linked to the amount of output. Intrinsically motivated employees on the other hand are found to be a better predictor of performance quality outcomes, for example, when the accuracy of output is measured (Cerasoli et al., 2014).

4 *Financial incentives increase performance of non-interesting tasks but decrease performance of interesting tasks (Level A).*

Financial incentives are found to have a strong positive effect on performance in the case of non-interesting tasks but tend to have a negative effect in the case of interesting tasks (Weibel et al., 2010). This effect could be explained by the fact that interesting tasks are linked to intrinsic motivation, whereas non-interesting tasks are linked to extrinsic motivation. The application of financial incentives erodes intrinsic motivation, which in turn will have a negative effect on performance.

5 *The effect on performance for equitably distributed rewards within teams is higher than for equally distributed rewards, but this effect decreases as the number of team members increases (Level A).*

Equitably distributed rewards—rewards that fairly differentiate among team members—tend to have a higher impact on performance than when rewards are distributed equally, that is, uniformly, among team members (Garbers & Konradt, 2014). A possible explanation for this finding is that equitably distributed rewards lead to higher individual motivation and as a result have a positive effect on performance. This effect, however, is found to decrease as the number of team members increases—in smaller teams, the individual effort is easier to identify, and the risk of freeloading is less significant (Garbers & Konradt, 2014).

Synthesis of Evidence

More than four decades of research and hundreds of studies have focused on the question whether, and under what circumstances, financial incentives have an effect on employees' motivation, behavior, and subsequent performance. After critical quality assessment of the scientific evidence, we can safely conclude that financial incentives have a positive impact on performance, also known as the *price effect*. However, direct financial incentives have a negative impact on the intrinsic motivation of employees, which is known as the *crowding-out effect*. The net result of these two opposing effects determines a possible gain or loss in performance. In addition, the net effect is influenced by several mediating and moderating variables. For instance, intrinsic motivation, often linked to executing interesting tasks, is critical when quality outcomes determine performance. However, intrinsic motivation is likely to be reduced by the use of direct financial incentives. Direct financial incentives, however, tend to have a positive effect on employees' quantity performance, associated with non-interesting tasks. Finally, when entire teams are incentivized, the evidence suggests that the rewards should be distributed equitably among team members, therefore strengthening employees in their motivation and diminishing the risk of free riding.

Conclusion

The scientific research literature strongly supports the claim that financial incentives are an effective way to encourage behavioral change and improve performance. However, the opposition of the price effect and crowding-out effect, which can occur under certain circumstances, requires a thoughtful approach as outcomes can vary widely when financial incentives are used. We therefore conclude that, based on the evidence found, this claim is very likely to be true, yet only under the described circumstances.

Practical Reflections

Financial incentives can be used to increase employee motivation and performance—something that is clearly needed in changing circumstances. However, managers should have a clear vision about the change in performance or behavior that they desire, as it requires different approaches to incentivizing. Intrinsically motivated employees executing interesting tasks where quality outcomes usually determine success could be encouraged by indirect incentives. Direct financial incentives are effective when extrinsic motivation and quantitative performance need to be stimulated. Managers should therefore continuously calculate the proposed net effect (positive price effect vs. negative crowding-out effect) when defining a pay plan. Ultimately, if the plan is designed to increase team performance, incentives should not be distributed equally, as this may harm individual motivation.

'Self-Managing Teams Perform Better in Realizing Change Than Traditionally Managed Teams'

Introduction

Even the more traditional organizations nowadays tend to seek 'salvation' by establishing self-managing teams. Laloux (2014), for instance, advocates self-managing teams in his best-selling book *Reinventing Organizations: A Guide to Creating Organizations Inspired by the Next Stage of Human Consciousness*. He states that to compete effectively in today's markets, organizations should focus on the creation of efficient, self-motivated teams and maximize the use of human talent. In fact, he considers self-management structures and self-managing teams as defining elements for success. From the Fortune 1000 it appears that in 2004, 79 percent of companies already deployed such 'empowered,' 'self-directed,' or 'autonomous' teams (Druskat & Wheeler, 2004). Scholars also advocate the use of self-managing teams, as the resulting autonomy should create the flexibility to be able to diagnose deficiencies in performance and instigate appropriate remedies (Johnson, Hollenbeck, DeRue, Barnes, & Jundt, 2013). At the same time, however, there are doubts whether these self-managing teams are really effective or just a contemporary reflection of employees' urge for freedom and flexibility, ignoring the real need for restraint, contextual knowledge, and accountability in organizations. According to Dembosky (2013, para 3), Evan Williams, the cofounder of Blogger, Twitter, and Medium, for example, argues that people romanticize the start-up culture and its lack of structure, in which there is, in fact, a great deal of anxiety and inefficiency. Some scholars also question the success of self-managing teams, where it is suggested that such teams are sometimes insufficiently aware of the needs of their environment and find it difficult to correctly pinpoint the cause of deficiencies in their performance (Johnson et al., 2013). Given this lack of consensus in the field, it is important to look at the contribution of self-managing teams and their impact in organizations and, more specifically, in the process of organizational change.

What Is Meant by Self-Managing Teams?

The concept of *self-managing teams* is referred to in various ways, using terms such as *autonomous groups*, *shared*, or *self-directed teams*; all of these terms refer to teams that are hallmarked by autonomy. We use the term *self-managing teams* to cover all of the different descriptions of this concept. Ingvaldsen and Rolfsen (2012) refer to the standard definition of *autonomous groups* as "groups responsible for a complete product or service, or a major part of a production process. They control members' task behavior and make decisions about task assignment and work methods" (Cummings & Worley, 2005, p. 341). Moreover, self-managing teams are seen as an option for organizational design, including teams that have the relatively broad authority to decide on how they execute certain tasks (Johnson et al., 2013).

How Does It Work?

The authors of numerous studies have investigated the relationship between self-managing teams and performance, generally expecting performance to be improved when teams are self-managed. Proponents generally build on the assumption that these teams are 'close to the action' and therefore should have more information about problems, suggesting that they will make appropriate changes to solve these problems (Johnson et al., 2013). Working with self-managing teams is also often expected to improve performance indirectly through positive relationships, with better attitudinal and behavioral outcomes such as quality of work life (Cohen & Ledford, 1994), attitude (Cordery, Mueller, & Smith, 1991), or job satisfaction (Pearson, 1992; Tata & Prasad, 2004; Wall, Kemp, Jackson, & Clegg, 1986; Workman, 2003). However, some scholars question these positive assumptions, arguing that self-managing teams might be insufficiently aware of their environment or make dysfunctional changes. The latter is likely to occur when self-managing teams experience a structural misalignment with their task environment. They are then more inclined to make dysfunctional changes in processes or personnel rather than changing their own structure as required (Johnson et al., 2013).

Search Strategy

We thoroughly searched relevant databases to find meta-analyses and studies, using the following key words: *self-managing teams, self-directing teams, self-regulating teams, self-organizing teams, self-leading teams, autonomous teams, empowered teams, autonomous task groups, autonomous work groups,* and *team leadership.* Studies were included for further analysis when they were related to organizational and behavioral components.

Assessing Quality and Relevance

Our initial search yielded a total of 345 studies. After screening the abstracts for relevance, 307 studies were excluded. Unfortunately, no relevant meta-analyses were found. Eventually, after a critical appraisal of the remaining 38 articles, a total of 25 single studies were identified. These studies, which were published between 1986 and 2015, varied considerably in methodological quality, ranging from good (randomized controlled studies) to poor (cross-sectional studies).

Main Findings

No relevant meta-analyses were found to investigate the current assumption. The main findings are therefore based on single studies that varied in quality. The findings have been formulated therefore only when a certain effect or result was seen and (1) based on numerous studies or (2) when a single study was considered to be of very good quality.

1   *The direct relationship between self-managing teams and performance is not clear and is influenced by several contextual factors.*

Several studies have found significant results that confirm a moderate positive direct relationship between self-managing teams and their performance (Cohen & Ledford, 1994; Erez, Lepine, & Elms, 2002; Fausing, Joensson, Lewandowski, & Bligh, 2015; Pearson, 1992), with levels varying from A to D, suggesting that self-managing teams are more effective than traditionally managed ones. However, several studies also did *not* find significant positive outcomes based on the overall performance of self-managing teams (Gupta, Huang, & Niranjan, 2010; Power & Waddell, 2004; Wall et al., 1986), with levels varying from B to D. In addition, several studies suggested that contextual factors greatly influence the relationship between self-managing teams and performance. For example, self-managing teams were found to be more effective under lower levels of authority hierarchy (micro-level centralization) and organizational formalization, and vice versa (Tata & Prasad, 2004), Level D. It was further found that conflicts within self-managing teams also negatively mediate the effect on performance (Gupta et al., 2010), Level C. Finally, it was found that the positive effect on performance is greatest for self-managing teams dealing with high-tech novelty and radical innovation (Patanakul, Chen, & Lynn, 2012), Level D. These findings suggest that the effect of self-managing teams on performance is far from clear and is mediated by several contextual factors.

2   *Self-managing teams show moderate positive effects on attitudinal and behavioral outcomes (Level A).*

There is strong evidence indicating that self-managing teams have moderate positive effects on the quality of work life, in terms of job satisfaction (Cohen, Chang, & Ledford, 1997; Pearson, 1992; Wall et al., 1986), social satisfaction, job feedback (Cohen et al., 1997; Cohen & Ledford, 1994), and work attitudes (Cordery et al., 1991). A possible explanation for this effect is that self-managing teams tend to foster self-control among employees, which in turn supports motivation due to the greater autonomy, identity, and feedback (Cohen & Ledford, 1994).

3   *Self-managing teams that experience structural misalignment with their task environment are more likely to choose dysfunctional process changes rather than functional structural changes (Level B).*

The evidence suggests that self-managing teams, when faced with structural problems, seek solutions in process and personnel interventions rather than applying the structural interventions that are needed (Johnson et al., 2013). It seems that self-managing teams tend to see their performance as a result of the team members and their actions, rather than the underlying structure, thereby risking an incorrect diagnosis of the problem. However, the evidence also suggests that when such a structurally misaligned team is given feedback about their situation, or when a diagnostic list of possible changes is provided, they are more likely to choose to change the structure of the team.

Synthesis of the Evidence

Scientific research on the effects of self-managing teams is still at an early stage. Hence, no meta-analyses were found on the current topic, and the main findings were formulated on the basis of the available single studies, which varied widely in quality. The available evidence shows that self-managing teams have both positive and negative effects on performance.

This ambiguous finding may be explained by several contextual factors that may mediate this relationship. For example, self-managing teams appear to perform better where there is no conflict and when the organizational structure exhibits high levels of decentralization and low levels of formalization (e.g., few or even no specific rules, policies, and procedures). Self-managing teams also appear to perform better in high-tech and radical innovation contexts. The research evidence, however, does suggest that there is a clear positive effect of self-managing teams on attitudinal and behavioral outcomes regarding the quality of employees' work lives. Finally, it appears that self-managing teams find it difficult to instigate structural changes when no dedicated feedback is provided in situations where there is a structural misalignment.

Conclusion

The research literature does not support the claim that self-managing teams perform better than traditionally managed teams and therefore make a greater contribution to the realization of change. The currently available evidence is ambiguous regarding the relationship between self-managing teams and performance. Based on the evidence found, we therefore conclude that this claim can be neither confirmed nor rejected.

Practical Reflections

Because the research evidence does not provide us with a decisive answer to the question of whether self-managing teams perform better, no clear recommendations for practice can be given on whether organizations should implement self-managing teams. Neither can it be said whether self-managing teams will help organizations to change more successfully. Nevertheless, we would encourage managers to be aware of the contextual factors that seem to play an important role in the success of self-managing teams. In this light, we suggest that organizations need to be careful about implementing self-managing teams when the organization has high levels of hierarchy (i.e., micro-level centralization) or organizational formalization. Organizations that are typically defined by high-tech novelty and radical innovation, however, do not need to be as cautious in implementing self-managing teams, although they do need to be aware of the potential for conflict within their teams and the negative impact that this could have on team performance. The available knowledge on these contextual factors is still limited due to the current embryonic state of research evidence on this subject. Any introduction of self-managing teams that may be planned should therefore be considered carefully as managers fulfill a vital function within organizations. This is for instance illustrated by the outcomes of our review of supervisory support, transformational leadership, and trust in the leader, all of which underline the important roles of management in organizational change. On the other hand, it is questionable to what extent self-managing teams are capable of fulfilling a wide range of functions and if this will lead to the most effective way of organizing (related to the goals of the organization). There may be therefore a lack of caution as managers can easily get carried away by the current popular appeal of self-managing teams.

Note

* Some of the ideas in these paragraphs are based on earlier research by Ernst Graamans as presented in:

    Graamans, E., Ten Have, S., & Ten Have, W. D. (2016). Een alternatief voor opportunistisch gebruik van het begrip 'cultuur' in organisaties. *Holland Management Review*, 165, 32–39.
    Graamans, E., Millenaar, L., & Ten Have, W. D. (2014). Dynamieken binnen het topmanagementteam van een grote zorgorganisatie: Een cultuurpsychologisch perspectief. *Management & Organisatie*, 68(3), 22–42.

References

Abrell-Vogel, C., & Rowold, J. (2014). Leaders' commitment to change and their effectiveness in change—a multilevel investigation. *Journal of Organizational Change Management*, 27(6), 900–921.

Acar, A. Z., & Acar, P. (2014). Organizational culture types and their effects on organizational performance in Turkish hospitals. *Emerging Markets Journal*, 3(3), 17–31.

Allaire, Y., & Firsirotu, M. E. (1984). Theories of organizational culture. *Organization Studies*, 5(3), 193–226.

Biswas, S. (2009). HR practices as a mediator between organizational culture and transformational leadership: Implications for employee performance. *Psychological Studies*, 54(2), 114–123.

Bouckenooghe, D., Schwarz, G. M., & Minbashian, A. (2015). Herscovitch and Meyer's Three Component model of commitment to change: Meta-analytic findings. *European Journal of Work and Organizational Psychology*, 24(4), 578–595.

Boyce, A. S., Nieminen, L. R. G., Gillespie, M. A., Ryan, A. M., & Denison, D. (2015). Which comes first, organizational culture or performance? A longitudinal study of causal priority with automobile dealerships. *Journal of Organizational Behavior*, 36(3), 339–359.

Büschgens, T., Bausch, A., & Balkin, D. B. (2013). Organizational culture and innovation: A meta-analytic review. *Journal of Product Innovation Management*, 30(4), 763–781.

Cameron, K., & Quinn, R. E. (2011). *Diagnosing and changing organizational culture: Based on the competing values framework*. Reading, MA: Addison Wesley Longman.

Cerasoli, C. P., Nicklin, J. M., & Ford, M. T. (2014). Intrinsic motivation and extrinsic incentives jointly predict performance: A 40-year meta-analysis. *Psychological Bulletin*, 140(4), 980–1008.

Chan, L. L. M., Schaffer, M. A., & Snape, E. (2004). In search of sustained competitive advantage: The impact of organizational culture, competitive strategy and human resource management practices on firm performance. *The International Journal of Human Resource Management*, 15(1), 17–35.

Christersson, M., & Rothe, P. (2012). Impacts of organizational relocation: A conceptual framework. *Journal of Corporate Real Estate*, 14(4), 226–243.
Clay-Williams, R., Nosrati, H., Cunningham, F. C., Hillman, K., & Braithwaite, J. (2014). Do large-scale hospital- and system-wide interventions improve patient outcomes: A systematic review. *BMC Health Services Research*, 14(1), 369–382.
Cohen, S. G., & Ledford, G. E. (1994). The effectiveness of self-managing teams: A quasi-experiment. *Human Relations*, 47(1), 13–43.
Cohen, S. G., Chang, L., & Ledford, G. E. (1997). A hierarchical construct of self-management leadership and its relationship to quality of work life and perceived work group effectiveness. *Personnel Psychology*, 50(2), 275–308.
Collins, J. C. (2001). *Good to great: Why some companies make the leap . . . and others don't*. New York, NY: HarperCollins Publishers.
Collins, J. C., & Porras, J. I. (1997). *Built to last: Successful habits of visionary companies*. New York, NY: Harper Business.
Conner, D. R. (1992). *Managing at the speed of change: How resilient managers succeed and prosper where others fail*. New York, NY: Random House.
Cooke, R. A., & Lafferty, J. C. (1989). *Organizational culture inventory*. Plymouth, MI: Human Synergistics.
Cordery, J. L., Mueller, W. S., & Smith, L. M. (1991). Attitudinal and behavioral effects of autonomous group working: A longitudinal field study. *Academy of Management Journal*, 34(2), 464–476.
Csikszentmihalyi, M. (1998). *Finding flow: The psychology of engagement with everyday life*. New York, NY: Basic Books.
Cummings, T. G., & Worley, C. G. (2005). *Organization development and change* (8th ed.). Mason, OH: South-Western.
Dauber, D. (2012). Opposing positions in M&A research: Culture, integration and performance. *Cross Cultural Management*, 19(3), 375–398.
De Waal, A. A. (2007). The characteristics of a high-performance organization. *Business Strategy Series*, 8(3), 179–185.
Dembosky, A. (2013, February 22). *Evan William on building a company mindfully*. Retrieved February 2, 2016, from http://blogs.ft.com/tech-blog/2013/02/evan-williams-on-holacracy-and-building-a-company-mindfully/
Denison, D. R. (1990). *Corporate culture and organizational effectiveness*. New York, NY: John Wiley & Sons.
Denison, D. R., & Neale, W. S. (1996). *Denison organizational culture survey*. Ann Arbor, MI: Aviat.
Druskat, V. U., & Wheeler, J. V. (2004). *How to lead a self-managing team*. Retrieved January 3, 2016, from http://sloanreview.mit.edu/article/how-to-lead-a-selfmanaging-team/
Erez, A., Lepine, J. A., & Elms, H. (2002). Effects of rotated leadership and peer evaluation on the functioning and effectiveness of self-managed teams: A quasi-experiment. *Personnel Psychology*, 55(4), 929–948.
Erez, M. (1977). Feedback: A necessary condition for the goal setting-performance relationship. *Journal of Applied Psychology*, 62(5), 624–627.
Farley, J. U., Hoenig, S., & Ismail, Z. (2008). Organizational culture, innovativeness, market orientation and firm performance in South Africa: An interdisciplinary perspective. *Journal of African Business*, 9(1), 59–76.
Faull, K., Kalliath, T., & Smith, D. (2004). Organizational culture: The dynamics of culture on organizational change within a rehabilitation center. *Organization Development Journal*, 22(1), 40–55.

Fausing, M. S., Joensson, T. S., Lewandowski, J., & Bligh, M. (2015). Antecedents of shared leadership: Empowering leadership and interdependence. *Leadership & Organization Development Journal, 36*(3), 271–291.

Garbers, Y., & Konradt, U. (2014). The effect of financial incentives on performance: A quantitative review of individual and team-based financial incentives. *Journal of Occupational and Organizational Psychology, 87*(1), 102–137.

Greene, R. J. (2011). *Rewarding performance: Guiding principles; custom strategies.* New York, NY: Routledge.

Greenwood, J. D. (1994). *Realism, identity and emotion: Reclaiming social psychology.* London, UK: Thousand Oaks.

Groves, P. S. (2014). The relationship between safety culture and patient outcomes: Results from pilot meta-analyses. *Western Journal of Nursing Research, 36*(1), 66–83.

Gupta, V. K., Huang, R., & Niranjan, S. (2010). A longitudinal examination of the relationship between team leadership and performance. *Journal of Leadership & Organizational Studies, 17*(4), 335–350.

Harrison, D. A., Newman, D. A., & Roth, P. L. (2006). How important are job attitudes? Meta-analytic comparisons of integrative behavioral outcomes and time sequences. *The Academy of Management Journal, 49*(2), 305–325.

Hartnell, C. A., Ou, A. Y., & Kinicki, A. (2011). Organizational culture and organizational effectiveness: A meta-analytic investigation of the competing values framework's theoretical suppositions. *Journal of Applied Psychology, 96*(4), 677–694.

Heracleous, L. (2001). An ethnographic study of culture in the context of organizational change. *The Journal of Applied Behavioral Science, 37*(4), 426–446.

Herscovitch, L., & Meyer, J. P. (2002). Commitment to organizational change: Extension of a three-component model. *Journal of Applied Psychology, 87*(3), 474–487.

Hofstede, G. (1980). *Culture's consequences: International differences in work-related values.* London, UK: Sage Publications.

Imran, R., Zahoor, F., & Zaheer, A. (2012). Leadership and performance relationship: Culture matters. *International Journal of Innovation, Management and Technology, 3*(6), 713–717.

Incentive. (n.d.). In *Merriam-Webster.* Retrieved February 2, 2016, from http://www.merriam-webster.com/dictionary/incentive

Ingvaldsen, J. A., & Rolfsen, M. (2012). Autonomous work groups and the challenge of intergroup coordination. *Human Relations, 65*(7), 861–881.

Jaros, S. (2010). Commitment to organizational change: A critical review. *Journal of Change Management, 10*(1), 79–108.

Johnson, M. D., Hollenbeck, J. R., DeRue, D. S., Barnes, C. M., & Jundt, D. (2013). Functional versus dysfunctional team change: Problem diagnosis and structural feedback for self-managed teams. *Organizational Behavior and Human Decision Processes, 122*(1), 1–11.

Kluger, A. N., & DeNisi, A. (1996). The effects of feedback interventions on performance: A historical review, a meta-analysis, and a preliminary feedback intervention theory. *Psychological Bulletin, 119*(2), 254–284.

Kotrba, L. M., Gillespie, M. A., Schmidt, A. M., Smerek, R. E., Ritchie, S. A., & Denison, D. R. (2012). Do consistent corporate cultures have better business

performance? Exploring the interaction effects. *Human Relations*, 65(2), 241–262.
Laloux, F. (2014). *Reinventing organizations: A guide to creating organizations inspired by the next stage of human consciousness*. Brussel, BE: Nelson Parker.
Latham, G. P. (2009). Motivate employee performance through goal setting. In E. A. Locke (Ed.), *Handbook of principles of organizational behavior* (pp. 161–178). Chichester, UK: John Wiley & Sons.
Leong, J., & Anderson, C. (2012). Fostering innovation through cultural change. *Library Management*, 33(8/9), 490–497.
Locke, E. A. (1968). Toward a theory of task motivation and incentives. *Organizational Behavior and Human Performance*, 3, 157–189.
Locke, E. A., & Latham, G. P. (1990). *A theory of goal setting and task performance*. Englewood Cliffs, NJ: Prentice-Hall.
McGregor, D. (1960). *The human side of enterprise*. New York, NY: McGraw-Hill.
Mento, A. J., Steel, R. P., & Karren, R. J. (1987). A meta-analytic study of the effects of goal setting on task performance: 1966–1984. *Organizational Behavior and Human Decision Processes*, 39(1), 52–83.
Meyer, J. P., Srinivas, E. S., Lal, J. B., & Topolnytsky, L. (2007). Employee commitment and support for an organizational change: Test of the three-component model in two cultures. *Journal of Occupational & Organizational Psychology*, 80(2), 185–211.
Motowildo, S. J., Borman, W. C., & Schmit, M. J. (1997). A theory of individual differences in task and contextual performance. *Human Performance*, 10(2), 71–83.
Mousavi, S. A., Hosseini, S. Y., & Hassanpour, N. (2015). On the effects of organizational culture on organizational performance: An Iranian experience in state bank branches. *Iranian Journal of Management Studies*, 8(1), 97–116.
Naor, M., Goldstein, S. M., Linderman, K. W., & Schroeder, R. G. (2008). The role of culture as driver of quality management and performance: Infrastructure versus core quality practices. *Decision Sciences*, 39(4), 671–702.
Neubert, M. J. (1998). The value of feedback and goal setting over goal setting alone and potential moderators of this effect: A meta-analysis. *Human Performance*, 11(4), 321–335.
Ng, T. W. H. (2015). The incremental validity of organizational commitment, organizational trust, and organizational identification. *Journal of Vocational Behavior*, 88, 154–163.
Patanakul, P., Chen, J., & Lynn, G. S. (2012). Autonomous teams and new product development. *Journal of Product Innovation Management*, 29(5), 734–750.
Pearson, C. A. (1992). Autonomous workgroups: An evaluation at an industrial site. *Human Relations*, 45(9), 905–936.
Peters, T. J., & Waterman, R. H. (1982). *In search of excellence: Lessons from America's best-run companies*. New York, NY: Harper & Row.
Pettigrew, A. M. (1979). On studying organizational cultures. *Administrative Science Quarterly*, 24(4), 570–581.
Pink, D. (2009, August). *The puzzle of motivation*. Retrieved February 2, 2016, from https://www.ted.com/talks/dan_pink_on_motivation?language=en#t-93360
Power, J., & Waddell, D. (2004). The link between self-managed work teams and learning organizations using performance indicators. *The Learning Organization*, 11(3), 244–259.

Prajogo, D., & McDermott, C. M. (2010). The relationship between multidimensional organizational culture and performance. *International Journal of Operations & Production Management, 31*(7), 712–735.

Quantum Health Resources & Associates. (n.d.). *Our services*. Retrieved February 2, 2016, from http://www.quantumhealthresources.com/services.htm

Quinn, R. E., & Rohrbaugh, J. (1981). A competing values approach to organizational effectiveness. *Public Productivity Review, 5*(2), 122–140.

Quinn, R. E., & Rohrbaugh, J. (1983). A spatial model of effectiveness criteria: Towards a competing values approach to organizational analysis. *Management Science, 29*, 363–377.

Riketta, M. (2002). Attitudinal organizational commitment and job performance: A meta-analysis. *Journal of Organizational Behavior, 23*(3), 257–266.

Rubera, G., & Kirca, A. H. (2012). Firm innovativeness and its performance outcomes: A meta-analytic review and theoretical integration. *Journal of Marketing, 76*(3), 130–147.

Ryan, R., & Deci, E. (2000). Intrinsic and extrinsic motivations: Classic definitions and new directions. *Contemporary Educational Psychology, 25*(1), 54–67.

Schein, E. H. (1990). Organizational culture. *American Psychologist, 45*(2), 109-119.

Schein, E. H. (1996). Culture: The missing concept in organization studies. *Administrative Science Quarterly, 41*(2), 229–240.

Seo, M., Taylor, M. S., Hill, N. S., Zhang, X., Tesluk, P. E., & Lorinkova, N. M. (2012). The role of affect and leadership during organizational change. *Personnel Psychology, 65*(1), 121–165.

Shier, V., Khodyakov, D., Cohen, L. W., Zimmerman, S., & Saliba, D. (2014). What does the evidence really say about culture change in nursing homes? *The Gerontologist, 54*(1), 6–16.

Shum, P., Bove, L., & Auh, S. (2008). Employee's affective commitment to change: The key to successful CRM implementation. *European Journal of Marketing, 42*(11/12), 1346–1371.

Smircich, L. (1983). Concepts of culture and organizational analysis. *Administrative Science Quarterly, 28*(3), 339–358.

Tata, J., & Prasad, S. (2004). Team self-management, organizational structure, and judgments of team effectiveness. *Journal of Managerial Issues, 16*(2), 248–265.

Tichy, N. M. (1982). Managing change strategically: The technical, political, and cultural keys. *Organizational Dynamics, 11*(2), 59–80.

Tubbs, M. E. (1986). Goal setting: A meta-analytic examination of the empirical evidence. *Journal of Applied Psychology, 71*(3), 474–483.

Turner, D. M. (2015). *Buy in is not enough*. Retrieved February 2, 2016, from http://thinktransition.com/articles/buy-in-is-not-enough/

Uzkurt, C., Kumar, R., Kimzan, H. S., & Eminoğlu, G. (2013). Role of innovation in the relationship between organizational culture and firm performance. *European Journal of Innovation Management, 16*(1), 92–117.

Verheggen, T. (2005). *Culture alt delete: On the misperception of culture in psychology* (Doctoral dissertation). Retrieved January 13, 2016, from http://www.ou.nl/Docs/Faculteiten/PSY/Onderzoek/Dissertation%20Theo%20Verheggen_Full%20Version%20(Final).pdf

Voestermans, P., & Verheggen, T. (2013). *Culture as embodiment: The social tuning of behavior*. Hoboken, NJ: John Wiley & Sons.

Wall, T. D., Kemp, N. J., Jackson, P. R., & Clegg, C. W. (1986). Outcomes of autonomous workgroups: A long-term field experiment. *Academy of Management journal*, *29*(2), 280–304.

Wegge, J., Jeppesen, H. J., Weber, W. G., Pearce, C. L., Silva, S. A., Pundt, A., Jonsson, T., Wolf, S., Wassenaar, C. L., Unterrainer, C., & Piecha, A. (2010). Promoting work motivation in organizations: Should employee involvement in organizational leadership become a new tool in the organizational psychologist's kit? *Journal of Personnel Psychology*, *9*(4), 154–171.

Weibel, A., Rost, K., & Osterloh, M. (2010). Pay for performance in the public sector-benefits and (hidden) costs. *Journal of Public Administration Research and Theory*, *20*(2), 87–412.

William Thomson. (n.d.). In *Wikipedia*. Retrieved November 11, 2015, from https://en.wikiquote.org/wiki/William_Thomson.

Workman, M. (2003). Results from organizational development interventions in a technology call center. *Human Resource Development Quarterly*, *14*(2), 215–230.

Wright, T. A., & Bonett, D. G. (2002). The moderating effects of employee tenure on the relation between organizational commitment and job performance: A meta-analysis. *Journal of Applied Psychology*, *87*(6), 1183–1190.

Zhang, M., Li, H., & Wei, J. (2008). Examining the relationship between organizational culture and performance: The perspectives of consistency and balance. *Frontiers of Business Research in China*, *2*(2), 256–276.

8 The Story of Change Reconsidered

"Act on the best evidence possible, and learn from your mistakes."

(Sutton [n.d.] in Pearlman, 2006)

At the start of our journey we presented the 'Story of Change'—a story that is built on the claims found in management books and statements made by other merchants of hope, such as management thinkers and consultants. The 'Story of Change' is based on a coherent set of 18 popular and widespread assumptions on managing change representing important beliefs, design guidelines, convictions, and practices among practitioners involved in change management. The 18 assumptions, which were distilled from the top best sellers in the management literature and the professional statements, assumptions and claims of reputed consulting firms and experts (see Chapter 3), can be seen as practical design guidelines for successful change management. They are reflected in the statements and credentials of leading consultants and consultancy firms.

The journey we set out on was an unpredictable one but also one with a mission: to reevaluate change management by taking an evidence-based approach with a strong emphasis on the available academic research and insights. From a learning perspective we hoped it would be a real journey, a voyage. Ibarra (2015) provided us with a metaphor in the story of Ulysses on his long and meandering journey to Ithaca. Ulysses's journey was beset with many challenges, uncertainties, crises, profound experiences, and temptations on the way. In the words of the poet C. P. Cavafy, it was "full of adventure, full of discovery" (Cavafy, 1992, p. 36). Our journey, too, was enriching, informative, and edifying. On this journey—defined by its evidence-based perspective—there is no such thing as a final destination. So this is not the end of our journey; we will keep on traveling and learning. But we can say that we have arrived at a stopping point, a place where we can share our experience and tell our story. This new 'Story of Change' reflects a detailed reexamination of change management. No doubt it will continue to grow and evolve as we embark on the next stage of our journey. Having said that, the story so far will influence what is to come. It provides a new starting point, a standard of sorts, and as such is our 'evidence-based' travel companion.

The Story of Change Reconsidered 177

Notwithstanding our critical reflection and comments on some of their statements and claims, we would like to emphasize the fact that the new story would not have been possible without the work of the authors and consultants who provided the elements for the initial 'Story of Change.' Their thinking and experience are vital to any serious discussion on evidence-based change management. Their contributions are important, and it should be noted that a significant proportion of their claims has proven to be of value in both research and practice.

It should also be noted, however, that important parts of the 'Story of Change' (see Chapter 3) turned out to be questionable. We therefore propose a new 'Story of Change,' one that has been reconsidered, enriched, fueled, and structured with the evidence we gathered. It contains the basic elements of evidence about managing change.

The common belief that 70 percent of all change interventions fail is unsubstantiated. More importantly, it is an inappropriate incentive for developing a professional framework needed to manage change. Blindly assuming that change initiatives have a high risk of failure is misleading and potentially harmful. Such an attitude may seriously hinder the change process by creating uncertainty, inhibiting innovation, and affecting organizational learning. As a result, it can lead to negative, self-fulfilling prophecies.

People need a sense of direction: a vision, a mission, a goal, or a dream that can provide, mobilize, and inspire and may even help to deal with uncertainties and fears. Change initiatives start for many reasons; they may be chosen, forced, or driven by ambition or crisis. A sense of urgency among employees is not essential for implementing successful change, and managers should therefore be encouraged not to establish an artificial crisis to force change.

Trust in leaders is indeed critical to successful change. What leadership style will be most effective depends on the context and the nature of the change. So transformational and transactional leadership styles may be appropriate in different types of organizational change. The performance outcomes will indicate the kind of leadership style that is most likely to be successful.

Emotional Intelligence influences job performance as well as the working environment and may therefore positively contribute to change processes. However, Emotional Intelligence alone does not provide a revolutionary approach to changing organizations and people. Supervisory support is critical to the success of change.

In leading change, it is important to know which characteristics contribute to performance separately, which should be embedded in,

> *for example, a guiding coalition or a strong leadership team. To build the change capacity needed, employees and organizational capabilities need to be developed. Critical levers here include strategy, structure, systems, purpose, social processes, and people, which should be applied in an orchestrated manner.*
>
> *Participation may help in certain situations; yet it is not the key to successful change. Particular attention should be paid to resistance as this may negatively influence, for instance, job satisfaction, goal accomplishment, or creative performance. But it is also important to pay attention, at the start of a change process, to the elements that might cause resistance. A fair change process is important to realize successful change as procedural justice positively influences organizational outcomes.*
>
> *Organizational culture, and its relationship to change and performance, has an intuitive appeal. Nevertheless, culture is an illusory concept. Users risk getting caught up in metaphorical descriptions with harmful stereotyping as a possible result, and good analysis and solutions may be blocked.*
>
> *Combining goal setting with feedback is a powerful tool that change leaders can use to influence employee behavior. Financial incentives can also be used to increase employee motivation and performance in changing circumstances. However, managers should have a clear vision about desired behavior as different methods of incentivizing may be required. Such incentives, when wrongly or insensitively applied, could stifle intrinsic motivation, initiative, and creativity. Also employee commitment to change objectives is critical to successful change, and such commitment is positively related to performance.*
>
> *Finally, any planned introduction of self-managing teams, as an alternative to traditionally managed teams, should be carefully considered as the current popularization of self-managing teams is not supported by scientific evidence.*

This new 'Story of Change' is, unlike its predecessor, an evidence-based one. Change management looked at from an evidence-based perspective is a positive development. Its application will contribute to economic growth as well as overall well-being and quality of life while avoiding unnecessary economic, social, and emotional damage. Our aim with this book is to contribute to professional development and craftsmanship. The main focus is on (scientific) knowledge. As Martins (2008) states:

> There are two parts to learning craftsmanship: knowledge and work. You must gain the knowledge of principles, patterns, practices, and heuristics that a craftsman knows, and you must also grind that knowledge into your fingers, eyes, and gut by working hard and practicing. (p. 26)

Change management is no different. It requires both knowledge and practice. As Robert I. Sutton once said, "Act on the best evidence possible, and learn from your mistakes" (Sutton [n.d.] in Pearlman, 2006, para 1). As in evidence-based medicine (EBM), evidence-based *change management* is founded on at least three principles: the wishes and needs of the informed user or client (i.e., the patient), the experiential knowledge of the professional, as well as systematic and validated (scientific) knowledge. Systematic, validated knowledge helps users become informed. In the context of EBM, Burgers (2015) argues for a return to the 'original EBM' or, in his words, the 'real EBM.' Burgers also points out the danger of the science perspective overshadowing practice (i.e., the experienced practitioner) and preference (i.e., the informed user) in EBM: The quality of the scientific evidence prevails at the expense of its practical application.

However, the main focus of this book is on knowledge and its quality. The essential basis of each profession lies in its *body of knowledge*—systematic, validated, formal knowledge (Abbott, 1996; Barber, 1963; Greenwood, 1957). As Wilensky (1964) concluded, systematic, formal knowledge in particular defines professional work. Professional effect and contribution are defined by the quality of knowledge and the quality of its application. But, however excellent the process of application may be, without correct knowledge the results will probably not be satisfactory. Sometimes the necessary knowledge does not exist or is not available. Practitioners are then forced to experiment, prototype, and work on the basis of trial and error—which can also be done in an evidence-based way. But when the knowledge does exist and can be accessed, not using it is unforgiveable from a professional perspective. In the practice of change management, this is too often the case, as the 18 popular assumptions we have reviewed illustrate.

Change management is an *Integrationswissenschaft*, a synoptic science (Nouelle-Neuman, Schultz, & Wilke, 1971). In the context of change management, *professional* means systematic and methodical, making use of the available knowledge, experience, and insights. As in other professions, evidence-based design guidelines are the foundation (Liedtka, 2000; Van Aken, 1994). The 18 assumptions selected can be seen as design guidelines. The comedian George Carlin once asked: "Isn't it a bit unnerving that doctors call what they do 'practice'?" (George Carlin, n.d.). It is worth thinking about that. The *Economist* (2015) recently stated that doctors use evidence when prescribing treatment and that policy makers should do the same. We, in turn, would like managers and other practitioners involved in change management to do so as well.

As stated in the introduction, we hope that this book and our research on evidence-based change management will help practitioners achieve their goals. This is not art for art's sake. *Reconsidering Change Management—Applying Evidence-Based Insights in Change Management Practice* is a new contribution to management technology. As Peter Drucker (1957) put it, the ability of employees to change determines an organization's capacity to change. Consequently, what we do need is a different framework for managing organizational change—most certainly not because 70 percent of all change initiatives fail. As we demonstrated in Chapter 5, it is highly unlikely that this claim is true, given that robust evidence is lacking. A different approach is needed because the development of our field has come to a halt. This dilemma can be overcome only by avoiding using highly subjective anecdotes and instead starting to apply more evidence-based change management principles.

We hope that every practitioner, manager, or consultant with a responsible position in a change process—as well as students and researchers—will take note of the progress and reflections in this book. However, it must be seen as just one step in a longer journey and not as an end in itself. We therefore hope that this book will serve as an inspiration for the future development of evidence-based change management as well as the discipline, experience, practice, and insights underlying this development. And, last but not least, we hope it provides a sound basis for initiating and implementing actions and interventions that will contribute to better change management.

References

Abbott, A. (1996). *The system of professions. An essay on the division of expert labor*. Chicago, IL: The University of Chicago Press.

Barber, B. (1963). Some problems in the sociology of professions. *Daedalus, 92*(4), 669–688.

Burgers, J. S. (2015). Opschudding over evidence-based medicine. Van reductionisme naar realisme in de toepassing van richtlijnen. *Nederlands Tijdschrift voor Geneeskunde, 159*, 1–5.

Cavafy, C. P. (1992). *Cavafy, collected poems*. Princeton, NJ: Princeton University Press.

Drucker, P. F. (1957). *Management in de praktijk*. Bussum, NL: G. J. A. Ruys Uitgeversmaatschappij.

The *Economist*. (2015, December 12). In praise of human guinea pigs. Retrieved January 14, 2016, from http://www.economist.com/news/leaders/21679799-doctors-use-evidence-when-prescribing-treatments-policymakers-should-too-praise-human

Greenwood, E. (1957). Attributes of a profession. *Social Work, 2*(3), 44–55.

Liedtka, J. (2000). In defense of strategy as design. *California Management Review, 42*(3), 8–30.

Martins, R. C. (2008). *Clean code. A handbook of agile software craftsmanship*. New York, NY: Pearson Education.

Nouelle-Neuman, E., Schultz, W., & Wilke, J. (1971). *Das Fischer Lexikon Publizistik*. Bonn, DE: Broschiert.

Pearlman, E. (2006, February 2). *Robert I. Sutton: Making a case for evidence-based management*. Retrieved January 14, 2016, from http://www.cioinsight.com/c/a/Expert-Voices/Robert-I-Sutton-Making-a-Case-for-EvidenceBased-Management

Van Aken, J. E. (1994). De bedrijfskunde als ontwerpwetenschap: De regulatieve en reflectieve cyclus. *Bedrijfskunde, 66*(1), 16–26.

Wilensky, H. L. (1964). The professionalization of everyone? *American Journal of Sociology, 70*(2), 137–158.

Appendix A
Overview of Authors and Researchers

Authors

Steven ten Have, PhD, is a full professor of strategy and change at the Vrije Universiteit Amsterdam, the Netherlands, visiting professor at the Nyenrode Business University, the Netherlands, chair of the Foundation, the CEBMa, and partner at TEN HAVE Change Management.

Wouter ten Have, PhD, is a full professor of organization and change at the Vrije Universiteit Amsterdam, the Netherlands, visiting university lecturer of change management (MBA health care management) at the Amsterdam Business School, the Netherlands, and partner at TEN HAVE Change Management.

Anne-Bregje Huijsmans, MSc, PhD candidate, is a consultant at TEN HAVE Change Management.

Maarten Otto, MSc, PhD candidate, is visiting university lecturer of organization and change (MS in management) at the Hague University of Applied Sciences, the Netherlands, and a consultant at TEN HAVE Change Management.

Researchers

Niels van der Eng, MSc, PhD candidate, is a university lecturer of organization and change at the Vrije Universiteit Amsterdam, the Netherlands, and head of research at TEN HAVE Change Management.

Ernst Graamans, MSc, PhD candidate, is a university lecturer of organization and change at the Vrije Universiteit Amsterdam, the Netherlands, and researcher at TEN HAVE Change Management.

Leonard Millenaar, MSc, is a consultant at TEN HAVE Change Management.

Lisa van Rossum, MSc, is a consultant at TEN HAVE Change Management.

Sjoerd Segijn, MSc, is a consultant at TEN HAVE Change Management.

Cornell Vernooij, MSc, is a consultant at TEN HAVE Change Management.

Joris Westhof, MSc, is a consultant at TEN HAVE Change Management.

Appendix B
Allocation of Researchers Per Assumption

Table B.1 Overview of Researchers Per Assumption

Assumption	Researchers
70 percent of all change initiatives fail.	Joris Westhof & Niels van der Eng
A clear vision is needed for successful change.	Niels van der Eng & Ernst Graamans
People will not change if there is no sense of urgency.	Cornell Vernooij & Ernst Graamans
Trust in the leader is needed for successful change.	Ernst Graamans & Sjoerd Segijn
When managing change, a transformational leadership style is more effective than a transactional one.	Lisa van Rossum & Sjoerd Segijn
Organizational change requires leaders with strong emotional intelligence.	Joris Westhof & Niels van de Eng
Supervisory support is critical for the success of change.	Cornell Vernooij & Leonard Millenaar
To realize change in organizations, a powerful guiding coalition is needed.	Sjoerd Segijn & Leonard Millenaar
Employees' capabilities to change determine the organization's capacity to change.	Niels van der Eng & Cornell Vernooij
Participation is key to successful change.	Sjoerd Segijn & Leonard Millenaar
Resistance to change is detrimental to the success of change.	Lisa van Rossum & Niels van der Eng
A fair change process is important in achieving successful change.	Leonard Millenaar & Cornell Vernooij
Changing organizational culture is time-consuming and difficult.	Ernst Graamans & Joris Westhof
Organizational culture is related to performance.	Ernst Graamans & Joris Westhof
Goal setting combined with feedback is a powerful tool for change leaders.	Sjoerd Segijn & Lisa van Rossum

(*Continued*)

Table B.1 (Continued)

Assumption	Researchers
Commitment to change is an essential component of a successful change initiative.	Joris Westhof & Cornell Vernooij
Financial incentives are an effective way to encourage change and improve performance.	Lisa van Rossum & Joris Westhof
Self-managing teams perform better in realizing change than traditionally managed teams.	Leonard Millenaar & Lisa van Rossum

Appendix C
List of Firms Referred to in Chapter 3

Accenture
Achievers
Agility Ladder
Bain & Company
Being First
Boston Consulting Group
Capillary Consulting
Change Leader's Network
Cleveland Consulting Group
Connerpartners
DeGarmo
KPMG
McKinsey & Company
LenCD
Liquidplanner
Meliorate
Performance Consultants International
PwC
RocheMartin
Saint Consulting Group
SCInc.—SafetyBUILT-IN
Scontrino-Powell
Select International
Sense of Urgency Consulting
TTG Consultants
Zark Consultancy

Appendix D
Bibliography

Abbott, A. (1996). *The system of professions. An essay on the division of expert labor.* Chicago, IL: The University of Chicago Press.

Abraham, M., Griffin, D., & Crawford, J. (1999). Organisation change and management decision in museums. *Management Decision, 37*(10), 736–751.

Abrell-Vogel, C., & Rowold, J. (2014). Leaders' commitment to change and their effectiveness in change—a multilevel investigation. *Journal of Organizational Change Management, 27*(6), 900–921.

Acar, A. Z., & Acar, P. (2014). Organizational culture types and their effects on organizational performance in Turkish hospitals. *Emerging Markets Journal, 3*(3), 17–31.

Accenture. (n.d.). *Create and communicate a strong vision.* Retrieved January 28, 2016, from https://www.accenture.com/cn-en/insight-radical-change-are-you-ready-lead-on-summary.aspx

Achievers. (n.d.). *The impact of employee engagement on performance.* Retrieved January 5, 2016, from http://www.achievers.com/resource/impact-employee-engagement-performance

Adams, J. S. (1965). Inequity in social exchange. In L. Berkowitz (Ed.), *Advances in experimental social psychology* (pp. 267–299). New York, NY: Academic Press.

Adamson, G., Pine, J., Van Steenhoven, T., & Kroupa, J. (2006). How storytelling can drive strategic change. *Strategy & Leadership, 34*(1), 36–41.

AFM & DNB. (n.d.). *Capacity for change in the financial sector.* Retrieved February 3, 2016, from https://www.afm.nl/~/profmedia/files/brochures/2014/verandervermogen-banken-verzekeraars-2.ashx

Agility Ladder. (n.d.). *Creating a leading coalition.* Retrieved December 5, 2015, from http://agilityladder.nl/leading-the-transformation/build-a-guiding-coalition/

Ahmad, H., & Jalil, J. (2013). Relationship between personality traits and sense of urgency: A study of Repso Malaysia. *IBIMA Business Review, 2013*, 1–22.

Akgün, A. E., Lynn, G. S., & Byrne, J. C. (2006). Antecedents and consequences of unlearning in new product development teams. *The Journal of Product Innovation Management, 23*, 73–88.

Albert Einstein Quotes. (n.d.). In *BrainyQuote.* Retrieved December 20, 2015, from http://www.brainyquote.com/quotes/quotes/a/alberteins125154.html

Allaire, Y., & Firsirotu, M. E. (1984). Theories of organizational culture. *Organization Studies, 5*(3), 193–226.

Allen, R. C. (2002). *Guiding change journeys: A synergistic approach to organization transformation.* San Francisco, CA: Jossey-Bass and Pfeiffer.

Anderson, L. A., & Anderson, D. (2010a). *Ensuring your organization's capacity to change*. Retrieved November 12, 2015, from http://www.beingfirst.com/resources/pdf/SR_EnsuringOrgsCapacityToChg_v3_101006.pdf

Anderson, L. A., & Anderson, D. (2010b). *Ten common mistakes in leading transformation*. Retrieved January 28, 2016, from http://changeleadersnetwork.com/wp-content/uploads/2010/09/PC_TenCommonMistakes_v1_101006.pdf

Anderson, L. A., & Anderson, D. (2010c). *The change leader's roadmap*. San Francisco, CA: Jossey-Bass.

Antman, E. M. (1992). A comparison of results of meta-analyses of randomized controlled trials and recommendations of clinical experts. *Journal of the American Medical Association, 286*(2), 240–248.

Appelbaum, S. H., Habashy, S., Malo, J. L., & Shafiq, H. (2012). Back to the future: Revisiting Kotter's 1996 change model. *Journal of Management Development, 31*(8), 764–782.

Argyris, C. (1960). *Understanding organizational behavior*. Homewood, IL: Dorsey Press.

Argyris, C. (1962). *Interpersonal competence and organizational effectiveness*. Homewood, IL: Dorsey Press.

Armenakis, A. A., Harris, S. G., & Mossholder, K. W. (1993). Creating readiness for organizational change. *Human Relations, 46*(6), 681–703.

Balliet, D., & Van Lange, P. A.M. (2013). Trust, conflict, and cooperation: A meta-analysis. *Psychological Bulletin, 139*(5), 1090–1112.

Barber, B. (1963). Some problems in the sociology of professions. *Daedalus, 92*(4), 669–688.

Barends, E., & Ten Have, S. (2008). Op weg naar evidence-based verandermanagement. *Holland Management Review, 120*, 15–21.

Barends, E., Janssen, B., Ten Have, W. D., & Ten Have, S. (2013). Effects of change interventions: What kind of evidence do we really have? *Journal of Applied Behavioral Science, 50*(1), 5–27.

Barends, E., Janssen, B., Ten Have, W. D., & Ten Have, S. (2014). Difficult but doable: Increasing the internal validity of organizational change management studies. *The Journal of Applied Behavioral Science, 50*(1), 50–54.

Barends, E., Rousseau, D. M., & Briner, R. B. (2014). *Evidence-based management: The basic principles*. Amsterdam, NL: Center for Evidence-Based Management.

Barends, E., Villanueva, J., Briner, R. B., & Ten Have, S. (2015). Managers' attitudes and perceived barriers to evidence-based management: An international survey. In E. Barends (Ed.), *In search of evidence. Empirical findings and professional perspectives on evidence-based management* (pp. 143–178). Amsterdam, NL: VU University Press.

Barge, J. K. (1994). *Leadership: Communication skills for organizations and groups*. New York, NY: St. Martin's Press.

Barker, R. (2010). No, management is not a profession. *Harvard Business Review, 88*(7/8), 52–60.

Barnett, K. (2011). System members at odds: Managing divergent perspectives in the higher education change process. *Journal of Higher Education Policy and Management, 33*(2), 131–140.

Barratt-Pugh, L., Bahn, S., & Gakere, E. (2013). Managers as change agents. *Journal of Organizational Change Management, 26*(4), 748–764.

Baskerville, R. F. (2003). Hofstede never studied culture. *Accounting, Organizations and Society, 28*(1), 1–14.

Bass, B. M. (1985). *Leadership and performance beyond expectations*. New York, NY: The Free Press.

Bass, B. M. (1991). From transactional to transformational leadership: Learning to share the vision. *Organizational Dynamics*, *18*(3), 19–31.

Batchelor, R. (2015, February 25). *Grow your organizational change capacity through high quality change agents*. Retrieved January 28, 2016, from http://www.capillaryconsulting.com/grow-organizational-change-capacity-high-quality-change-agents/

Baum, J. R., Locke, E. A., & Kirkpatrick, S. A. A. (1998). Longitudinal study of the relation of vision and vision communication to venture growth in entrepreneurial firms. *Journal of Applied Psychology*, *83*(1), 43–54.

Beaujean, M., Davidson, J., & Madge, S. (2006, February). *The 'moment of truth' in customer service*. Retrieved March, 19, 2015, from http://www.mckinsey.com/insights/organization/the_moment_of_truth_in_customer_service

Beer, M., & Nohria, N. (2000). Cracking the code of change. *Harvard Business Review*, *78*(3), 133–141.

Belasco, J. A. (1990). *Teaching the elephant to dance. Empowering change in your organization*. New York, NY: Crown Publishers.

Bennebroek Gravenhorst, K. M., Werkman, R. A., & Boonstra, J. J. (2003). The change capacity of organisations: General assessment and five configurations. *Applied Psychology*, *52*(1), 3–105.

Bernerth, J. B., Armenakis, A. A., Field, H. S., & Walker, H. J. (2007). Justice, cynicism, and commitment: A study of important organizational change variables. *The Journal of Applied Behavioral Science*, *43*(3), 303–326.

Bierly, C., & Shy, E. (2013, December 9). *U.S. school systems miss the mark for developing talent into leadership roles*. Retrieved November 15, 2015, from http://www.bain.com/about/press/press-releases/us-school-systems-miss-the-mark-for-developing-talent-into-leadership-roles.aspx

Biswas, S. (2009). HR practices as a mediator between organizational culture and transformational leadership: Implications for employee performance. *Psychological Studies*, *54*(2), 114–123.

Blumer, H. (1969). *Symbolic interactionism: Perspective and method*. Englewood Cliffs, NJ: Prentice-Hall.

Bouckenooghe, D., Schwarz, G. M., & Minbashian, A. (2015). Herscovitch and Meyer's Three Component model of commitment to change: Meta-analytic findings. *European Journal of Work and Organizational Psychology*, *24*(4), 578–595.

Bower, J. L. (2000). The purpose of change: A commentary on Jensen and Senge. In M. Beer, & N. Nohria (Eds.), *Breaking the code of change* (pp. 83–95). Boston, MA: Harvard Business School Press.

Bowling, N. A. (2007). Is the job satisfaction-job performance relationship spurious? A meta-analytic examination. *Journal of Vocational Behavior*, *71*(2), 167–185.

Bowman, D. (n.d.). *The five best ways to build—and—lose trust in the workplace*. Retrieved January 29, 2016, from http://www.ttgconsultants.com/articles/trust-workforce.html

Boyce, A. S., Nieminen, L. R. G., Gillespie, M. A., Ryan, A. M., & Denison, D. (2015). Which comes first, organizational culture or performance? A longitudinal study of causal priority with automobile dealerships. *Journal of Organizational Behavior*, *36*(3), 339–359.

Bridges, W. (1991). *Managing transitions: Making the most of change*. Reading, MA: Perseus Books.

Briner, R. (2015, November 27). *Why the CEBMa model is misleading—further comments* [Blog post]. Retrieved January 4, 2016, from https://groups.google.com/forum/#!msg/evidence-based-management/Gjj2B_Qeav4/uG8pDs_rCAAJ

Brockner, J. (2006). Why it's so hard to be fair. *Harvard Business Review, 84*(3), 122–129.

Brockner, J., & Wiesenfeld, B. M. (1996). An integrative framework for explaining reactions to decisions: The interactive effects of outcomes and procedures. *Psychological Bulletin, 120*(2), 189–208.

Brown, K. G., Charlier, S. D., Rynes, S. L., & Hosmanek, A. (2013). What do we teach in organizational behavior? An analysis of MBA syllabi. *Journal of Management Education, 37*(4), 447–472.

Brown, S., & Eisenhardt, K. (1995). Product development: Past research, present findings, and future directions. *The Academy of Management Review, 20*(2), 343–378.

Brown, T. (2009). *Change by design: How design thinking transforms organizations and inspires innovation*. Broadway, NY: HarperCollins Publishers.

Brownell, K. D., & Rodin, J. (1994). The dieting maelstrom: Is it possible and advisable to lose weight? *American Psychologist, 49*(9), 781–791.

Buick, F., Blackman, D. A., O'Donell, M. E., O'Flynn, J. L., & West, D. (2015). Can enhanced performance management support sector change? *Journal of Organizational Change Management, 28*(2), 271–289.

Buono, A. F., & Kerber, K. W. (2009, June). *Building organizational change capacity*. Unpublished paper presented at the Management Consulting Division International Conference. Vienna, Austria.

Burfisher, M. E., Robinson, S., & Thierfelder, K. (2001). The impact of NAFTA on the United States. *Journal of Economic perspectives, 15*(1), 125–144.

Burgers, J. S. (2015). Opschudding over evidence-based medicine. Van reductionisme naar realisme in de toepassing van richtlijnen. *Nederlands Tijdschrift voor Geneeskunde, 159*, 1–5.

Burns, J. M. (1978). *Leadership*. New York, NY: Harper & Row.

Burpitt, W. (2009). Exploration versus exploitation: Leadership and the paradox of administration. *Journal of Behavioral and Applied Management, 10*(2), 227–246.

Busato, V. (2014). *Psychologie al dente*. Amsterdam, NL: Uitgeverij Fosfor.

Büschgens, T., Bausch, A., & Balkin, D. B. (2013). Organizational culture and innovation: A meta-analytic review. *Journal of Product Innovation Management, 30*(4), 763–781.

Bushman, B. J., & Wells, G. L. (2001). Narrative impressions of literature: The availability bias and the corrective properties of meta-analytic approaches. *Personality and Social Psychology Bulletin, 27*(9), 1123–1130.

Butler, M. J. R. (2003). Managing from the inside out: Drawing on 'receptivity' to explain variation in strategy implementation. *British Journal of Management, 14*(1), 47–60.

Caldwell, D. F., Chatman, J., O'Reilly, A. C., Ormitson, M., & Lapiz, M. (2008). Implementing strategic change in a health care system: The importance of leadership and change readiness. *Health Care Manage Review, 33*(2), 124–133.

Cameron, K., & Quinn, R. E. (2011). *Diagnosing and changing organizational culture: Based on the competing values framework*. Reading, MA: Addison Wesley Longman.

Cândido, C. J. F., & Santos, P. (2015). Strategy implementation: What is the failure rate? *Journal of Management & Organization, 21*(2), 237–262.

Carless, S. A., Rasiah, J., & Irmer, B. E. (2009). Discrepancy between human resource research and practice: Comparison of industrial/organisational psychologists and human resource practitioners' beliefs. *Australian Psychologist, 44*(2), 105–111.

Carlock, R., & Blondel, C. (2004, September 1). *Fair process and family business.* Retrieved May 17, 2015, from http://www.campdenfb.com/article/fair-process-and-family-business-governance

Cavafy, C. P. (1992). *Cavafy, collected poems.* Princeton, NJ: Princeton University Press.

Center for Evidence-Based Management. (CEBMa). (n.d. a). *What is evidence-based management?* Retrieved January 14, 2016, from http://www.cebma.org/frequently-asked-questions/evidence-based-management/

Center for Evidence-Based Management. (CEBMa). (n.d. b). *Resources and tools.* Retrieved January 14, 2016, from http://www.cebma.org/resources-and-tools/

Cerasoli, C. P., Nicklin, J. M., & Ford, M. T. (2014). Intrinsic motivation and extrinsic incentives jointly predict performance: A 40-year meta-analysis. *Psychological Bulletin, 140*(4), 980–1008.

Chalmers, I., Enkin, M., & Keirse, M. J. (1993). Preparing and updating systematic reviews of randomized controlled trials of health care. *The Milbank Quarterly, 71*(3), 411–437.

Chan, L. L. M., Schaffer, M. A., & Snape, E. (2004). In search of sustained competitive advantage: The impact of organizational culture, competitive strategy and human resource management practices on firm performance. *The International Journal of Human Resource Management, 15*(1), 17–35.

Changing Minds. (n.d.). *Transformational leadership.* Retrieved November 20, 2015, from http://changingminds.org/disciplines/leadership/styles/transformational_leadership.htm

Charlier, S. D., Brown, K. G., & Rynes, S. L. (2011). Teaching evidence-based management in MBA programs: What evidence is there? *Academy of Management Learning & Education, 10*(2), 222–236.

Chauvin, B., Rohmer, O., Spitzenstetter, F., Raffin, D., Schimchowitsch, S., & Louvet, E. (2014). Assessment of job stress factors in a context of organizational change. *European Review of Applied Psychology, 64*(6), 299–306.

Chiaburu, D. S., Smith, T. A., Wang, J., & Zimmerman, R. D. (2015). Relative importance of leader influences for subordinates' proactive behaviors, prosocial behaviors, and task performance. *Journal of Personnel Psychology, 13*(2), 70–86.

Chiocchio, F., & Essiembre, H. (2009). Cohesion and performance: A meta-analytic review of disparities between project teams, production teams, and service teams. *Small Group Research, 40*(4), 382–420.

Christersson, M., & Rothe, P. (2012). Impacts of organizational relocation: A conceptual framework. *Journal of Corporate Real Estate, 14*(4), 226–243.

Clark, T. (2013, May 22). *How to create a sense of urgency with your team.* Retrieved February 4, 2016, from http://www.liquidplanner.com/blog/team-urgency/

Clark, T., & Greatbach, D. (2004). Management fashion as image-spectacle: The production of best-selling management books. *Management Communication Quarterly, 17*(3), 396–424.

Clay-Williams, R., Nosrati, H., Cunningham, F. C., Hillman, K., & Braithwaite, J. (2014). Do large-scale hospital- and system-wide interventions improve patient outcomes: A systematic review. *BMC Health Services Research, 14*(1), 369–382.

Cleveland Consulting Group. (n.d.). *Developing emotional intelligence: Studies show success of programs designed to increase EI*. Retrieved January 28, 2015, from http://www.clevelandconsultinggroup.com/pdfs/rb_Developing_EI.pdf

Coch, L., & French, J. R. P. (1948). Overcoming resistance to change. *Human Relations, 1*(4), 512–532.

Coffman, J., & Neuenfeldt, B. (2014). *Everyday moments of truth: Frontline managers are to women's career aspirations*. Retrieved January 28, 2016, from http://www.bain.com/Images/BAIN_REPORT_Everyday_moments_of_truth.pdf

Cohen, J. (1988). *Statistical power analysis for the behavioral sciences* (2nd ed.). New York, NY: Routledge.

Cohen, S. G., & Ledford, G. E. (1994). The effectiveness of self-managing teams: A quasi-experiment. *Human Relations, 47*(1), 13–43.

Cohen, S. G., Chang, L., & Ledford, G. E. (1997). A hierarchical construct of self-management leadership and its relationship to quality of work life and perceived work group effectiveness. *Personnel Psychology, 50*(2), 275–308.

Cohen-Charash, Y., & Spector, P. E. (2001). The role of justice in organizations: A meta-analysis. *Organizational Behavior and Human Decision Processes, 86*(2), 278–321.

Collins, J. C. (2001). *Good to great: Why some companies make the leap . . . and others don't*. New York, NY: HarperCollins Publishers.

Collins, J. C. (2009). *How the mighty fall: And why some companies never give in*. New York, NY: HarperCollins Publishers.

Collins, J. C., & Porras, J. I. (1996). Building your company's vision. *Harvard Business Review, 74*(5), 65–77.

Collins, J. C., & Porras, J. I. (1997). *Built to last: Successful habits of visionary companies*. New York, NY: Harper Business.

Colquitt, J. A., Scott, B. A., & LePine, J. A. (2007). Trust, trustworthiness, and trust propensity: A meta-analytic test of their unique relationships with risk taking and job performance. *Journal of Applied Psychology, 92*(4), 909–927.

Colquitt, J. A., Scott, B. A., Rodell, J. B., Long, D. M., Zapata, C. P., Conlon, D. E., & Wesson, M. J. (2013). Justice at the millennium, a decade later: A meta-analytic test of social exchange and affect-based perspectives. *Journal of Applied Psychology, 98*(2), 199–236.

Conner, D. R. (1992). *Managing at the speed of change: How resilient managers succeed and prosper where others fail*. New York, NY: Random House.

Conner, D. R. (2006). *Managing at the speed of change: How resilient managers succeed and prosper where others fail*. New York, NY: Random House.

Conner, D. R. (2012, July 12). *The dirty little secret behind the 70% failure rate of change projects*. Retrieved September 16, 2015, from http://www.connerpartners.com/how-challenging-is-the-change/the-dirty-little-secret-behind-the-70-failure-rate-of-change-projects

Connors, R., & Smith, T. (2011). *Change the culture, change the game: The breakthrough strategy for energizing your organization and creating accountability for results*. New York, NY: Random House.

Cooke, R. A., & Lafferty, J. C. (1989). *Organizational culture inventory*. Plymouth, MI: Human Synergistics.

Cordery, J. L., Mueller, W. S., & Smith, L. M. (1991). Attitudinal and behavioral effects of autonomous group working: A longitudinal field study. *Academy of Management Journal, 34*(2), 464–476.

Cotton, J. L., Vollrath, D. A., Froggatt, K. L., Lengnick-Hall, M. L., & Jennings, K. R. (1988). Employee participation: Diverse forms and different outcomes. *Academy of Management Review, 13*(1), 8–22.

Covington, J. (2001). Leading successful, sustainable change. *Executive Excellence, 18*(12), 15–16.

Critical Appraisal Skills Programme. (CASP). (n.d.). *CASP checklists.* Retrieved January 29, 2015, from http://www.casp-uk.net/#!casp-tools-checklists/c18f8

Croon, De E. M., Sluiter, J. K., Kuijer, P. P., & Frings-Dresen, M. H. (2005). The effect of office concepts on worker health and performance: A systematic review of the literature. *Ergonomics, 48*(2), 119–134.

Csikszentmihalyi, M. (1998). *Finding flow: The psychology of engagement with everyday life.* New York, NY: Basic Books.

Cummings, T. G., & Worley, C. G. (2005). *Organization development and change* (8th ed.). Mason, OH: South-Western.

Dauber, D. (2012). Opposing positions in M&A research: Culture, integration and performance. *Cross Cultural Management, 19*(3), 375–398.

Davidson, J. (2002). *The complete idiot's guide to change management.* Indianapolis, IN: Alpha Books.

De Croon, E. M., Sluiter, J. K., Kuijer, P. P., & Frings-Dresen, M. H. (2005). The effect of office concepts on worker health and performance: A systematic review of the literature. *Ergonomics, 48*(2), 119–134.

DeGroot, T., Kiker, D. S., & Cross, T. C. (2000). A meta-analysis to review organizational outcomes related to charismatic leadership. *Canadian Journal of Administrative Sciences, 17*(4), 356–372.

Dembosky, A. (2013, February 22). *Evan William on building a company mindfully.* Retrieved February 2, 2016, from http://blogs.ft.com/tech-blog/2013/02/evan-williams-on-holacracy-and-building-a-company-mindfully/

Denison, D. R. (1990). *Corporate culture and organizational effectiveness.* New York, NY: John Wiley & Sons.

Denison, D. R., & Neale, W. S. (1996). *Denison organizational culture survey.* Ann Arbor, MI: Aviat.

Denning, S. (2011, July 23). *How do you change an organizational culture?* Retrieved April 12, 2015, from http://www.forbes.com/sites/stevedenning/2011/07/23/how-do-you-change-an-organizational-culture/#30231eac3baa

Detert, J. R., & Pollock, T. G. (2008). Values, interests, and the capacity to act understanding professionals' responses to market-based improvement initiatives in highly institutionalized organizations. *The Journal of Applied Behavioral Science, 44*(2), 186–214.

Deutsch, M. (1975). Equity, equality, and need: What determines which value will be used as the basis for distributive justice? *Journal of Social Issues, 31*(3), 137–149.

De Waal, A. A. (2007). The characteristics of a high-performance organization. *Business Strategy Series, 8*(3), 179–185.

De Wit, B., & Meyer, R. (1999). *Strategy synthesis: Resolving strategy paradoxes to create competitive advantage.* London, UK: International Thompson Business Press.

Diab, S. M. (2014). The impact of leadership styles on selection the areas of organizational change (An empirical study on the Jordanian pharmaceutical companies). *International Journal of Business and Management, 9*(8), 140–154.

Dirks, K. T., & Ferrin, D. L. (2002). Trust in leadership: Meta-analytic findings and implications for research and practice. *Journal of Applied Psychology, 87*(4), 611–628.

Doucouliagos, C. (1995). Worker participation and productivity in labor-managed and participatory capitalist firms: A meta-analysis. *Industrial and Labor Relations Review, 49*(1), 58–77.

Dougherty, J. (2013, December 3). *The best way for new leaders to build trust*. Retrieved November 11, 2015, from https://hbr.org/2013/12/the-best-way-for-new-leaders-to-build-trust/

Drucker, P. F. (1957). *Management in de praktijk*. Bussum, NL: G. J. A. Ruys Uitgeversmaatschappij.

Drucker, P. F. (1996). *Your leadership is unique. Good news: There is no one "leadership personality"*. Retrieved December 12, 2015, from http://boston.goarch.org/assets/files/your%20leadership%20is%20unique.pdf

Drucker, P. F. (2010). *Technology, management, and society*. Boston, MA: Harvard Business Press.

Druskat, V. U., & Wheeler, J. V. (2004). *How to lead a self-managing team*. Retrieved January 3, 2016, from http://sloanreview.mit.edu/article/how-to-lead-a-selfmanaging-team/

Dunnette, M., & Brown, Z. (1968). Behavioral science research and the conduct of business. *Academy of Management Journal, 11*(2), 177–188.

Eagan, O. (2012, December 12). *Strategic comms 50: Importance of fair process in entitlement*. Retrieved February 2, 2015, from http://tscg.biz/2012/12/strategic-comms-50-importance-of-fair-process-in-entitlement.html

Eckes, G. (2001). *Making Six Sigma last: Managing the balance between cultural and technical change*. New York, NY: John Wiley & Sons.

The *Economist*. (2015, December 12). *In praise of human guinea pigs*. Retrieved January 14, 2016, from http://www.economist.com/news/leaders/21679799-doctors-use-evidence-when-prescribing-treatments-policymakers-should-too-praise-human

Edmondson, D. R., & Boyer, S. L. (2013). The moderating effect of the boundary spanning role on perceived supervisory support: A meta-analytic review. *Journal of Business Research, 66*(11), 2186–2192.

Elias, S. M., & Mittal, R. (2011). The importance of supervisor support for a change initiative: An analysis of job satisfaction and involvement. *International Journal of Organizational Analysis, 19*(4), 305–316.

EPPI-Centre. (n.d.). *Guidelines for the reporting of primary empirical research studies in education (The REPOSE Guidelines)*. Retrieved January 29, 2015, from https://eppi.ioe.ac.uk/cms/Portals/0/PDF%20reviews%20and%20summaries/EPPI%20REPOSE%20Guidelines%20A4%202.1.pdf

Erez, A., Lepine, J. A., & Elms, H. (2002). Effects of rotated leadership and peer evaluation on the functioning and effectiveness of self-managed teams: A quasi-experiment. *Personnel Psychology, 55*(4), 929–948.

Erez, M. (1977). Feedback: A necessary condition for the goal setting-performance relationship. *Journal of Applied Psychology, 62*(5), 624–627.

Erwin, D. G., & Garman, A. N. (2010). Resistance to organizational change: Linking research and practice. *Leadership & Organization Development Journal, 31*(1), 39–56.

Ewenstein, B., Smith, W., & Sologar, A. (2015, July). *Changing change management*. Retrieved January 1, 2016, from http://www.mckinsey.com/insights/leading_in_the_21st_century/changing_change_management?cid=other-eml-ttn-mip-mck-oth-1512

Farley, J. U., Hoenig, S., & Ismail, Z. (2008). Organizational culture, innovativeness, market orientation and firm performance in South Africa: An interdisciplinary perspective. *Journal of African Business*, 9(1), 59–76.

Farmer, B. A., Slater, J. W., & Wright, K. S. (1998). The role of communication in achieving shared vision under new organizational leadership. *Journal of Public Relations Research*, 10(4), 219–235.

Faull, K., Kalliath, T., & Smith, D. (2004). Organizational culture: The dynamics of culture on organizational change within a rehabilitation center. *Organization Development Journal*, 22(1), 40–55.

Fausing, M. S., Joensson, T. S., Lewandowski, J., & Bligh, M. (2015). Antecedents of shared leadership: Empowering leadership and interdependence. *Leadership & Organization Development Journal*, 36(3), 271–291.

Fink, A. (1998). *Conducting research literature reviews: From the Internet to paper*. London, UK: Sage Publications.

Fitzgerald, L., Ferlie, E., Addicott, R., Baeza, J., Buchanan, D., & McGivern, G. (2007). Service improvement in healthcare: Understanding change capacity and change context. *Clinician Management*, 15(2), 61–74.

Folger, R., & Skarlicki, D. (1999). Unfairness and resistance to change: Hardship as Mistreatment. *Journal of Organizational Change Management*, 12(1), 35–50.

Franke, R. H., & Kaul, J. D. (1978). The Hawthorne experiments: First statistical interpretation. *American Sociological Review*, 43(5), 623–643.

Fredberg, T., Beer, M., Eisenstat, R., Foote, N., & Norrgren, F. (2008). *Embracing commitment and performance: CEOs and practices to manage paradox*. Retrieved October 17, 2015, on http://www.hbs.edu/faculty/Publication%20Files/08–052_18284f5a-c48b-45e9-acfd-8b3d3242514e.pdf

Frese, M. (2015, November 27). *Re: Why the CEBMa model may, for some people, be misleading—some suggestions for improvement* [Blog post]. Retrieved December 15, 2015, from https://groups.google.com/forum/#!msg/evidence-based-management/Gjj2B_Qeav4/eKV65–7sCAAJ

Fuchs, S., & Prouska, R. (2014). Creating positive employee change evaluation: The role of different levels of organizational support and change participation. *Journal of Change Management*, 14(3), 361–383.

Gabriel, H., Kottasz, R., & Bennett, R. (2006). Advertising planning, ad-agency use of advertising models, and the academic practitioner divide. *Marketing Intelligence & Planning*, 24(5), 505–527.

Gabris, G. T., Golembiewski, R. T., & Ihrke, D. M. (2001). Leadership credibility, board relations, and administrative innovation at the local government level. *Journal of Public Administration Research & Theory*, 11(1), 89–108.

Garbers, Y., & Konradt, U. (2014). The effect of financial incentives on performance: A quantitative review of individual and team-based financial incentives. *Journal of Occupational and Organizational Psychology*, 87(1), 102–137.

Gardner, J. W. (1993). *On leadership*. New York, NY: Free Press.

Gates, B. (1995). *The road ahead*. New York, NY: Viking Press.

Georgle Carlin (n.d.). In *Goodreads*. Retrieved February 4, 2016, from http://www.goodreads.com/quotes/81562-isn-t-it-a-bit-unnerving-that-doctors-call-what-they

Gersick, C. J. (1988). Time and transition in work teams: Toward a new model of group development. *Academy of Management Journal, 31*(1), 9–41.

Ghoshal, S. (2005). Bad management theories are destroying good management practices. *Academy of Management Learning & Education, 4*(1), 75–91.

Gilley, A., Dixon, P., & Gilley, J. W. (2008). Characteristics of leadership effectiveness: Implementing change and driving innovation in organizations. *Human Resource Development Quarterly, 19*(2), 153–169.

Goleman, D. (1995). *Emotional intelligence: Why it can matter more than IQ*. New York, NY: Bantam Dell.

Goleman, D. (1998). *Working with emotional intelligence*. New York, NY: Bantam Dell.

Goleman, D. (2015). *On emotional intelligence*. Boston, MA: Harvard Business Review Press.

Goleman, D. (n.d.). *Emotional intelligence*. Retrieved January 14, 2016, from http://www.danielgoleman.info/topics/emotional-intelligence/

Goodie, A. S., & Crooks, C. L. (2004). Time-pressure effects on performance in a base-rate task. *The Journal of General Psychology, 131*(1), 18–28.

Gray, J. R. (1999). A bias toward short-term thinking in threat-related negative emotional states. *Personality and Social Psychology Bulletin, 25*(1), 65–75.

Greenberg. (1987). A Taxonomy of organizational justice theories. *Academy of Management Review, 12*(1), 9–22.

Greene, R. J. (2011). *Rewarding performance: Guiding principles; custom strategies*. New York, NY: Routledge.

Greenwood, E. (1957). Attributes of a profession. *Social Work, 2*(3), 44–55.

Greenwood, J. D. (1994). *Realism, identity and emotion: Reclaiming social psychology*. London, UK: Thousand Oaks.

Groves, P. S. (2014). The relationship between safety culture and patient outcomes: Results from pilot meta-analyses. *Western Journal of Nursing Research, 36*(1), 66–83.

Gupta, V. K., Huang, R., & Niranjan, S. (2010). A longitudinal examination of the relationship between team leadership and performance. *Journal of Leadership & Organizational Studies, 17*(4), 335–350.

Gupta, Y. P., & Somers, T. M. (1992). The measurement of manufacturing flexibility. *European Journal of Operational Research, 60*(2), 166–182.

Hammer, M., & Champy, J. (1993). *Reengineering the corporation: A manifesto for business revolution*. London, UK: Nicholas Brearly.

Hammer, M., & Stanton, S. A. (1995). *The reengineering revolution: A handbook*. New York, NY: HarperCollins.

Harari, O. (1995). U2D2: The Rx for leadership blues. *Management Review, 84*(8), 34–36.

Harms, P. D., & Credé, M. (2010). Emotional intelligence and transformational and transactional leadership: A meta-analysis. *Journal of Leadership & Organizational Studies, 17*(1), 5–17.

Harrison, D. A., Newman, D. A., & Roth, P. L. (2006). How important are job attitudes? Meta-analytic comparisons of integrative behavioral outcomes and time sequences. *The Academy of Management Journal, 49*(2), 305–325.

Hartnell, C. A., Ou, A. Y., & Kinicki, A. (2011). Organizational culture and organizational effectiveness: A meta-analytic investigation of the competing values framework's theoretical suppositions. *Journal of Applied Psychology, 96*(4), 677–694.

Hay Group. (n.d.). *Emotional intelligence training.* Retrieved January 14, 2016, from http://www.haygroup.com/leadershipandtalentondemand/your-challenges/emotional-intelligence/index.aspx

Heath, C., & Heath, D. (2010). *Switch: How to change things when change is hard.* New York, NY: Broadway Books.

Heckmann, N., Steger, T., & Dowling, M. (2016). Organizational capacity for change, change experience, and change project performance. *Journal of Business Research, 69*(2), 777–784.

Hedges, L., & Olkin, I. (1980). Vote-counting methods in research synthesis. *Psychological Bulletin, 88*(2), 359–369.

Heifetz, R. A., Grashow, A., & Linsky, M. (2009). *The practice of adaptive leadership: Tools and tactics for changing your organization and the world.* Boston, MA: Harvard Business Press.

Heller, J. (1998). *Essential managers: Managing change.* New York, NY: D. K. Publishing.

Henderson, B. (n.d.). *Why change is so difficult.* Retrieved August 1, 2015, from https://www.bcgperspectives.com/content/Classics/why_change_is_so_difficult/

Heracleous, L. (2001). An ethnographic study of culture in the context of organizational change. *The Journal of Applied Behavioral Science, 37*(4), 426–446.

Herrmann, D., & Felfe, J. (2013). Moderators of the relationship between leadership style and employee creativity: The role of task novelty and personal initiative. *Creativity Research Journal, 25*(2), 172–181.

Herscovitch, L., & Meyer, J. P. (2002). Commitment to organizational change: Extension of a three-component model. *Journal of Applied Psychology, 87*(3), 474–487.

Hesselbein, F. (2000). The key to cultural transformation. In F. Hesselbein, & R. Johnston (Eds.), *On leading change: A leader to leader guide* (pp. 1–6). San Francisco, CA: Jossey-Bass.

Hesselbein, F., & Johnston, R. (2002). *On leading change: A leader to leader guide.* San Francisco, CA: Jossey-Bass.

Higgins, J. P. T., & Green, S. (2006). *Cochrane handbook for systematic reviews of interventions 4.2.6* [updated September 2006]. Retrieved September 1, 2015, from http://community.cochrane.org/sites/default/files/uploads/Handbook4.2.6Sep2006.pdf

Hoch, D. J., Roeding, C., Purkert, G., & Lindner, S. K. (1999). *Secrets of software success: Management insights from 100 software firms around the world.* Boston, MA: Harvard Business Review Press.

Hofstede, G. (1980). *Culture's consequences: International differences in work-related values.* London, UK: Sage Publications.

Hoheb, C. (2014, January 29). *Lessons learned from France Telecom: Stress in the workplace.* Retrieved January 13, 2016, from http://www.corporatewellnessmagazine.com/focused/france-telecom-layoffs/

Holt, D. T., Armenakis, A. A., Feild, H. S., & Harris, S. G. (2007). Readiness for organizational change: The systematic development of a scale. *The Journal of Applied Behavioral Science, 43*(2), 232–255.

Hon, A. H. Y., Bloom, M., & Crant, J. M. (2014). Overcoming resistance to change and enhancing creative performance. *Journal of Management, 40*(3), 919–941.

Hope-Hailey, V., & Balogun, J. (2002). Devising context sensitive approaches to change: The example of Glaxo Wellcome. *Long Range Planning, 35,* 153–178.

Howells, J., Nedeva, M., & Georghiou, L. (1998). *Industry academic links in UK*. Retrieved February 8, 2016, from https://www.google.nl/url?sa=t&rct=j&q=&esrc=s&source=web&cd=2&ved=0ahUKEwjG4Kv79ufKAhXGwxQKHYqbC3AQFggnMAE&url=http%3A%2F%2Fwww.ibrarian.net%2Fnavon%2Fpaper%2FIndustry_Academic_Links_in_the_UK.pdf%3Fpaperid%3D13710593&usg=AFQjCNFWk8qk5QNnVSE-MRJYRbznTr3Gnw&cad=rja

Hughes, M. (2011). Do 70 per cent of all organizational change initiatives really fail? *Journal of Change Management, 11*(4), 451–464.

Hülsheger, U. R., Anderson, N., & Salgado, J. F. (2009). Team-level predictors of innovation at work: A comprehensive meta-analysis spanning three decades of research. *Journal of Applied Psychology, 94*(5), 1128–1145.

Humble, J., Molesky, J., & O'Reilly, B. (2015). *Lean enterprise: How high performance organizations innovate at scale*. Sebastopol, CA: O'Reilly Media.

Hunter, J., & Schmidt, F. (1990). *Methods of meta-analysis: Correcting error and bias in research findings*. Thousand Oaks: CA: Sage Publications.

Ibarra, H. (2015). *Act like a leader, think like a leader*. Boston, MA: Harvard Business Review Press.

Imran, R., Zahoor, F., & Zaheer, A. (2012). Leadership and performance relationship: Culture matters. *International Journal of Innovation, Management and Technology, 3*(6), 713–717.

Incentive. (n.d.). In *Merriam-Webster*. Retrieved February 2, 2016, from http://www.merriam-webster.com/dictionary/incentive

Ingvaldsen, J. A., & Rolfsen, M. (2012). Autonomous work groups and the challenge of intergroup coordination. *Human Relations, 65*(7), 861–881.

Isern, J. & Pung, C. (2007, November). *Driving radical change*. Retrieved January 28, 2015, from http://www.mckinsey.com/insights/organization/driving_radical_change

Jackman, J. M., & Strober, M. N. (2003). Fear of feedback. *Harvard Business Review, 81*(4), 101–108.

Jaros, S. (2010). Commitment to organizational change: A critical review. *Journal of Change Management, 10*(1), 79–108.

Jarrett, S. (n.d.). *How to change employee behavior*. Retrieved January 28, 2015, from http://www.selectinternational.com/blog/bid/188077/How-to-Change-Employee-Behavior

Job satisfaction. (2016, January 27). In *Wikipedia*. Retrieved January 27, 2016, from http://en.wikipedia.org/wiki/Job_satisfaction

Johnson, M. D., Hollenbeck, J. R., DeRue, D. S., Barnes, C. M., & Jundt, D. (2013). Functional versus dysfunctional team change: Problem diagnosis and structural feedback for self-managed teams. *Organizational Behavior and Human Decision Processes, 122*(1), 1–11.

Joseph, D. L., Jin, J., Newman, A., & O'Boyle, E. H. (2015). Why does self-reported emotional intelligence predict job performance? A meta-analytic investigation of mixed EI. *Journal of Applied Psychology, 100*(2), 298–342.

Joseph, D. L., & Newman, D. A. (2010). Emotional intelligence: An integrative meta-analysis and cascading model. *Journal of Applied Psychology, 95*(1), 54–78.

Judge, W., & Douglas, T. (2009). Organizational change capacity: A systematic development of a scale. *Journal of Organizational Change Management, 22*(6), 635–649.

Judge, W. Q., & Elenkov, D. (2005). Organizational capacity for change and environmental performance: An empirical assessment of Bulgarian firms. *Journal of Business Research, 58*(7), 893–901.

Judge, W. Q., Naoumova, I., & Douglas, T. (2009). Organizational capacity for change and firm performance in a transition economy. *The International Journal of Human Resource Management, 20*(8), 1737–1752.

Judge, T. A., Thoresen, C. J., Bono, J. E., & Patton, G. K. (2001). The job satisfaction-job performance relationship: A qualitative and quantitative review. *Psychological Bulletin, 127*(3), 376–407.

Karmakar, A., & Datta, B. (2012). *Principles and practices of management and business communication.* New Delhi, IN: Dorling Kindersley.

Katzenbach, J. R., & Smith, D. K. (1992). Why teams matter. *McKinsey Quarterly, 3,* 3–27.

Kegan, R., & Lahey, L. (2001). *How the way we talk can change the way we work.* New York, NY: John Wiley & Sons.

Kegan, R., & Lahey, L. (2009). *Immunity to change: How to overcome it and unlock the potential in yourself and your organization.* Boston, MA: Harvard Business Press.

Keller, S., & Aiken, C. (2009). *The inconvenient truth about change: Why it isn't working and what to do about it.* Retrieved July 10, 2015, from http://www.aascu.org/corporatepartnership/McKinseyReport2.pdf

Keller, S., & Aiken, C. (2014). *On performance culture.* Retrieved November 28, 2015, from http://www.oncourse.com.au/articles/McKinsey%20On%20Performance%20Culture.pdf

Kerber, K., & Buono, A. F. (2005). Rethinking organizational change: Reframing the challenge of change management. *Organizational Development Journal, 23*(3), 23–38.

Khurana, R., Nohria, N., & Penrice, D. (2005). Management as a profession. In J. W. Lorsch, L. Berlowitz, & A. Zelleke (Eds.), *Restoring trust in American business* (43–62). Cambridge, MA: Massachusetts Institute of Technology Press.

Kickul, J., Lester, S. W., & Finkl, J. (2002). Promise breaking during radical organizational change: Do justice interventions make a difference? *Journal of Organizational Behavior, 23*(4), 469–488.

Kirk, D. (1992). *World-class teams.* Retrieved November 11, 2015, from http://www.mckinsey.com/insights/organization/world-class_teams

Klarner, P., Probst, G., & Soparnot, R. (2007). *From change to the management organizational change capacity: A conceptual approach.* Retrieved February 3, 2015, from http://archive-ouverte.unige.ch/unige:5739

Kleingeld, A., Van Mierlo, H., & Arenas, L. (2011). The effect of goal setting on group performance: A meta-analysis. *Journal of Applied Psychology, 96*(6), 1289–1304.

Klonsky, E. J. (2010, September 10). *How to support your staff.* Retrieved November 16, 2015, from http://www.inc.com/guides/2010/09/how-to-support-your-staff.html

Kluger, A. N., & DeNisi, A. (1996). The effects of feedback interventions on performance: A historical review, a meta-analysis, and a preliminary feedback intervention theory. *Psychological Bulletin, 119*(2), 254–284.

Knight, R. (n.d.). *Resistance to change.* Retrieved January 29, 2016, from http://www.zarkconsultancy.com/wp-content/uploads/2015/07/resistance_to_change.pdf

Kong, D. T., Dirks, K. T., & Ferrin, D. L. (2014). Interpersonal trust within negotiations: Meta-analytic directions, critical contingencies, and directions for future research. *Academy of Management Journal, 57*(5), 1235–1255.

Kotrba, L. M., Gillespie, M. A., Schmidt, A. M., Smerek, R. E., Ritchie, S. A., & Denison, D. R. (2012). Do consistent corporate cultures have better business performance? Exploring the interaction effects. *Human Relations, 65*(2), 241–262.

Kotter, J. P. (1982). *The general managers.* New York, NY: Free Press.
Kotter, J. P. (1995). Leading change: Why transformation efforts fail. *Harvard Business Review, 73*(2), 59–67.
Kotter, J. P. (1996). *Leading change.* Boston, MA: Harvard Business Review Press.
Kotter, J. P. (2008). *A sense of urgency.* Boston, MA: Harvard Business Review Press.
Kotter, J. P. (2011a, June 7). *How to create a powerful vision for change.* Retrieved October 14, 2015, from http://www.forbes.com/sites/johnkotter/2011/06/07/how-to-create-a-powerful-vision-for-change/#14c411932a3c
Kotter, J. P. (2011b, July 12). *Change management vs. change leadership—What's the difference?* Retrieved November 20, 2015, from http://www.forbes.com/sites/johnkotter/2011/07/12/change-management-vs-change-leadership-whats-the-difference/#45ed310618ec
Kotter, J. P. (2012). *Leading change.* Boston, MA: Harvard Business Review Press.
Kotter, J. P., & Schlesinger, L. A. (1979). Choosing strategies for change. *Harvard Business Review, 86*(7/8), 130–139.
Kouzes, J., & Posner, B. (2012). *The leadership challenge: How to make extraordinary things happen in organizations.* San Francisco, CA: Jossey-Bass.
KPMG. (n.d.). *Strategy and operations.* Retrieved February 4, 2016, from http://www.kpmg.com/in/en/services/advisory/performance-technology/pages/businesseffectivenessstrategy.aspx
Kriegel, R. J., & Brandt, D. (1996). *Sacred cows make the best burgers.* New York, NY: Warner Books, Inc.
Kunze, F., Boehm, S., & Bruch, H. (2013). Age, resistance to change, and job performance. *Journal of Managerial Psychology, 28*(7/8), 741–760.
Laloux, F. (2014). *Reinventing organizations: A guide to creating organizations inspired by the next stage of human consciousness.* Brussel, BE: Nelson Parker.
Landau, D., Drori, I., & Porras, J. (2006). Vision change in a governmental R&D organization. *The Journal of Applied Behavioral Science, 42*(2), 145–171.
Langley, G. J., Moen, R., Nolan, K. M., Nolan, T. W., Norman, C. L., & Provost, L. P. (2009). *The improvement guide: A practical approach to enhancing organizational performance.* San Francisco, CA: Jossey-Bass.
Larkin, T., & Larkin, S. (1994). *Communicating change: Winning employee support for new business goals.* New York, NY: McGraw-Hill.
Latham, G. P. (2009). Motivate employee performance through goal setting. In E. A. Locke (Ed.), *Handbook of principles of organizational behavior* (pp. 161–178). Chichester, UK: John Wiley & Sons.
Lawrence, P. R. (1954). How to deal with resistance to change. *Harvard Business Review, 32*(3), 49–57.
LenCD. (n.d.). *How to work with incentives to stimulate change.* Retrieved May 15, 2015, from http://www.lencd.org/learning/howto-incentives
Leong, J., & Anderson, C. (2012). Fostering innovation through cultural change. *Library Management, 33*(8/9), 490–497.
Leventhal, G. S. (1980). What should be done with equity theory? New approaches to the study of fairness in social relationships. In K. Gergen, M. Greenberg, & R. Willis (Eds.), *Social exchange: Advances in theory and research* (pp. 27–55). New York, NY: Plenum Press.
Lewin, K., Lippitt, R., & White, R. K. (1938). Patterns of aggressive behavior in experimentally created "social climates." *The Journal of Social Psychology, 10*(2), 271–299.

Lewis, L. K., Schmisseur, A. M., Stephens, K. K., & Weir, K. E. (2006). Advice on communicating during organizational change. The content of popular press books. *Journal of Business Communication, 43*(2), 113–137.

Liedtka, J. (2000). In defense of strategy as design. *California Management Review, 42*(3), 8–30.

Lilienfeld, S. O., Lynn, S. J., Ruscio, J., & Beyerstein, B. L. (2010). *50 great myths of popular psychology. Shattering widespread misconceptions about human behavior.* Chichester, UK: Wiley-Blackwell.

Lines, R. (2007). Using power to install strategy: The relationships between expert power, position power, influence tactics and implementation success. *Journal of Change Management, 7*(2), 143–170.

Lippitt, L. L. (1999). Preferred futuring: The power to change whole systems of any size. In P. Holman, & T. Devane (Eds.), *The change handbook* (pp. 159–174). San Francisco, CA: Berrett-Koehler.

Llopis, G. (2012, July 16). *6 things that will make you (and your manager) a better leader.* Retrieved November 16, 2015, from http://www.forbes.com/sites/glennllopis/2012/07/16/6-things-that-will-make-you-and-your-manager-a-better-leader/

Locke, E. A. (1968). Toward a theory of task motivation and incentives. *Organizational Behavior and Human Performance, 3,* 157–189.

Locke, E. A., & Latham, G. P. (1990). *A theory of goal setting and task performance.* Englewood Cliffs, NJ: Prentice-Hall.

Loeser, H., O'Sullivan, P., & Irby, D. M. (2007). Leadership lessons from curricular change at the University of California, San Francisco, School of Medicine. *Academic Medicine, 82*(4), 324–330.

Logan, M. S., & Ganster, D. C. (2007). The effects of empowerment on attitudes and performance: The role of social support and empowerment beliefs. *Journal of Management Studies, 44*(8), 1523–1550.

Lowe, K. B., Kroeck, K. G., & Sivasubramaniam, N. (1996). Effectiveness correlates of transformational and transactional leadership: A meta-analytic review of the MLQ literature. *The Leadership Quarterly, 7*(3), 385–425.

Luchman, J. N., & González-Morales, M. G. (2013). Demands, control and support: A meta-analytic review of work characteristics interrelationships. *Journal of Occupational Health Psychology, 18*(1), 37–52.

Luo, Y., & Jiang, H. (2014). Effective public relations leadership in organizational change: A study of multinationals in mainland China. *Journal of Public Relations Research, 26*(2), 134–160.

Mabin, V. J., Forgeson, S., & Green, L. (2001). Harnessing resistance: Using the theory of constraints to assist change management. *Journal of European Industrial Training, 25*(2/3/4), 168–191.

Mansell, A., Brough, P., & Cole, K. (2006). Stable predictors of job satisfaction, psychological strain, and employee retention: An evaluation of organizational change within the New Zealand customs service. *International Journal of Stress Management, 13*(1), 84–107.

Mario Andretti Quotes. (n.d.). In *BrainyQuote.* Retrieved December 18, 2015, from http://www.brainyquote.com/quotes/quotes/m/marioandre130613.html

Markey, R. (2014). *Energetic, enthusiastic and creative employees.* Retrieved January 28, 2016, from http://www.bain.com/Images/BAIN_BRIEF_Loyalty_Insights_16_Energetic_enthusiastic_and_creative.pdf

Martins, R. C. (2008). *Clean code. A handbook of agile software craftsmanship*. New York, NY: Pearson Education.

Maurer, R. (2010). *Beyond the wall of resistance: Why 70% of all changes still fail—and what you can do about it*. Austin, TX: Bard Press.

Maxwell, J. C. (2013). *The 17 indisputable laws of teamwork: Embrace them and empower your team*. Nashville, TN: Thomas Nelson Inc.

Mayer, J. D., Caruso, D. R., & Salovey, P. (2000). Selecting a measure of emotional intelligence: The case for ability scales. In R. Bar-On, & J. D. A. Parker (Eds.), *The handbook of emotional intelligence* (pp. 320–342). New York, NY: Jossey-Bass.

Mayer, R. C., Davis, J. H., & Schoorman, F. D. (1995). An integrative model of organizational trust. *Academy of Management Review, 20*, 709–734.

Mayo, E. (1933). *The human problems of an industrial civilization*. New York, NY: Macmillan.

McCracken, M., & McIvor, R. (2013). Transforming the HR function through outsourced shared services: Insights from the public sector. *The International Journal of Human Resource Management, 24*(8), 1685–1707.

McGregor, D. (1960). *The human side of enterprise*. New York, NY: McGraw-Hill.

McGregor, D. (1967). *The professional manager*. New York, NY: McGraw-Hill.

McGuiness, T., & Morgan, R. E. (2005). The effect of market and learning orientation on strategy dynamics: The contributing effect of organisational change capability. *European Journal of Marketing, 39*(11/12), 1306–1326.

McKinsey & Company. (2010, March). *What successful transformation share: McKinsey global Surevy results*. Retrieved July 17, 2015, from http://www.mckinsey.com/insights/organization/what_successful_transformations_share_mckinsey_global_survey_results

McQuarrie, F. A. E. (2005). How the past is present(ed): A comparison of information on the Hawthorne studies in Canadian management and organizational behavior textbooks. *Canadian Journal of Administrative Sciences, 22*(3), 230–242.

Melcher, K. (n.d.). *Employee relations: Understanding employee commitment to change*. Retrieved January 29, 2016, from http://www.degarmo.com/understanding-employee-commitment-to-change

Mento, A. J., Steel, R. P., & Karren, R. J. (1987). A meta-analytic study of the effects of goal setting on task performance: 1966–1984. *Organizational Behavior and Human Decision Processes, 39*(1), 52–83.

Meyer, C., & Stensaker, I. (2006). Developing capacity for change. *Journal of Change Management, 6*(2), 217–230.

Meyer, J. P., Srinivas, E. S., Lal, J. B., & Topolnytsky, L. (2007). Employee commitment and support for an organizational change: Test of the three-component model in two cultures. *Journal of Occupational & Organizational Psychology, 80*(2), 185–211.

Micklethwait, J., & Wooldridge, A. (1998). *The witch doctors: Making sense of the management gurus*. New York, NY: Three Rivers Press.

Miller, C., Cardinal, L. B., & Glick, W. H. (1997). Retrospective reports in organizational research. A reexamination of recent evidence. *Academy of Management Journal, 40*(2), 189–204.

Miller, K. (2002). *The change agent's guide to radical improvement*. Milwaukee, WI: American Society for Quality.

Miller, K. I., & Monge, P. R. (1986). Participation, satisfaction, and productivity: A meta-analytic review. *Academy of Management Journal, 29*(4), 727–753.

Moher, D., Liberati, A., Tetzlaff, J., Altman, D. G., & PRISMA Group. (2009). Reprint—preferred reporting items for systematic reviews and meta-analyses: The PRISMA statement. *Physical Therapy*, 89(9), 873–880.

Moher, D., Schulz, K. F., & Altman, D. G. (2001). The CONSORT statement: Revised recommendations for improving the quality of reports of parallel-group randomised trials. *The Lancet*, 357(9263), 1191–1194.

Moore, T. J. (1995). *Deadly medicine: Why tens of thousands of heart patients died in America's worst drug disaster*. New York, NY: Simon & Schuster.

Mor Barak, M. E., Travis, D. J., Pyun, H., & Xie, B. (2009). The impact of supervision on worker outcomes: A meta-analysis. *Social Service Review*, 83(1), 3–32.

Motowildo, S. J., Borman, W. C., & Schmit, M. J. (1997). A theory of individual differences in task and contextual performance. *Human Performance*, 10(2), 71–83.

Mourier, P., & Smith, M. R. (2001). *Conquering organizational change. How to succeed where most companies fail*. Atlanta, GA: CEP Press.

Mousavi, S. A., Hosseini, S. Y., & Hassanpour, N. (2015). On the effects of organizational culture on organizational performance: An Iranian experience in state bank branches. *Iranian Journal of Management Studies*, 8(1), 97–116.

Naor, M., Goldstein, S. M., Linderman, K. W., & Schroeder, R. G. (2008). The role of culture as driver of quality management and performance: Infrastructure versus core quality practices. *Decision Sciences*, 39(4), 671–702.

Nasche, M. (n.d.). *Sense of urgency consulting*. Retrieved February 4, 2016, from http://senseofurgencyconsulting.com/

Neubert, M. J. (1998). The value of feedback and goal setting over goal setting alone and potential moderators of this effect: A meta-analysis. *Human Performance*, 11(4), 321–335.

Neves, P. (2011). Building commitment to change: The role of perceived supervisor support and competence. *European Journal of Work and Organizational Psychology*, 20(4), 437–450.

Newman, M., & Elbourne, D. (2005). Improving the usability of educational research: Guidelines for the REPOrting of primary empirical research Studies in Education (the REPOSE guidelines). *Evaluation and Research in Education*, 18(4), 201–212.

Ng, T. W. H. (2015). The incremental validity of organizational commitment, organizational trust, and organizational identification. *Journal of Vocational Behavior*, 88, 154–163.

Ng, T. W. H., & Sorensen, K. L. (2008). Toward a further understanding of the relationships between perceptions of support and work attitudes. *Group & Organization Management*, 33(3), 243–268.

Nouelle-Neuman, E., Schultz, W., & Wilke, J. (1971). *Das Fischer Lexikon Publizistik*. Bonn, DE: Broschiert.

Novak, D. (2012). *Taking people with you: The only way to make big things happen*. New York, NY: Portfolio and Penguin.

O'Boyle, E. H., Humphrey, R. H., Pollack, J. M., Hawver, T. H., & Story, P. A. (2011). The relation between emotional intelligence and job performance: A meta-analysis. *Journal of Organizational Behavior*, 32(5), 788–818.

O'Leary-Kelly, A. M., Martocchio, J. J., & Frink, D. D. (1994). A review of the influence of group goals on group performance. *Academy of Management Journal*, 37(5), 1285–1301.

Oreg, A. (2006). Personality, context, and resistance to organizational change. *European Journal of Work and Organizational Psychology, 15*(1), 73–101.
Oreg, S. (2003). Resistance to change: Developing an individual differences measure. *Journal of Applied Psychology, 88*(4), 680–693.
Oswald, S. L., Mossholder, K. W., & Harris, S. G. (1997). Relations between strategic involvement and managers' perceptions of environment and competitive strengths: The effect of vision salience. *Group and Organization Management, 22*(3), 343–365.
Oxtoby, B., McGuiness, T., & Morgan, R. (2002). Developing organizational change capability. *European Management Journal, 20*(3), 310–320.
Patanakul, P., Chen, J., & Lynn, G. S. (2012). Autonomous teams and new product development. *Journal of Product Innovation Management, 29*(5), 734–750.
Pearlman, E. (2006, February 2). *Robert I. Sutton: Making a case for evidence-based management*. Retrieved January 14, 2016, from http://www.cioinsight.com/c/a/Expert-Voices/Robert-I-Sutton-Making-a-Case-for-EvidenceBased-Management
Pearson, C. A. (1992). Autonomous workgroups: An evaluation at an industrial site. *Human Relations, 45*(9), 905–936.
Performance Consultants International. (n.d.). *Our values and vision*. Retrieved January 28, 2016, from http://www.performanceconsultants.com/values-vision
Peters, G. J. Y., Ruiter, R. A., & Kok, G. (2013). Threatening communication: A critical re-analysis and a revised meta-analytic test of fear appeal theory. *Health Psychology Review, 7*(1), 8–31.
Peters, T. J. (2001, December). *Tom Peters' true confessions*. Retrieved January 12, 2016, from http://www.fastcompany.com/44077/tom-peterss-true-confessions
Peters, T. J., & Waterman, R. H. (1982). *In search of excellence: Lessons from America's best-run companies*. New York, NY: Harper & Row.
Petrosino, A., Turpin-Petrosino, C., Hollis-Peel, M. E., Lavenberg, J. G., & Stern, A. (2004). *Scared straight and other juvenile awareness programs for preventing juvenile delinquency*. Retrieved July 19, 2015, from http://www.campbellcollaboration.org/lib/download/13/Scared+Straight_R.pdf
Pettigrew, A. M. (1979). On studying organizational cultures. *Administrative Science Quarterly, 24*(4), 570–581.
Petticrew, M., & Roberts, H. (2006). *Systematic reviews in the social sciences: A practical guide*. Malden, MA: Blackwell.
Pettit, R. (2006, December 3). *The agile manager: It might make the car go faster, but does it make the car more competitive?* Retrieved January 12, 2016, from http://www.rosspettit.com/2006/12/it-might-make-car-go-faster-but-does.html?m=1
Pfeffer, J. (2012). Foreword. In D. M. Rousseau (Ed.), *The Oxford handbook of evidence-based management* (pp. VII–X). New York, NY: Oxford University Press.
Pfeffer, J. (2015). *Leadership BS: Fixing workplaces and careers one truth at a time*. New York, NY: Harper Business.
Pfeffer, J., & Sutton, R. I. (2006a). *Hard facts, dangerous half-truths, and total nonsense: Profiting from evidence-based management*. Boston, MA: Harvard Business School Press.
Pfeffer, J., & Sutton, R. I. (2006b). Treat your organization as a prototype: The essence of evidence-based management. *Design Management Review, 17*(3), 10–14.
Piderit, S. K. (2000). Rethinking resistance and recognizing ambivalence: A multidimensional view of attitudes toward an organizational change. *Academy of Management Review, 25*(4), 783–794.

Pillai, R., Kohles, J. C., Bligh, M. C., Carsten, M. K., & Brodowsky, G. (2011). Leadership in "Confucian Asia": A three-country study of justice, trust, and transformational leadership. *Organization Management Journal*, 8(4), 242–259.

Pink, D. (2009, August). *The puzzle of motivation*. Retrieved February 2, 2016, from https://www.ted.com/talks/dan_pink_on_motivation?language=en#t-93360

Posner, A. Z., & Kouzes, J. M. (1988). Relating leadership and credibility. *Psychological Reports*, 63, 527–530.

Powel, J. (2011, April 8). *Supervisor support*. Retrieved on December 16, 2015, from http://www.scontrino-powell.com/2011/supervisor-support-a-key-ingredient-in-effective-leadership/

Power, J., & Waddell, D. (2004). The link between self-managed work teams and learning organizations using performance indicators. *The Learning Organization*, 11(3), 244–259.

Prajogo, D., & McDermott, C. M. (2010). The relationship between multidimensional organizational culture and performance. *International Journal of Operations & Production Management*, 31(7), 712–735.

PWC. (n.d. a). *People & change: How can you make change stick and manage human resources?* Retrieved May 8, 2015, from https://www.pwc.ch/en/our_services/advisory/consulting/people_change.html

PWC. (n.d. b) *People & change*. Retrieved February 4, 2016, from http://www.pwc.be/en/services/consulting/people-change.html

Quantum Health Resources & Associates. (n.d.). *Our services*. Retrieved February 2, 2016, from http://www.quantumhealthresources.com/services.htm

Quinn, R. E., & Rohrbaugh, J. (1981). A competing values approach to organizational effectiveness. *Public Productivity Review*, 5(2), 122–140.

Quinn, R. E., & Rohrbaugh, J. (1983). A spatial model of effectiveness criteria: Towards a competing values approach to organizational analysis. *Management Science*, 29, 363–377.

Quote Investigator. (n.d.). *When the facts change, I change my mind. What do you do, sir?* Retrieved December 14, 2015, from http://quoteinvestigator.com/2011/07/22/keynes-change-mind/

Rechtbank Amsterdam. (2009, June 12). *ECLI:NL:RBAMS:2009:BI7370*. Retrieved January 12, 2016, from http://deeplink.rechtspraak.nl/uitspraak?id=ECLI:NL:RBAMS:2009:BI7370

Richa. (2014, June 12). *Team structure: Creating and managing great teams*. Retrieved November 10, 2015, from https://blog.udemy.com/team-structure/

Rick, T. (2011, May 23). *Top 12 reasons why people resist change*. Retrieved June 6, 2015, from http://www.torbenrick.eu/blog/change-management/12-reasons-why-people-resist-change/

Rick, T. (2013, March 8). *Change is not the problem—Resistance to change is the problem*. Retrieved June 6, 2015, from http://www.torbenrick.eu/blog/change-management/change-is-not-the-problem-resistance-to-change-is-the-problem/

Riketta, M. (2002). Attitudinal organizational commitment and job performance: A meta-analysis. *Journal of Organizational Behavior*, 23(3), 257–266.

Robbins, S. R., & Duncan, R. B. (1988). The role of the CEO and top management in the creation and implementation of strategic vision. *The Executive Effect: Concepts and Methods for Studying Top Managers*, 2, 205–236.

Robertson, B. J. (2015). *Holacracy: The new management system for a rapidly changing world*. New York, NY: Henry Holt and Company.

RocheMartin. (n.d.). *Emotional intelligence*. Retrieved January 3, 2016, from http://www.rochemartin.com/about/emotional-intelligence.html

Rogers, P., & Tierney, T. (2004). Leadership without control. *European Business Journal*, 78–82. Retrieved November 8, 2015, from http://www.bain.com/Images/EBJ_Leadership_without_control.pdf

Rogers, R. W. (1975). A protection motivation theory of fear appeals and attitude change. *Journal of Psychology, 91*(1), 93–114.

Rooy, Van D. L., & Viswesvaran, C. (2004). Emotional intelligence: A meta-analytic investigation of predictive validity and nomological net. *Journal of Vocational Behavior, 65*(1), 71–95.

Rosenzweig, P. (2007). *The halo effect . . . and the eight other business delusions that deceive managers*. New York, NY: Free Press.

Ross, L., & Ward, A. (1996). Naive realism in everyday life: Implications for social conflict and misunderstanding. In T. Brown, E. S. Reed, & E. Turiel (Eds.), *Values and knowledge* (pp. 103–135). Hillsdale, NJ: Erlbaum.

Rousseau, D. M. (1989). Psychological and implied contracts in organizations. *Employee Responsibilities and Rights Journal, 2*(2), 121–139.

Rubera, G., & Kirca, A. H. (2012). Firm innovativeness and its performance outcomes: A meta-analytic review and theoretical integration. *Journal of Marketing, 76*(3), 130–147.

Ryan, R., & Deci, E. (2000). Intrinsic and extrinsic motivations: Classic definitions and new directions. *Contemporary Educational Psychology, 25*(1), 54–67.

Rynes, S. L., Colbert, A. E., & Brown, K. G. (2002). HR professionals' beliefs about effective human resource practices: Correspondence between research and practice. *Human Resource Management, 41*(2), 149–174.

Sagan, C. (1996). *The demon-haunted world: Science as a candle in the dark*. New York, NY: Random House.

Salovey, P., & Mayer, J. D. (1990). Emotional intelligence. *Imagination, Cognition and Personality, 9*(3), 185–211.

Samuelson, R. J. (1993, September 15). *Scare talk about NAFTA*. Retrieved January 12, 2016, from https://www.washingtonpost.com/archive/opinions/1993/09/15/scare-talk-about-nafta/82a1c705-732c-499c-80bc-e63fd74e5942/

Sanders, K., Van Riemsdijk, M., & Groen, B. (2008). The gap between research and practice: A replication study on the HR professionals' beliefs about effective human resource practices. *The International Journal of Human Resource Management, 19*(10), 1976–1988.

Saruhan, N. (2014). The role of corporate communication and perception of justice during organizational change process. *Business and Economics Research Journal, 5*(4), 143–166.

Schein, E. H. (1990). Organizational culture. *American Psychologist, 45*(2), 109–119.

Schein, E. H. (1996). Culture: The missing concept in organization studies. *Administrative Science Quarterly, 41*(2), 229–240.

Schein, E. H. (2009). *The corporate culture survival guide*. San Francisco, CA: John Wiley & Sons.

Schramade, P. W. J. (2006). Tussen providence- en evidence-based HRD. *Opleiding & Ontwikkeling, 19*(3), 10.

Schramade, P. W. J. (2014). Laveren tussen Evidence- en providence-based management. *Holland Management Review, 157*(Sep-Oct), 3.

Seo, M., Taylor, M. S., Hill, N. S., Zhang, X., Tesluk, P. E. and Lorinkova, N. M. (2012). The role of affect and leadership during organizational change. *Personnel Psychology*, 65(1), 121–165.

Shadish, W. R., Cook, T. D., & Campbell, D. T. (2002). *Experimental and quasi-experimental designs for generalized causal inference*. Boston, MA: Wadsworth Cengage Learning.

Shermon, G. (2012). *Creating and optimized organization: Key opportunities and challenges*. Retrieved January 28, 2015, from https://www.kpmg.de/docs/India_OptimizedOrganisation.pdf

Shier, V., Khodyakov, D., Cohen, L. W., Zimmerman, S., & Saliba, D. (2014). What does the evidence really say about culture change in nursing homes? *The Gerontologist*, 54(1), 6–16.

Shum, P., Bove, L., & Auh, S. (2008). Employee's affective commitment to change: The key to successful CRM implementation. *European Journal of Marketing*, 42(11/12), 1346–1371.

Slater, R. (2015). *Leadership genius: 40 insights from the science of leading*. Abingdon, UK: Teach Yourself.

Smircich, L. (1983). Concepts of culture and organizational analysis. *Administrative Science Quarterly*, 28(3), 339–358.

Smith, M. E. (2002). Success rates for different types of organizational change. *Performance Improvement*, 41(1), 26–33.

Smollan, R., & Parry, K. (2011). Follower perception of the emotional intelligence of change leaders: A qualitative study. *Leadership*, 7(4), 435–462.

Soparnot, R. (2011). The concept of organizational change capacity. *Journal of Organizational Change Management*, 24(5), 640–661.

Staber, U., & Sydow, J. (2002). Organizational adaptive capacity: A structuration perspective. *Journal of Management Inquiry*, 11(4), 408–424.

Stinglhamber, F., & Vandenberghe, C. (2003). Organizations and supervisors as sources of support and targets of commitment: A longitudinal study. *Journal of Organizational Behavior*, 24(3), 251–270.

Stuhlmacher, A. F., Gillespie, T. L., & Champagne, M. V. (1998). The impact of time pressure in negotiation: A meta-analysis. *The International Journal of Conflict Management*, 9(2), 97–116.

Sutton, B. (2007, September 17). *Why management is not a profession*. Retrieved February 8, 2016, from http://bobsutton.typepad.com/my_weblog/2007/09/more-evidence-t.html

Sutton, R. I., & Staw, B. M. (1995). What theory is not. *Administrative Science Quarterly*, 40(3), 371–384.

Svendsen, E. (2015, June 22). *The role of a "guiding coalition" when leading safety-culture change*. Retrieved October, 25, 2015, from http://safetybuiltin.com/2015/06/22/the-role-of-a-guiding-coalition-when-leading-safety-culture-change/

Sverke, M., Hellgren, J., Näswall, K., Göransson, S., & Öhrming, J. (2008). Employee participation in organizational change: Investigating the effects of proactive vs. reactive implementation of downsizing in Swedish hospitals. *Zeitschrift für Personalforschung*, 22(2), 111–129.

Tata, J., & Prasad, S. (2004). Team self-management, organizational structure, and judgments of team effectiveness. *Journal of Managerial Issues*, 16(2), 248–265.

Team based organization. (n.d.). In *BusinessDictionary.com*. Retrieved January 28, 2016, from http://www.businessdictionary.com/definition/team-based-organization-TBO.html

Ten Broeke, A. (2015). *De verleiding van de TED-cultuur*. Retrieved January 2, 2016, from https://blendle.com/i/de-volkskrant/de-verleiding-van-de-ted-cultuur/bnl-vkn-20150102-3826828

Ten Have, S., Ten Have, W. D., & Janssen, B. (2009). *Het Veranderboek: 70 vragen van managers over organisatieverandering*. Amsterdam, NL: Mediawerf.

Ten Have, S., Ten Have, W. D., Huijsmans, A. B., & Van der Eng, N. (2015). *Change competence: Implementing effective change*. New York, NY: Routledge.

Ten Have, S., & Visser, C. (2004). Naar een productief veranderperspectief: Van mislukking naar succes. *Holland Management Review, 98*, 32–47.

Thibaut, J. W., & Walker, L. (1975). *Procedural justice: A psychological analysis*. Hillsdale, NJ: Erlbaum.

Thorbecke, W., & Eigen-Zucchi, C. (2002). Did NAFTA cause a "giant sucking ground?" *Journal of Labor Research, 23*(4), 647–658.

Tichy, N. M. (1982). Managing change strategically: The technical, political, and cultural keys. *Organizational Dynamics, 11*(2), 59–80.

Tichy, N. M. (1983). *Managing strategic change: Technical, political, and cultural dynamics*. New York, NY: John Wiley & Sons.

Tichy, N. M., & DeVanna, M. A. (1986). *The transformational leader*. New York, NY: John Wiley & Sons.

Toolpack. (n.d.). *Why cultural change can fail*. Retrieved January 28, 2016, from http://www.toolpack.info/articles/cultural-change-failure.html

Transformational leadership. (n.d.). In *BusinessDictionairy.com*. Retrieved January 30, 2016, from http://www.businessdictionary.com/definition/transformational-leadership.html

Tsoukas, H., & Chia, R. (2002). On organizational becoming: Rethinking organizational change. *Organization Science, 13*(5), 567–582.

Tubbs, M. E. (1986). Goal setting: A meta-analytic examination of the empirical evidence. *Journal of Applied Psychology, 71*(3), 474–483.

Turner, D. M. (2015). *Buy in is not enough*. Retrieved February 2, 2016, from http://thinktransition.com/articles/buy-in-is-not-enough/

Tyler, T. R., & De Cremer, D. (2005). Process-based leadership: Fair procedures and reactions to organizational change. *The Leadership Quarterly, 16*(4), 529–545.

Urgency. (n.d.). In *American heritage® dictionary of the English language, fifth edition*. Retrieved January 30, 2016, from http://www.thefreedictionary.com/urgency

Uzkurt, C., Kumar, R., Kimzan, H. S., & Eminoğlu, G. (2013). Role of innovation in the relationship between organizational culture and firm performance. *European Journal of Innovation Management, 16*(1), 92–117.

Vaccaro, I. G., Jansen, J. J., Van den Bosch, F. A., & Volberda, H. W. (2012). Management innovation and leadership: The moderating role of organizational size. *Journal of Management Studies, 49*(1), 28–51.

Van Aken, J. E. (1994). De bedrijfskunde als ontwerpwetenschap: De regulatieve en reflectieve cyclus. *Bedrijfskunde, 66*(1), 16–26.

Van Bokhoven, M. A., Koch, H., Dinant, G. J., Bindels, P. J. E., Grol, R. P. T. M., & Van der Weijden, T. (2008). Exploring the black box of change in improving test-ordering routines. *Family Practice, 25*(3), 139–145.

Van Dierendonck, D., & Jacobs, G. (2002). Survivors and victims, a meta-analytical review of fairness and organizational commitment after downsizing. *British Journal of Management, 23*(1), 96–109.

Van Rooy, D. L., & Viswesvaran, C. (2004). Emotional intelligence: A meta-analytic investigation of predictive validity and nomological net. *Journal of Vocational Behavior*, 65(1), 71–95.

Verheggen, T. (2005). *Culture alt delete: On the misperception of culture in psychology* (Doctoral dissertation). Retrieved January 13, 2016, from http://www.ou.nl/Docs/Faculteiten/PSY/Onderzoek/Dissertation%20Theo%20Verheggen_Full%20Version%20(Final).pdf

Vestergard, B. (n.d.). *Fair process change*. Retrieved November 23, 2015, from http://www.fairprocesschange.com

Vidal, M. (2007). Manufacturing empowerment? 'Employee involvement' in the labour process after Fordism. *Socio-economic Review*, 5, 197–232.

Vilet, J. (2013, November 4). *Why it's so difficult to really change a company culture*. Retrieved January 10, 2015, from http://www.eremedia.com/tlnt/why-its-so-difficult-to-really-change-a-company-culture/

Vision. (n.d.). In *Dictionary.com*. Retrieved January 30, 2016, from http://dictionary.reference.com/browse/vision?s=t

Viswesvaran, C., & Ones, D. S. (2002). Examining the construct of organizational justice: A meta-analytic evaluation of relations with work attitudes and behaviors. *Journal of Business Ethics*, 38(3), 193–203.

Voestermans, P., & Verheggen, T. (2007). *Cultuur en lichaam: Een cultuurpsychologisch perspectief op patronen in gedrag*. Malden, MA: Blackwell Publishing.

Voestermans, P., & Verheggen, T. (2013). *Culture as embodiment: The social tuning of behavior*. Hoboken, NJ: John Wiley & Sons.

Wagner, J. A. (1994). Participation's effects on performance and satisfaction: A reconsideration of research evidence. *Academy of Management Review*, 19(2), 312–330.

Wagner, J. A., & Lepine, J. A. (1999). Effects of participation on performance and satisfaction: Additional meta-analytic evidence. *Psychological Reports*, 84(3), 719–725.

Wagner, J. A., Leana, C. R., Locke, E. A., & Schweiger, D. M. (1997). Cognitive and motivational frameworks in U.S. research on participation: A meta-analysis of primary effects. *Journal of Organizational Behavior*, 18(1), 49–65.

Wall, T. D., Kemp, N. J., Jackson, P. R., & Clegg, C. W. (1986). Outcomes of autonomous workgroups: A long-term field experiment. *Academy of Management journal*, 29(2), 280–304.

Wang, G., Oh, I. S., Courtright, S. H., & Colbert, A. E. (2011). Transformational leadership and performance across criteria and levels: A meta-analytic review of 25 years of research. *Group & Organization Management*, 36(2), 223–270.

Watkins, M. D. (2013). *The first 90 days: Proven strategies for getting up to speed faster and smarter, updated and expanded*. Boston, MA: Harvard Business Review Press.

Wegge, J., Jeppesen, H. J., Weber, W. G., Pearce, C. L., Silva, S. A., Pundt, A., Jonsson, T., Wolf, S., Wassenaar, C. L., Unterrainer, C., & Piecha, A. (2010). Promoting work motivation in organizations: Should employee involvement in organizational leadership become a new tool in the organizational psychologist's kit? *Journal of Personnel Psychology*, 9(4), 154–171.

Weibel, A., Rost, K., & Osterloh, M. (2010). Pay for performance in the public sector-benefits and (hidden) costs. *Journal of Public Administration Research and Theory*, 20(2), 87–412.

Weick, K. E. (1995). *Sensemaking in organizations*. Thousand Oaks, CA: Sage.

West, M. A. (1990). The social psychology of innovation in groups. In M. A. West, & J. L. Farr (Eds.), *Innovation and creativity at work* (pp. 309–333). Chichester, UK: Wiley.

White, J. (2011, March 17). *Born to run: Haile Gebrselassie interview*. Retrieved January 18, 2016, from http://www.telegraph.co.uk/sport/othersports/athletics/8373361/Born-to-run-Haile-Gebrselassie-interview.html

Wilensky, H. L. (1964). The professionalization of everyone? *American Journal of Sociology, 70*(2), 137–158.

William Thomson. (n.d.). In *Wikipedia*. Retrieved November 11, 2015, from https://en.wikiquote.org/wiki/William_Thomson

Workman, M. (2003). Results from organizational development interventions in a technology call center. *Human Resource Development Quarterly, 14*(2), 215–230.

Wright, T. A., & Bonett, D. G. (2002). The moderating effects of employee tenure on the relation between organizational commitment and job performance: A meta-analysis. *Journal of Applied Psychology, 87*(6), 1183–1190.

Zaffron, S., & Logan, D. (2009). *The three laws of performance: Rewriting the future of your organization and your life*. San Francisco, CA: Jossey-Bass.

Zagoršek, H., Dimovski, V., & Škerlavaj, M. (2009). Transactional and transformational leadership impacts on organizational learning. *Journal for East European Management Studies, 14*(2), 144–165.

Zhang, M., Li, H., & Wei, J. (2008). Examining the relationship between organizational culture and performance: The perspectives of consistency and balance. *Frontiers of Business Research in China, 2*(2), 256–276.

Zuckerman, H. S., Kaluzny, A. D., & Ricketts, T. C. (1995). Alliances in health care: What we know, what we think we know, and what we should know. *Health Care Management Review, 20*(1), 54–64.

Index

assumptions in change practice: change capacity 43–4, 112–17, 177; vision 34–5, 73–8, 176, 177; commitment 177; commitment to change 53–5, 156–61; emotional intelligence 38–40, 92–6, 176; financial incentives 55–6, 161–5, 177; goal setting with feedback 52–3, 151–6, 177; fair change process 47–8, 125–31, 177; resistance 45–7, 121–5, 177; leadership styles 37–8, 87–92, 176; powerful guiding coalition 41–2, 107–11, 177; organizational culture challenges 48–50, 138–45, 177; organizational culture performance 50–2, 145–51, 177; participation 44–5, 117–21, 177; supervisory support 40–1, 102–7, 176; self-managing teams 56–8, 165–70, 177; sense of urgency 36, 78–83, 176; failure rate change initiatives 33–4, 70–3, 176; trust in leadership 36–7, 83–7, 110, 176
Argyris, C. 104
autonomy 165

Bass, Bernard 89
Beer, Michael 70
business process reengineering (BPR) management approach 18
Burns, James MacGregor 88
business process redesign 7
business schools 8–9

change capacity: definitions and concepts 112–7; key assumption 43–4, 177
change management: academic roots and pragmatic orientation of 10–12; activist approach 10; challenges 7–8, 15; development and maturation of 6–7; eminence-based approach 3, 17, 19–21; evidence-based approach 10; evidence-based perspective 178; exposing quacks 10; goals 9; Integrationswissenschaft 179; leading assumptions 29–58; providence-based approach 3, 17, 22–4
change-oriented performance 89–90
change readiness 116
Collins, Jim 5, 15, 20
commitment: affective (attitudinal) commitment 157, 158–9; continuance commitment 157; definitions and concepts 156–7; effect on support for change 159–61; employee satisfaction 24; key assumption 53–5, 177; normative commitment 157, 159; participation 117; performance 158–9
Competing Values Framework 142, 148
confidence 53
conflicts 86, 130
consensus building 39
critical appraisal: effect sizes 67; methodological appropriateness 65–6; methodological quality 66–7
crowding-out effect 163, 164
culture: definitions and concepts 136–8, 140, 150–1, 177; organizational culture challenges 48–50, 138–45; organizational culture performance 50–2, 145–51; team-based culture 57
culture change: organizational culture challenges 48–50; engagement 45
culture–performance dynamic 146–7
culture-producing phenomena 139

decision making 118, 121
Denison Organizational Culture Survey 148

downsizing 51, 128
Drucker, Peter 179

Einstein, Albert 83
eminence-based approach 3, 17, 19–21
emotional intelligence (EI): construct 93–4; definitions and concepts 93–4; effects of 96; concept 15, 93; empathy 39; key assumption 38–40, 176; motivation 39; performance 95, 176; self-awareness 39, 94; self-regulation 39, 94; social skill 39
emotional support 103
employees: change capacity 43–4, 112–17; change/non-change-oriented performance 89–90; commitment 160–1; employee satisfaction 23–4; engagement 45, 55; fear appeal 81–2; feedback 52–3, 103, 151–6; financial incentives 162, 164–5; goal setting 52–3, 151–6; fair change process 47–8; voice and participation of 44–5, 118; job performance 158–9; motivation 163; organizational culture challenges 145; perceived supervisory support 103; reciprocity 103–4; relationship between supervisor 107; transformational leadership style 91, 92
engagement 45, 54
evidence-based change management 179
evidence-based management: academic roots and pragmatic orientation 10–12; exposing quacks 10; guiding principle 10–11; managers favoring 7; movement ix–x
evidence-based medicine (EBM) 179
evidence-based paradigm 2–3
evidence-based practice (EBP) x, 6
executives: employee engagement 55; employee satisfaction 23; levels of executive capabilities 37; role of 8

failure rate 34
fair change process: definitions and concepts 125–7; effects 128–9; key assumption 47–8, 177
fairness 125
fear appeal 81–2
feedback: consistency 53; definitions and concepts 151–3; key assumption 52–3, 177; outcome-related feedback 153, 155; ongoing regard 53; performance 152; process-related feedback 153, 155; reinforcement 53; supervisory support 103; underlying mechanisms 153
financial incentives: definitions and concepts 161–2; effect on performance 163–4; key assumption 55–6, 177; performance 163–4
first-line supervisors 40
future-based language 35

Gates, Bill 79
Gideon's mob approach 41–2
goals: accomplishment 123; big, hairy, audacious goals (BHAGs) 75; common goals 110, 111
goal setting: definitions and concepts 151–3; key assumption 52–3, 177; SMART 152, 154–5; underlying mechanisms 153; goal-setting theory 77, 152
Goleman, Daniel 15, 93
guiding coalition: definitions and concepts 108; characteristics 108, 111; key assumption 41–2, 177; Kotter's eight-step change model 73; trust 108; steps in establishing successful 109

Hawthorne studies 19
high-performance organizations (HPO) 145, 146, 151
Hofstede, Geert 19
Hofstede's cultural dimensions 19, 20–1
human resource managers 23

incentives: aligning 56; general 161–2; direct 163–4; extrinsic 56, 163; indirect 163; intrinsic 163; performance-salient 162; price effect 164; recognition 36, 161
integrative behaviors 86
involvement 24

job performance 158–9
job satisfaction 24, 86, 123
justice: distributive justice 126; equity theory 126; general 125–7; organizational justice 125–6, 129; procedural justice 126, 129–30

Keynes, John Maynard 12
Kotter, John 16, 42, 70, 78, 107, 117
Kotter's eight-step change model 73, 78–9

Latham, Gary 152
leadership: authoritarian leadership style 88; autocratic leadership style 88; change readiness 116; clear vision 34–5; definitions and concepts 83; delegative leadership style 88; democratic leadership style 88; emotional intelligence 38–40, 92–6; goal setting with feedback 52–3; good-to-great leaders 44; guiding coalitions 108, 110; fair change process 47–8; key assumption 37–8, 176; laissez-faire leadership style 88; levels of executive capabilities 37; participative leadership style 88; supervisory support 40–1; transactional leadership style 37, 176; transformational leadership style 37–8, 176; trust 36–7, 83–7, 110
leader vision 74
lean management 7, 18, 51
level-five leadership 15
Locke, Edwin 152
loyalty 39

management 7–8
management improvement strategies 51–2
managers: capacity issues 117; challenges facing 15–7; characteristics 15–6; lack of trust 124–5; organizational culture challenges 145; organizational culture performance 151; role 8–9; self-managing teams 170; SMART project management 152; supervisory support 102, 107; transactional leadership style 37; evidence-based approach 17
McGregor, Douglas 161
medical practitioners 8
medical schools 8
mergers and acquisitions (M&A) 148
middle management 107
motivation: intrinsic 162–4; extrinsic 162; general 39, 94, 162, 165
motivational theory 103
mutual trust 108

negotiations 86
new way of working 22–3
Nieuwe Leren (New Learning) 2
Nixon, Richard 118
Nohria, Nitin 70

non-change-oriented performance 89–90
non-interesting tasks 162, 164

open-plan offices 22–3
organizational architect 57
organizational culture challenges: definitions and concepts 138–9; key assumption 48–50, 177
organizational culture performance: culture–performance dynamic 146–7; definitions and concepts 145–7, 150–1; high-performance organizations 145–6, 151; key assumption 50–2, 177
organizational formalization 169
organizational hierarchy 169
ownership 36

participation: definitions and concepts 117–9; effect 119–20; key assumption 44–5, 177; theoretical models 118–9, 120–1; typology in decision making 118
perception and memory 18
performance: change capacity 116; commitment to change 55, 158–9; emotional intelligence 95, 176; employee satisfaction 23–4; equitably distributed rewards 164; feedback 52–3, 152, 154; financial incentives 163–4; high-performance organizations 145–6, 151; leadership styles 89; mergers and acquisitions 149; motivation 162; new way of working 22–3; organizational culture performance 50–2, 145–51; resistance to change 123; self-managing team performance 56–8, 165–70; self-managing teams 167–8
personality traits 94
Peters, Tom 5–6, 20
position power 108, 110
process fairness 48
providence-based approach 3, 17, 22–4
psychological contract 104, 129
purposive change 114

quality of work life 166, 168

Rapid Evidence Assessments (REAs): change capacity 112–7; clear vision as essential for successful change 73–8; commitment to change 156–61; emotional intelligence

92–6; financial incentives 161–5; goal setting with feedback 151–6; importance of fair change process 125–31; importance of understanding resistance 121–5; leadership styles 87–92; methodology 62–8, 138; necessity of powerful guiding coalition 107–11; organizational culture challenges 138–45; organizational culture performance 145–51; role of participation 117–21; role of supervisory support 102–7; self-managing team performance 165–70; sense of urgency 78–83; seventy percent change initiative failure rate 70–3; trust in leadership 83–7
re-engineering 52
resistance to change: definitions and concepts 121–2; goal accomplishment 123; job satisfaction 123; key assumption 45–7, 177; lack of trust in management 124; performance 123
rewards: general 36, 53, 55–6, 126, 161–2, 164; equitably distributed rewards 164; intrinsic rewards 56
Rousseau, D.M. 104

safety culture 51
Sagan, Carl 111
Salmon, Felix 19
Schlessinger, Leonard 117
self-determination theory 162
self-managing teams: autonomous groups 165; definitions and concepts 165–7; effects on attitudinal and behavioral outcomes 168; implementing 169–70; key assumption 56–8, 177; micro-level centralization 169; performance 167–8; role of contextual factors 169–70; self-directed teams 165; shared teams 166; structural problems 168
seventy percent change initiative failure rate 179–80; definitions and concepts 70–1; key assumption 33–4, 176
social exchange theory: general 103, 104; reciprocity 103
start-up culture 56, 166
Strategy 39
structural problems 57, 166–8, 168
Studiehuis (Independent Self-Study) 2
supervisors 40–1

supervisory support: definitions and concepts 102–4; key assumption 40–1, 176; perceived supervisory support, 103, 105–6
Sutton, Robert I. 178–9

team-based organization (TBO) 58
teams 56–8, 91, 108, 165–70
TED culture 19
tell-and-sell strategy 120
ten Broeke, Asha 18–19
Theory X 161
Theory Y 161
time pressure 81
total quality management (TQM) 18, 51
traditionally managed teams 56–8, 167, 177
transactional leadership style: change/non-change-oriented performance 90–1; definitions and concepts 88–9, 176; effectiveness 89–90; managers 37; positive effects 92
transformational leadership style: change/non-change-oriented performance 90–1; definitions and concepts 88–9, 176; effectiveness 89–90; positive effects 91
trust: ability 84; benefits 87; benevolence 84; definitions and concepts 83–4; dispositional trust 85; integrity 84; key assumption 36–7, 176; lack of 124; models for underlying mechanisms 84; mutual trust 108; role in resolution of conflicts and negotiations 86; trust propensity 84–5, 87
trustworthiness 37

urgency: burning-platform situations 36; definitions and concepts 79; feedback 53; key assumption 36, 176; Kotter's eight-step change model 78–9; level 80; sense of urgency 36, 53, 78–83, 176

vision: change vision 74, 77–8, 114; definitions and concepts 74; effectiveness of 75; goals 74–5; key assumption 34–5, 176; shared vision 45, 73, 75, 77; vision clarity 34–5, 73–8
visionary companies 75

Waterman, R.H. 5–6, 20
Welch, Jack 17
Williams, Evan 56, 166